Original Artwork and Cover design by

Steve Woodhouse

© Steven Woodhouse 2023

The Icarus Game

Critical Acclaim

"What the hell am I supposed to do with this?"

Publishing agent. (Name withheld)

Top Amazon reviews from United Kingdom

5.0 out of 5 stars. **Amusing and witty, a must for aviation enthusiasts.**

Reviewed in the United Kingdom on 4 May 2023
Verified Purchase

As an ex-freight dog, it brought back a lot of memories and made me chuckle. Seems like there was never a dull moment on the Electra or with Atlantic. An easy book to read, the author is self-deprecating, humble, and very tongue in cheek. Dog had it coming!

5.0 out of 5 stars. **An amazing life story**

Reviewed in the United Kingdom on 3 August 2023
Verified Purchase

An amazing life story told with both passion and irony. You seem to make the most of what ever life throws at you and have worked and played with some characters. Written from the heart a cracking read. Anyone thinking or writing their own story should read this first.

The Icarus Game

Steve Woodhouse

First Published 2023

Back From The Shed Publishing

© Steven Woodhouse 2023

The right of Steven Woodhouse to be identified as the author of this work has been asserted in accordance with The Copyright, Designs and Patents Act 1988. All rights reserved. No part of this book may be reproduced, stored in, or entered into a retrieval system, or transmitted, in any form or by any means (electronic, mechanical, photocopying, recording or otherwise) without the written permission of the publisher. Any unauthorised act in relation to this publication may be liable to criminal prosecution and civil claims for damages.

ISBN 978-1-7395181-0-3 (paperback)

First Edition (2023)

Typeset in 11pt Calibri.

Back From The Shed Publishing.

The Icarus Game

Steve Woodhouse

Thank you to my long-suffering wife Gay,

Who, despite knowing that I am an idiot,

Forgives me. Because I'm her idiot.

Many thanks also go to my

family and friends for all their support.

The Icarus Game

Steve Woodhouse

When obstructive people try to make what you want to do sound impossible, the reasoning process is logical.

What's the worst that can happen?

It's not rocket science.

How hard can it be?

Any idiot can do it.

LOC/WOO Circa 2005

The Icarus Game

The Icarus Game

On The Fringes Of Legality

(First Edition 2023)

Steve Woodhouse

The Icarus Game

Contents

	Page
Introduction	19.
Chapter 1. My life systematically dismantled.	23.
Chapter 2. Growing up.	32.
Chapter 3. Lympstone.	41.
Chapter 4. Between jobs.	49.
Chapter 5. Coningsby.	56.
Chapter 6. Marham.	67.
Chapter 7. Laarbruch.	79.
Chapter 8. Decimomanu.	87.
Chapter 9. 20 Squadron.	94.
Chapter 10. Changing times.	103.
Illustrations.	110.
Chapter 11. Coming home.	114.
Chapter 12. My war.	125.
Chapter 13. Tabuk.	133.
Chapter 14. Civvy street.	141.
Chapter 15. Flog it.	151.
Chapter 16. In at the deep end.	161.

The Icarus Game

Contents

	Page
Chapter 17. Opa Locka.	173.
Chapter 18. On line.	181.
Chapter 19. Ad hoc-ing	290.
Chapter 20. Guardian angels.	200.
Chapter 21. Marseilles.	209.
Illustrations.	217.
Chapter 22. Mile high club.	219.
Chapter 23. The end is nigh.	228.
Chapter 24. The end is here.	238.
Chapter 25. Flight training.	247.
Chapter 26. Recon'.	257.
Chapter 27. Around the coast.	266.
Chapter 28. Electra training.	275.
Chapter 29. You can take the kid out of the council estate…	284.
Chapter 30. Fishy fingers.	292.
Chapter 31. Smart quips and cockups.	301.
Chapter 32. Benny the ball.	312.

The Icarus Game

Contents

	Page
Chapter 33. Mr Woo.	321.
Illustrations.	330.
Chapter 34. Odd jobs.	334.
Chapter 35. Hassi Messaoud.	344.
Chapter 36. Second time around.	353.
Chapter 37. End of the Atlantic Line.	362.
Chapter 38. I love passengers.	370.
Chapter 39. New start.	379.
Chapter 40. Heart attack.	388.
Chapter 41. Sick leave.	396.
Chapter 42. Back to work.	405.
Chapter 43. That bloody dog.	411.
Chapter 44. Epilogue.	420.
Note From the Author	429.
What Goes Around Comes Around	431.
Annex 1.	432.
Illustration.	441/443.
Thanks	445.

The Icarus Game

Introduction.

Shooting the breeze with mates over breakfast, would usually result in the conversation being directed towards our respective favourite 'War Stories'. Pull up a sandbag and swing that lamp.

Leading a nomadic life, I have never shirked the challenges that come my way. Sometimes they are tackled begrudgingly, sometimes with a passion. I seem to have collected more than my fair share of anecdotes. "You should write a book" is a comment I've heard frequently over the years. I didn't know whether there was an actual book in me. Writing it would take a lot of effort, rummaging in the most entrenched areas of my memory, resurrecting the secrets I'd kept repressed for decades. To extract something close to the full story was going to be demanding.

My favourite tales revolve around cock ups, and I've made plenty of those. The times when things could, and by rights should have gone a lot better. But when your Gods conspire against you, there is little you can do other than to accept, calamity and chaos are the only realistic outcomes. Nobody wants to hear stories of cruising to success, that's just bragging. Overcoming adversity, rising from the smouldering wreckage of life, beating the odds, are the things that for me, make the endeavour worthwhile.

Those times when your meticulous planning evaporates, and your world implodes on itself, make for the most compelling yarns. My problem was, writing stories down has never come naturally. I'd spent endless hours in classrooms at school, sat staring vacantly at a blank sheet of A4 paper, with absolutely no idea how to express the thoughts in my head. My teachers said that I would never amount to anything, they may well have been right. But for me getting nowhere has been the most exciting and challenging stumble in the dark imaginable.

Achieving the highly improbable, is a place I am as amazed as anybody to find myself. Dredging through the slimy depths of abject failure, then scaling heights that nobody would have predicted for me. I've tried to do this with a spirit of good humour and honesty, and when that hasn't worked, underhand scheming and direct action has been used. That's called life. When I can, I'll say what's on my mind clearly and politely. If that misses the mark, I resort to fluent council house Anglo Saxon. In the end, I treat people in the same fashion that they treat me. Decently, or with contempt, it makes little difference, I simply reflect what I receive.

My life took an unexpected turn a few years ago, and the outcome was as dramatic as it was unforeseen. I collected a criminal conviction for an unfortunate incident that sparked an international storm on the internet, and in the press. It should have caused little more than a row between neighbours. Instead, it exploded into a global media circus fuelled by mass hysteria on social networking sites. Years later it is still front and centre if you Google my name.

This internet persona means that even if I want to, I can't brush my past under the carpet and carry on as normal. The caricature of me that has been created on the world wide web, by the cyber lynch mob, now resides embedded in every search engine in my name. It will remain there in perpetuity. That only leaves one option, challenge it head on. Or as my mate 'Mick the

Plumber' always said, 'If you can't hide it, make a feature of it.' And he was the most artistic plumber I ever knew; he could transform any bodge up into a creative centre piece.

At the time, there was an absolute tsunami of comment and abuse in the media. This meant that any statement I made was simply going to be lost in the howling hurricane of armchair opinion. So, I made no comments then. This book doesn't try to justify or condone what I did, that was undoubtedly wrong. Its purpose is to put my life and actions into context. It's my response to the highly opinionated, media obsessed world that we now inhabit. Some will not want to read it. Others will.

Starting this project with a conscience, I tried to obscure the identities of individuals and organisations. I didn't wish to embarrass anybody, or face the possibility of litigation, again. Then I worked out that nobody had paid me the same courtesy. Ok, I may have been guilty, but really, the do-gooders had absolutely no sense of proportion. If anybody recognises themselves from the descriptions in the stories I tell, then the story must be accurate. Here rests the case for the defence m' lord.

Foremost it is written to give a balanced account of my life and attitudes, I hope it succeeds in that. I firmly believe that having friends makes you comfortable, having enemies shows that you have occasionally stood up for yourself. For all those people who over the years have remained solid friends, thank you. For all those people who abused me or turned their backs on me, you gave me the impetus to put my experiences down in writing. So, thank you too.

When I started to think about the events of the last fifty odd years, I was keeping short notes of just a word or two, trying the best I could to get them in the correct chronological order. The more I noted down, the more of my little mishaps and adventures came to mind. I wrote them all up as essays. Good, bad, and criminal. The stories in this book represent the bits of my life that I feel are worth sharing. As my lifetime passed by, it became a diverse and occasionally riotous adventure.

Chapter 1

My Life Systematically Dismantled.

When you know that your life expectancy is very limited, it puts a whole new angle on your attitudes. 'You've got cancer. It's started in your stomach with a tumour the size of a hen's egg, now it's spread to your liver.' The consultant glances across at the image on the screen in front of him. He didn't need to; he knew exactly how many tumours had erupted in my liver. 'There's about half a dozen tumours in there.'. There was seven, but hey, what's the odd stray malignant tumour between friends.

In a futile effort to see the positive in this shitty situation, he then came out with a comment that still echoes with irony. 'Of all the cancers you could have, this one's actually not so bad. Lots of my patients live four or five years.'. Doctors humour, I could have died laughing.

Emotional expression wasn't something that was encouraged in our household during my childhood. "If you think crying is going to get you out of this, think again young man." "Quit your snivelling, you're behaving like a bloody girl." "Big boys don't cry." All a bit harsh when you're only four.

This was pretty much the mantra of my childhood, and it's probably a familiar set of phrases for a lot of people. I'm sure it still happens.

The Icarus Game

The consulting room was packed, half a dozen random medics and student doctors, sat neatly lined up along the wall. Watching curiously as the bad news was broken to the unlucky patient. As the unlucky patient all I could think was 'Fuck, that's just typical.'

My wife, Gay is not nearly as uptight as me and was gripping my hand fiercely, she sobbed her heart out for both of us. I was fifty-five and unlikely to get a bus pass.

To be fair my upbringing didn't do me that much harm. Going through school, showing emotion was viewed as weakness, this would quickly turn you into the playground punchbag.

Serving my way through a career in the Royal Air Force, then working my way up the corporate greasy pole, showing empathy wasn't seen as a desirable trait. It stifled productivity; it wasn't efficient.

For most of my working life this wasn't an issue. Others came and went, rose, and fell. I kept my eye on the ball and did just fine, thank you. I had a permanent smile on my face, a positive demeanour. It worked for me. A mask to hide behind. Nobody knows what's going on behind smiling eyes.

It's a strategy that works quite well, while your star is ascending. It's not so helpful when things start going seriously wrong. I'd done well, exceeded everybody's expectations, even my own.

When things started going wrong, I really wasn't equipped to deal with it. I'd had a lifetime of suppressing my feelings. Tits and teeth darling. For the most part that's what people saw. I was fifty-two, when I discovered that life wasn't all beer and skittles. I made a mistake. It happened during the summer of 2014. The toll I paid for it was heavy.

Standing in front of the magistrates, charged with 'Causing unnecessary suffering to my next-door neighbour's dog, the use of a single word changed the rest of my life.

"Guilty."

With that plea, I lit the touch paper that inflamed every self-righteous armchair zealot to the point of apoplexy.

My rash action was undoubtedly wrong, it was a callous act of selfishness, intended to end years of harassment. Instead, it started a maelstrom of vindictiveness that ran feverishly around the globe. Enabled by the World Wide Web, totally unregulated, out of control. Social Media went into a frenzied state of hysteria. The local, national, and global press gave credibility to the story. Implausible, lurid accusations and theories ran amok.

The spite demonstrated by the cyber bully's knew no bounds, and why should it. After all they were for the most part unidentifiable. That's how it works, a social media influencer makes a comment and posts it online, they may even put their name to it. Then the glowing embers that they have ignited are fanned by hordes of fanatical, but anonymous disciples.

These troops that follow the 'Social Opinion Makers', the low-end muck-rakers, are more than happy to do the dirty work. They will enthusiastically try to improve their own online standing, their chance to profit, by exaggerating, misrepresenting or plain lying about events and inflating the negative consequences of their target's actions.

The Icarus Game

Pre-internet, these tactics were frequently used by toxic individuals to advance their own position in social situations, be it at school, in the workplace or a social environment. Trampling over others to get ahead.

With the advent of the internet the effectiveness of these tactics is now massively amplified. The level of humiliation and fear that can be generated is colossal. The consequences for some people, the individuals on the receiving end of this targeted and structured abuse can be dire.

Remember these targets are people, they are not faceless, lifeless punchbags for the bitchy, vexatious under-achievers to kick, simply because they are down. Playthings to make the embittered feel worthwhile. They are living, breathing people, with hopes, fears, responsibilities, families. With souls.

The right to free speech may be the chant of the internet, but until it is balanced with a requirement for accountability, compassion, and responsibility, it will continue to be the weapon of choice for the ill-informed, the easily led, or more pertinently, the easily miss-led.

Their aim is to crush their victim, total humiliation, total social exclusion. In my case it cost me the loss of many friends, rejection from social events. The loss of my career. The loss of my home. No possibility of recovering any of these things, ever.

This by any assessment is not a proportionate set of consequences for my action, this is not by any measure, justice. This was pure revenge. Simple vengeance on a massive, collective, and global scale. Thousands of screaming, swivel eyed jihadists, clamouring for the moral high ground, all coalescing to form an overwhelming online lynch mob.

I knew then, and accept, what I did was wrong, it was not the well-considered action of a responsible, balanced mind. It was the result of a great deal of stress. The result of knowing that my situation was untenable, but I had no idea how to initiate the changes my life needed for me to retain my sanity.

My breakdown was one that suddenly manifested itself, the threads holding the stability of my mind in place started to break, at first one, then the next. The strain on the remaining ties became excessive and before I knew what was happening, they all failed in rapid succession. My reality became incoherent fragments of memories, the result of insidious creeping pressures. One day my mind short circuited and I simply couldn't comprehend the world I found myself in.

The people around me, my closest friends, my family, even my wife were totally oblivious to my struggle. Until it was too late.

I'd kept all the plates spinning for years, apparently effortlessly. But when one wobbled and fell, the rest followed exponentially, cascading under the influence of gravity. Before I knew it, my life was disintegrating before my eyes. The things that once were a source of pleasure, a source of pride, those things that identified me as the person I was, suddenly become liabilities. Millstones that had to be discarded if I was to make any sense of my existence.

This is a scary place to be, dark does not do the feelings I experienced the justice they deserve. Curling up on the sofa with the curtains closed in the middle of the day, unable to move, unable to think, unable to make any sense of where I was. How did I end up here? Where do I go now? How do I get there? Will the raging noise that surrounds me ever stop? These, and other questions would have to wait a long time for answers.

The Icarus Game

The questions themselves had not formed in my mind at that point. That space in my brain was just humming, a dull monotonous drone of nothing. Black noise. Receiving no stimuli from my senses. Blanking out the world as it speculated about my future. As it speculated about the rest of my life. As it speculated about the profit to be gained from my downfall.

The targets for the online trolls shifted. From me to my family, to my friends, then to my employers. Some were able to ignore it, some argued my corner for me, hallelujah for them. Most capitulated to the swamp life that saturated the discussion. Smothering reason with their own selfish, heavily politicised brand of commotion.

This very modern blood sport is practiced by a repugnant band of proponents, a sizable and highly vocal minority of social media users. They demand that their narrow viewpoint be accepted. The problem with this being their acceptance comes at somebody else's detriment. They are happy to use abuse, threats, and violence to get their own way.

Their exploitation of the freedoms we all enjoy, is used to drive their victims into social isolation, character assassination on an industrial scale. Something that despots throughout history have not had the means to achieve so efficiently. The serious emotional damage that results, and even tragically, frequent suicides, is viewed by these pernicious troglodytes as a bonus. More likes. More clicks. More profit. More kudos.

Skulking in the darkest recesses of anonymity is their only defence, without this privilege they would be impotent. Reform to the laws regarding online abuse is long overdue, the authorities, sadly, are a long way behind the curve relating to this rapidly evolving technology.

The small amount of support I received was my lifeline. Against the hurricane of abuse, it was apparently futile, but it was all I had to cling to. "Mate, I know you're a twat, but I'm still here for you." These sentiments may not seem much like help in the normal run of life, but from where I was, they were ringing endorsements.

It was going to be a long struggle to recover, and to be honest I was in no fit state to take on anything. Rebuilding a life of any sort was out of the question from the despair I had descended into.

The psychologists, (note that's in plural), were mostly interested in proving their own pet theories, writing me up as a case study in their latest paper. Deciding whether I was sane enough to stand trial, to plead my case. Deciding for me, whether I should continue with my career or find another way to pay the bills.

The mist before my eyes and the humming between my ears were going to take a long time to clear. They were there in part, because of the relentless interest in me, online and in the press. They were there in part because of the pressure I put myself under in my work life and my home life. I had genuinely believed I was indestructible.

Able to succeed at anything I turned my hand to. So far this had been the case. I was an archetypal over achiever. No challenge was too daunting. No mountain too high, or treacherous to scale. My ambition outstripped my ability by a long way. By the time this became apparent, I was in so deep, backing down was not an option. This was going to change. It had to. If I was to stand any chance of recovering what remained of my mind.

The Icarus Game

It had never occurred to me that my sanity would be the weak link in my life. As far as I know, my judgement has always been as dubious as everybody else's around me. We all make wrong choices as we stumble through life. Most of these cockups can be resolved, mitigated against. I've made some shocking decisions, but I always managed to scramble back onto my feet.

This time though, the core reason for my crass decision making was the instability in my logical thinking, and that was going to stop me in my tracks. How can you recover if you don't know what's wrong with you? The only thing in my favour was a strong sense of self preservation.

It was going to take years, not months or weeks to recover from the dismal place I found myself inhabiting. No amount of Selective Serotonin Reuptake Inhibitors (SSRI's) was going to be the panacea to my situation. The handful of short therapy sessions may have helped some, but they gave me few answers. I still had to fathom out the questions before that would happen. The drugs did eventually give my mind the space to begin working again. Mapping out a path from the darkness that engulfed me. There was no light at the end of the tunnel, but in time, a faint glow just below the horizon began to grow in intensity.

Recovery is not a story of overcoming adversity, it's not a heroic tale of beating the odds, it's a slog. A daily grind of waking up, moving, doing the simple things to get through to bedtime. With a lot of support from my wife, and our friends and family, I can now see a way through, but the path has been littered with obstacles, none of which could have been predicted.

What you can still read about me on the internet is just a small facet of my life. A carefully selected microcosm of reality. The story as told by other people, most of whom have never met me. It will remain in cyber space in perpetuity.

Chapter 2

Growing Up.

Looking down at my feet, I soon work out that I am horizontal, flat on my back and falling. My ankles are either side of the trunk of a very tall, dead, and rotten fir tree. As I'm plunging earthwards, the branches my legs are crashing through are flying off the trunk and following me down towards the manicured lawn of a smart Devonshire hotel. I was with a friend playing in the gardens of his parent's business in Devon. We had raided the hotel beer store, which was a garage full of crates, and after sharing a bottle of Watney's finest, I had decided climbing the biggest tree in the garden was a good idea.

The resulting thud as my shoulder blades hit the grass is testimony to the flaw in my plan. I was about seven years old, creating my own crater on earth at the same time man was landing on the moon. I knocked every bit of wind out of my body, I couldn't even manage to talk for over a week. Mum was sufficiently concerned about her mute son that she took me to the doctors, he couldn't work out what the problem was. I couldn't speak to let on.

My childhood was a happy time. I am the eldest of two children, my sister Angie is a little over a year younger than me. My father was a Royal Air Force technician, he worked on radar installations. I didn't know him very well; he was never much of a feature in my life. He spent a lot of time away from home working. Mum on the other hand has always been there. Revelling in my successes and sucking her teeth at my failures.

We moved about a lot as a young armed forces family. My earliest recollections are from living at Winterberg in Germany. Winterberg is a winter holiday town. A ski resort with terrific facilities including a ski jump and a bobsleigh track. I learnt to ski at about the same time as I learnt to walk. During the day I spent a lot of time with the elderly German couple in the flat above ours, I knew them as Nan and Pop. They spoke no English, so I spoke with them in German. It was as natural to me as talking to my parents in English. I don't ever remember distinguishing between the two languages; it was just one big vocabulary to me.

After three years in Germany, we returned to the UK and settled down in Galmpton, a small rural Devonshire village. It was a picture book perfect, idyllic place. After we left Germany, I had no need to use my German, so like any skill that's not routinely practiced it was soon lost.

Entertaining myself with friends building campfires, climbing trees, and playing around the river Dart. None of these activities was approved of by mum, she was convinced that I wouldn't survive until teatime, let alone into adulthood. During one woodland playing session, me and my mates found a vine hanging out of a tree. All of us were fans of Tarzan, so there was clearly only one thing to be done. Getting hold of the vine, involved leaping out over a small ravine and grabbing it in mid-flight, then swinging heroically back.

I ran, I leapt, I caught the vine, my grip slipped, and I crashed down into the ravine. Me and gravity seem to have an ongoing issue. That would have been painful enough, but to add insult to injury the ground was covered in huge stinging nettles. They were bigger than I was. Being dressed in only shorts and a T-shirt the resulting mass of stings was really messy. When I arrived home, I looked like a plague victim. After a severe rollicking for my ape-man stupidity, mum painted me from head to toe in calamine lotion.

Summer holidays were great in Devon, the walk to the huge sandy beach at Broadsands was only about half an hour, it was the best place by far for a child to spend hot, sunny afternoons. I think mum took me and my sister to the beach so often, out of concern for what I would do if I was left to my own devices.

Being a Royal Air Force family, we moved home every few years, it was time to move on again, so we packed our belongings into a removal van and headed north for Yorkshire. Scarborough is a Victorian seaside town on North Yorkshire's east coast. In the winter it's bitterly cold, wet, and windy. In the summer it's packed with tourists. I loved the place as soon as we arrived.

We settled into our new home and a new school; things went along smoothly for a couple of years. During these years my interests were focussed on schoolboy engineering. I loved Meccano and building model aeroplanes from balsa wood and tissue paper. If I wanted something, the only way I was likely to get it was to make it myself. These hobbies kept me occupied most of the time, but I have always had a short attention span, if I'm not doing something that grabs my interest then I get bored. When I'm bored there's no telling what might happen.

It was at this time that my father who was still serving in the RAF was posted away to RAF Bishops Court in County Down, Northern Ireland. This was early in the 1970's and during the height of the troubles. For our family it was a worrying time. He was going to be away from us for two years.

Looking back, the apparently quiet Yorkshire village where we lived was far from a tranquil place. Fighting in the playground, on the bus or in the street was commonplace. When I went out with my mates, there was a good chance of getting into a scrape of some sort. Me and my mate were always into something. It started with campfires, then moved on to knives and bows and arrows. As our technological knowledge improved these morphed into explosives and guns.

Pleasant and polite I may have been, encumbered by scruples I wasn't. We were heading towards the local quarry with our latest weapon of choice. The plan was simple, we were going to make the biggest bang we could. Our improvised explosive device was a cocktail of disassembled fireworks and the petrol out of my mates' dad's lawnmower. We tucked our bomb under a rock, lit the fuse and retreated. The explosion was huge, it echoed around the quarry. Smoke and flames followed the rocks our explosives had propelled high into the Yorkshire sky. We were delighted with the success of our efforts as we sprinted into the woods, what a result, I was about eleven.

The Icarus Game

I've always known the difference between right and wrong. Applying this concept, that was forced on me by my parents and teachers was an altogether different thing. It seemed to be very restrictive and got in the way of a lot of fun. I'd tucked my airgun into the back of my jeans, as had my mate, and we headed into the local woods. This was a regular sport for us, we had done it hundreds of times before, we would wander into the woods and take pot shots at trees, stones and virtually anything else we found lying around. Tin cans were always fun, shooting holes in them was just a bit more exciting if they were balanced on my own, or my mates head.

We were knelt by a tree, shooting at a stone on the path, taking it in turns to make it jump progressively further away from us. There was a click and a phizz from the trunk of the tree between us. It was the unmistakeable sound of an airgun pellet, the telltale fresh scar in the tree's bark confirmed it, but it wasn't one of ours. We looked around, stood on the path behind us were two lads of about our age. One was holding an air pistol. The gun's barrel was broken, and he was feeling around in his pocket for another pellet.

My gun was loaded, so was my mates. We had the upper hand and we knew it. We turned and ran towards the other boys with our guns levelled at the armed kids face. By our standards his head was a huge target. We stopped a yard or two short of them, with my gun pointing directly into his right eye, I opened the dialogue. 'You're a crap shot.' I looked down at his gun, it was a Diana target pistol. I tucked my gun back into my belt. 'Gizza look.' I reached out my hand. He gave me his gun and I popped a pellet into the open breech and closed the barrel, took aim at a small stone on the path and squeezed the trigger. The stone jumped into the air. 'There's nothing wrong with that' I said as I handed it back to him. 'How did you miss us?' He said, he was running when he took his shot.

Tensions were reduced and it was clear the immediate threat had gone. This kid knew only too well that he still had two eyes, only because I'd decided not to take my revenge on him for shooting at me. Armed boy asked if he could see my gun. I took it out of my belt and passed it to him. 'It's a Webley, and it's still loaded' I told him. He pointed my gun straight at his friend's chest and pulled the trigger. Whack, unarmed boy clutched his chest and gasped for air. 'That's got a kick to it.' He observed.

We all watched curiously as a bloody bruise developed on unarmed boys' chest. I had no idea why he'd shot his friend and not me or my mate. Maybe he just didn't like him that much. More likely he just fancied shooting 'somebody' that day and he ruled out me and my mate because we were likely to turn into a bit of a handful. Out of the four of us in the woods that afternoon, three of us had guns. The only lad injured was the unarmed one.

It turned out that whilst my father was away, he was having an affair with a local Irish woman whom he subsequently married. Although I'd had very little contact with him over the preceding two years, this was in practical terms the end of my relationship with him. The breakdown of my parents' marriage thrust our family into a period of huge uncertainty. Another new home, new friends, new school, financial stress were just the start of it.

After my parents divorced, we moved from this 'sleepy, quiet' village onto a large, local council estate. This came as a shock for all of us, but we soon settled into our new house and school. It's fair to say that neither me nor my sister were model pupils. I don't recall attending any lessons on a Friday afternoon for the last year or two that I was at school, skiving was endemic. We are both independent thinkers. Rebellious according to our teachers.

Mum worked as a casual farm labourer to make ends meet. Out in the fields picking potatoes or brussels sprouts in the bitterest of weathers. She's a tough lady my mum. It was working on the farm where she met my stepdad, Chris.

The local Air Cadets was a regular diversion for me. This is a fantastic organisation that presented me with opportunities that would mould the rest of my adult life. It was during one summer camp at RAF Linton-on-Ouse in Yorkshire I had my first flight in a military aeroplane. An experience I still recall clearly some forty-odd years later.

I was one of a small group of excited teenage Air Cadets. We were sat in the briefing room contained within a wartime hut, alongside the aircraft dispersal. Stood in front of the blackboard in true aviation briefing style was an RAF squadron leader. He was straight out of 'Boys Own' magazine, resplendent in his RAF flying suit and sporting a fantastic moustache. He even spoke just like a character out of the Dam Busters. He told us in detail about the aircraft, the weather, and the various types of exercise we could elect to try. The whole room was captivated by this gentleman.

My turn came to fly, and with a parachute strapped to my backside I waddled out to the de Havilland Chipmunk waiting on the dispersal. Being helped to climb into the cockpit I was strapped into my seat by the ground crew, sitting on my parachute gave me a good view out of the windscreen. Putting on the headset I was talking directly to the same officer who had briefed us earlier about our flight and the aircraft.

'Well young man, what's it going to be.' 'Aero's (aerobatics), please sir.' I think this was one of the first occasions in my young life that somebody in authority had spoken to me as though my wishes actually counted.

We taxied out to the runway and took off. I was well and truly hooked on all thing's aeroplane related. During the entire flight I listened transfixed as the officer detailed what we were doing, how we were going to do it, explaining how the aeroplane worked. We did loops, rolls and stall turns for the whole of my half hour slot. On the way back to the airfield I even had a go on the controls myself. That was it, in my dream's aeroplanes were going to be part of my future.

The truth is, growing up on a North Yorkshire council estate is not the most inspirational of environments to start out life from. Petty crime, high rates of unemployment and low-level violence were daily realities. Options for a council house kid like me during the eighties were limited. I was surrounded at school and elsewhere by people who ensured my aspirations were maintained at a suitably low level. Career opportunities in a small seaside town were few and far between.

My school life had been undistinguished. I could see little reason at the time to put any effort into my studies, what would I do with a handful of GCE's. I was destined to join the ranks of factory fodder, churned out by our comprehensive system. I left school at sixteen with a handful of low-level qualifications. After a few labouring and factory jobs, a chance meeting with a friend's brother spurred me into looking beyond my immediate surroundings for a more invigorating career.

Dave had just completed his basic training with the Royal Marines, and it sounded a world apart from the factory drudgery I was employed in at the time. He reckoned I could never get selected. "You're under weight and puny" said the tough guy who had just collected his Green Beret. He had every right to feel superior. That was just the sort of challenge I needed. I went straight to the career's office and enlisted.

Joining the marines was delayed after I fell off my newly acquired moped and broke my ankle. After the crash I'd climbed back onto my Honda and ridden it to A&E. There my swollen ankle was x-rayed and plastered up. I then rode myself home, sat on the seat astride a pair of crutches.

A few months later, with a newly healed ankle, I stepped off the train at Exeter St David's station, to join a group of young men all heading for Lympstone.

Chapter 3

Lympstone.

Stepping off the train at CTCRM (Commando Training Centre Royal Marines) Lympstone with the muddy river Clyst estuary on one side of the railway lines and the assault course on the other was a moment of revelation. I looked across the grass up to the barrack blocks that I would be calling home for the next six months, I couldn't wait to get stuck in. Youthful exuberance was gushing through my veins. It was 1978 and this was my first time away from home.

Immediately we were rounded up by an NCO, taken to the accommodation block and allocated a bed space. This was my little patch of Devon and had to be kept immaculate. I very soon discovered that my idea of ship shape, and the training team's idea of spotless differed wildly. I worked at it and took my cues from the other men on the course. We all wanted this opportunity to work out for us. As soon as you arrive at Lympstone you are aware that you are trying to become part of something very special.

We were about to be undergoing the basic training of a Royal Marines Commando. This culminates in the award of the most prestigious insignia in the military world. The 'Green Beret' and 'Globe and Laurel'. To say this training was going to be tough was a massive understatement, it was, and still is brutal. Less than half the new recruits that enlist are expected to finish the course.

There were six men to a room and around thirty on the training troop. We were 131 troop. The other guys in my room were a very mixed bunch. Nev was in his twenties and from Norfolk. In the next bed was another Steve from Tyneside. Danny was from Wiltshire. Todd like me was from Yorkshire and Kev was from the Northeast. Job backgrounds covered everything from factory labourer, building labourer, working on a poultry farm artificially inseminating turkeys, and painting wheelbarrows.

At first basic training was very basic. Lots of running, sit-ups, squat thrusts. Daily marching, drill, and kit preparation. There was no free time at all. The standards were set high. From day one the pressure to maintain yourself and your kit in pristine condition was intense. Push-ups were the normal currency for mistakes. "Down and give me ten" was a phrase we were hearing a lot of. If you were lucky, you'd just be wearing a shirt, then ten press-ups took as many seconds. If you were unlucky, you would be carrying a kitbag on your back, then ten was a real struggle.

These are the fundamentals of any military training and lasted the first six weeks. We were then tested on the skills we had been drilled into learning and assessed whether we were fit to continue. Those who were not left the course along with those who elected to quit at this stage. Our numbers began to deplete.

We now spent less time in PT kit and more time in combat fatigues. It felt great not to stand out as raw 'Nods' anymore. The endless sessions in the gym, leaping over a vaulting horse or climbing ropes, were augmented with road runs and time on the assault course. I was light and fit at this time and loved the speed marches. I could go all day. I did struggle with the strength exercises though.

One of these involved getting into pairs, putting your partner and both sets of kit in a fireman's lift on your shoulders and running the length of the assault course in a prescribed time. I always ended up with a large muscular and very heavy partner. They had it easy with a racing snake like me on their shoulders.

Mud runs were a favourite punishment of the training team, and reserved for more serious derelictions of duty, I hated them. It usually involved wearing kit that had to be kept immaculately clean and running out onto the estuary at low tide. The sticky mud made moving incredibly hard work as it clawed its way up your legs, and it stank. Just for good measure a few sit-ups and press-ups would be introduced to increase the fatigue. This particularly special form of reprimand had a hidden sting in the tail. Turn up on parade the next morning looking like anything but a new pin, and you'd be doing it again at the end of the day. It was not uncommon to spend all night scrubbing, drying, and pressing your kit.

We spent a lot of time learning to shoot. The personal weapon issued at that time was the 7.62mm Self Loading Rifle (SLR). We became very well acquainted with this weapon and could literally strip, clean and reassemble it blindfolded. We spent a lot of time learning to point it straight.

We would practice endlessly controlling our breathing, aiming, and pulling the trigger with a penny balanced on the foresight. If the coin fell off you had snatched the trigger, and not squeezed it. Accuracy required concentration and a light touch. Your personal weapon was something you literally became attached to. It accompanied you everywhere. It could be reassuring, heavy and a lot of work to clean. Something of a mixed blessing.

Training with other weapons kept the learning curve steep, the SMG (Sub Machine Gun) and GPMG (General Purpose Machine Gun) being among them. The SMG was a small lightweight and extremely simple weapon, used for close quarter fighting.

I had my first near miss on the range with one of these guns. The trainee on the firing point to my left didn't cock his weapon fully when ordered to. This resulted in the working parts and the attached firing pin inadvertently flying forwards, collecting a round from the magazine and discharging it. The bullet passed in front of my eyes missing me by inches. I felt the breeze from it quite literally.

The response from the training team was instant and decisive. The trainee was disarmed and felled to the ground in one movement. He then had the undesirability of a 'negligent discharge' whispered into his ear in a way that he was unlikely to ever forget.

One of the exercises that I really excelled at was close quarter fighting, I've always quite enjoyed a scrap. On this occasion it was bayonet practice. We took on straw stuffed sandbags, in every conceivable situation. I found this to be the best cure for stress and pent-up teenage angst available anywhere. Run flat out, scream 'till your lungs burst and use all your body weight to drive the bayonet blade up to the hilt into your enemy. Twist it round, pull it out, and then stab the fucker again.

Some people were a bit squeamish about the idea, but at the time I felt great about it. Just thinking back on the process some forty odd years later, still makes me look back to those simpler days and smile. The trainer on the practice ground pointed me out to the rest of the training team and said, "watch out for that vicious little bastard.". I had really thrown myself into it, and was proud that my efforts stood out in such accomplished company.

When we weren't in CTCRM training, we would be in the wilderness of Woodbury Common, or on Dartmoor learning how to look after ourselves in inhospitable surroundings. You had to be able to take care of the basics, food, water, shelter, navigation, first aid and camouflage wherever you found yourself. The Marines specialise in urban, jungle, arctic and amphibious warfare, so there is a lifetime's worth of learning to do, if that's your chosen career.

The exercise we were engaged in was on Dartmoor, it was a tactical night navigation exercise. Speed marching in small teams of four or five from 'a to b', in the dark, to coordinates on a map. Trying our best to evade capture by the training team, whilst avoiding injury on the rough terrain. The main incentive for all of us was the promise of a square meal on successful completion of the exercise.

Eventually the troop was reunited at the bivvy site, having reached the end of the night march. It was in an isolated wooded area. One of the training team appeared with a flapping chicken in his hand and gathered the troop around. He then demonstrated how to kill and prepare dinner. No special equipment needed. Encouraging words of wisdom like, 'This is how you wring its neck, then ram your hand up its arse and pull its guts out' were echoing around the wood that evening. It's fair to say that Michelin Stars were not going to be awarded for this meal.

The trainers then appeared with a wriggling canvass sack and emptied its contents onto the ground. This led to a chaotic, hilarious few minutes of mayhem, with a mass of hungry recruits chasing their dinner around the woods. The combined commotion of free running would be marines in amongst a flock of squawking chickens had to be seen to be believed.

Soon the woods quietened down, and the sweet smell of chicken cooked a dozen different ways on hexy burners wafted through the air. There's something very satisfying about catching and preparing your dinner quite literally from scratch.

A vital part of any organizations training program, is to instil in its new starters a clear sense of the development and history of that establishment, and what career paths may become available to its members as their service progresses. The marines have a wide range of specializations, but the top of the pile must be the SBS, the Special Boat Service. These are a remarkable and very select group of people.

As a sixteen-year-old, the exploits of this cadre were truly astounding to me, what's more we got to spend a week in their company as part of our basic training. This involved lectures about general tactics and some specialist techniques they had pioneered over the years. Lots of stories describing courageous and innovative actions the unit had been involved in. Along with descriptions of the mass of decorations the squadron had fought for and won. We were also able to talk freely with serving members. Mind-blowing doesn't begin to describe this elite unit.

The highlight of the week on the south coast for me was a full-blown night raid on an island in a vast natural harbour. The troop was briefed on our objective, kitted out in light fighting order and joined by our section commanders. We climbed aboard a fleet of rigid raider landing craft. A lightweight open speedboat powered by a couple of big outboard motors. The Cox was wearing night vision goggles and stood behind the helm. The members of the unit were crouched down in our positions along either side of the boat. We then headed off at full throttle across the smooth waters of the bay. The water and wind rushed past, and the engines roared as the tight group of rigid raiders tore across the darkness in formation towards our target. With the assistance of a lot of blank ammunition and thunder flashes the raid was successful. Mission completed, and we returned exhausted but elated to our billet.

Completing these exercises marked the end of the first phase of our training and we were winding down for the mid-course break. Two weeks home leave. We continued with the regular drill and fitness training of course, no slacking off there. During one of the final sessions on the assault course, I landed a jump awkwardly. The pain was instant and severe. My ankle was broken, again. How ridiculous, after weeks of hard graft such a small incident brought my aspirations of becoming a Royal Marine to an instant impasse. I was sent to the medical centre where the injury was x-rayed and confirmed as a fracture. I was to go home on leave, with my leg plastered up, again.

Before leaving Lympstone on leave, I talked to the training team and was given a choice. Take it easy for a few months to allow my ankle to heal up, then join the next intake, to start my training again from the beginning. Alternatively, call it a day and return to civvy street. I went home to my parents with a lot to think about, returning to Lympstone two weeks later. After a lot of soul searching, I had decided to call it a day. This was the second time inside a year I'd broken my ankle and felt it was going to be a weakness for me for the foreseeable future. I spent a couple of days 'clearing'. This involved handing back all my kit and a few interviews with the obligatory form filling. Then with my travel warrant in hand I climbed aboard the train back home to Scarborough.

This all to brief experience of independence had sparked something in me. I knew I wasn't cut out to follow a conventional career path. Keep your nose clean, suck up to the boss, get the odd promotion, scraps from the table. This was not going to be my way through life. I didn't know at this time what was in store for me, but I was certain that my adventures had only just started.

Chapter 4

Between Jobs.

Returning to the red brick council estate in Scarborough, with my leg in plaster was a real disappointment. But the cast came off after a few weeks and I slipped back into my old habits. It was like the previous couple of months had never happened. Old friendships and acquaintances were rekindled. Life returned to a round of hanging out with mates, punctuated by occasional Friday and Saturday night highlights.

Finding myself a job that would allow my leg to heal, nothing too physical, proved easy. It was in the local abattoir. I was working as a clerk in the office preparing the payment forms for the farmers who were bringing their livestock to be slaughtered. This job proved very popular with my family. I would go into work with my sandwiches in a Tupperware box and come home with that same box filled with cut price pork chops or steak.

The meat that was prepared in the abattoir, would be checked by a government ministry inspector for quality and graded accordingly. This grading would govern the level of payments to the farmer, and the price at which it was sold to the local butchers, restaurants, and hotels.

The Slaughtermen and butchers were a very genial group, but like all manual workers they liked a laugh and a practical joke. To be considered humane, the smaller animals like pork pigs and lambs that were slaughtered, first had to be stunned using an electric shock before they were dispatched. The shock was administered using an instrument like a large pair of tongs with electrodes on one end, and insulated handles with a switch on the other. The electrodes went either side of the animal's head where a burst of high voltage left the creature senseless prior to slaughter.

The slaughterhouse was always awash with water, and the different areas separated with steel railings, just what you need when you are playing with high voltage electrical currents. Anybody seen leaning on the railings or worse, sitting on them could be certain that the man with the stunner would notice them, then apply the electrodes to the rails. An electric shock through the seat of your pants will elicit a hilarious result for everybody, except the unfortunate victim, who would leap into the air yelling obscenities. I quickly became very wary of my workmates.

Spring was approaching, and the daily nine to five in the office was starting to feel very hum drum. I felt fully fit again and needed to spread my wings. My long-standing enthusiasm for aeroplanes inevitably drew me towards the Royal Air Force careers office. I made enquiries about the opportunities the RAF had to offer. I've always tinkered with mechanical things so that was the direction I wanted to pursue.

The recruitment officer told me that my lack of academic qualifications was an issue. But it could be overcome if I passed the Air Forces own entrance exams. The time I'd spent in the Air Cadets also counted heavily in my favour. I sat tests in mathematics, mechanics, logical reasoning, English, and a personality profile type exam. He also suggested that finding a job with a technical aspect would help my cause. By this time my leg was fully healed, but I was still sent for a series of additional medical checks on it, to be sure.

I went back to the abattoir and worked my notice. Within a week I was working in one of the amusement arcades on the foreshore. I was employed to repair the slot machines and oversee what was going on in the amusement arcade around me, I learned a lot about electrics, gambling, and people. Most punters using the arcade simply enjoyed a flutter on the slot machines, some were there for less honest reasons.

They wanted to steal the money from within the machines. If you want to catch dishonest people, fiddling the arcade slot machines, then you need to know all about the scams and tactics the crooked visitors are likely to use. The guys I was working with had seen most of them, they even dreamt up a few ruses of their own. It's amazing what can be done with a little technical knowledge and the simplest of equipment. As the regular offenders were well known to the arcade staff, we kept a look out for them. If they came in, I'd make a point of standing next to them and engage them in some pointless chat. They didn't have time for this and needed privacy for their plans to work, so they would usually move on.

The sea front attracts all kinds of folk, from holidaying families, works outings, stag and hen parties, destitute drunks, and outright criminals. I met them all. The job was fun and sometimes a bit scary. Try explaining to a bunch of drunks at chucking out time, that tipping a slot machine upside-down to get at the cash inside, is the worst idea they've come up with so far that day. It takes a certain amount of cockiness.

One of my most enduring passions has been motorbikes. I've always ridden them, tinkered with them and lusted after them. So, moving back to Scarborough had one huge benefit, Oliver's Mount racing circuit. This is a brilliant, technical road racing circuit, full of tight corners and steep hills. As a teenager I regularly jumped over the fence into this place to watch my boyhood hero's, Barry Sheene, Giacomo Agostini, and a host of other international stars that all raced there. In more recent times I've bought a ticket and followed the current road racers.

Oliver's Mount continues to be exciting and challenging, and still attracts the world's best riders.

When racing was not taking place, the track is a public road. So, all the local kids knew the circuit as well as the riders. They would compare their latest bike against the quickest in the world. A cat and mouse game was regularly played out between the local police and exuberant teenagers. Thirty miles an hour on a racetrack is never going to catch on.

I may have been the motorbike nut, but mum was the families football fan. As a lifelong supporter of West Ham, she made Alf Garnett look non-committal and tame. Living in Yorkshire, regular trips to Upton Park were clearly out of the question. Instead, she was a long-time, passionate season ticket holder at Scarborough FC. Seeing my sixty-year-old mum tearing into players for dirty tackles or ripping into the referee for being a totally biased, short sighted little fascist, was something to behold. Even after a wayward shot at goal hit her on the head and laid her out cold, she was back on the touchline the

following Saturday. She was sent a bunch of flowers from the player and featured in the local paper for that one.

Although I was living with my friends and family, I still felt trapped in my own familiar surroundings, I had a real desire to get away from the constraints of living with my parents. Love them as I do, home life still felt claustrophobic. As time passed the desire to get out, to live my own life grew in intensity. I had been hanging about with my old school mates, their ambition seemed limited, to say the least. The general attitude among my friends around the estate at the time was, 'I'm going to find a job, join the union and go on strike. That'll be mint.' It really wasn't for me.

During the sixties there was a lot of talk among the stars of the day about emancipation, free love, and drugs, which led to a lot of great music. The seventies, however, was an era when more equality was starting to be demanded by working people. It became a time of immense social change. I'd grown up watching Arthur Scargill and other union leaders stirring up discontentment among the massed ranks of the labour force. This was a good time for union leaders, there was a groundswell of bitterness in the workplace.

Working people in all industries saw their bosses amassing huge wealth, whilst they were working for what they felt were subsistence wages. The politicians were from equally privileged, well-educated stock as the leaders of industry. It seemed that the wealthy few were preoccupied arguing the toss about the inequality of life amongst themselves, while normal hard-working people paid their taxes and picked up the bill.

Step in the unions, these organisations have huge pots of money, paid in by their members subscriptions. All the leaders had to do, was get themselves on the telly, banging the downtrodden worker's drum.

They then had all they needed to justify bottomless expenses accounts, and a fat cat salary, just like the other protagonists in the labour wars of the seventies and eighties. Battles were fought between the unions and the management on picket lines up and down the country. This came to a head in the early eighties when King Arthur and the miners took on Maggie Thatcher's government.

This dispute was verging on civil war, the unions against the state. They simply could not be allowed to win, if the government wanted to remain in power. Along with the rest of my generation I watched from the side-lines, knowing the outcome, one way or another was going to be seismic. I was not a fan of socialism as a kid and I'm still not.

The day I was looking forward to eventually came, a letter arrived on Her Majesties Service, I had been accepted into the Royal Air Force, to train as an 'Aircraft Technician - Airframes'. I was to report for basic training at RAF Swinderby in Lincolnshire during August 1980.

Arriving at Swinderby was reminiscent of turning up at Lympstone. The attitudes, sounds, smells, and routine were much the same. I felt in familiar surroundings and had no trouble at all slotting straight in. For a few recruits it was their first time away from home, but we were all in the same boat, with the same desire to succeed. The training staff were very encouraging and gave all the help they could to get us into shape. With regular kit preparation, lectures about the formation and history of the Air Force, and lots of marching. Most of the training flight were on the passing out parade six weeks later.

After passing out (graduating) from Swinderby, I went to RAF Halton, in Buckinghamshire for nine months of trade training. This was a very different environment. There was still the usual kit inspections and morning parades, but there was a lot more fascinating stuff to learn.

Chapter 5

Coningsby.

The Royal Air Force took up twelve years of my life. I hadn't forgotten the physicality of serving in the Marines, but the Air Force was an altogether different environment in which to work and live. It was going to provide plenty of challenges of its own special variety. Six weeks square bashing in Lincolnshire and nine months trade training as an Airframe Technician took care of the first year.

Trade training at RAF Halton in Buckinghamshire, was done along the same lines as technical college. The other trainees on the course were a mixed group with all sorts of different backgrounds. This time though, it was clear that a more specific selection criteria had been used.

A lot of the course members had college backgrounds or had done other technical training. I felt distinctly behind the curve. The course consisted of a mixture of lessons in the classroom, practical experience in the workshop, long hours of self-study and working on the assortment of training rigs and former service aircraft that were available at the school.

This was broken up with regular physical activities, in the gymnasium, swimming pool or on the football or rugby pitch. My intake, AAD78 had developed a very good team spirit, and rarely lost on the sports field against the other trainees. One exception was a hockey match against the girls of the WRAF, we played like gentlemen and the girls fought like cats. You can't win them all. Friday and Saturday nights tended to be intense times too.

Young men with a lot of energy looking for a release, mixed with a skin full of beer is always going to be messy. I lost count of the number of times we had to re-assemble the furniture in our barrack room after a weekend of late-night drunken games.

Not all nights were intoxicated and riotous. One quiet night drinking in the NAAFI bar was made more interesting, when we noticed we had company. The area by our table was filling up with cockroaches. This provided an opportunity for amusement, so we started racing them up the wall by chasing them with cigarette lighters. Us, betting coppers and cheering on our roach, attracted the attention of the bar manager. He was apparently more concerned for the welfare of his resident invertebrates than the hygiene of his bar.

We pointed out his managerial shortcomings, just before we were invited to leave. We were not the only ones to feel he lacked the ability to run a bar, because he was soon replaced, and equilibrium was restored.

Obviously, there was also a military aspect to RAF training. Regular kit inspections and marching to and from classes reminded you where you were. So, did the occasional night in the mess scrubbing pans or pealing spuds if you happened to transgress the many rules, and come to the attention of the Disciplinary Staff. At least I wasn't an apprentice and didn't have to fall in behind the regimental goat and drum for the march to work.

The Icarus Game

One of the more memorable highlights from my training was the annual RAF Halton show. The station open day. Whilst all my colleagues were detailed to organise car parks or sell entrance tickets, I was designated as the VIP gofer. This was to involve ensuring that the VIP guests were fed and watered all day, and in the right place at the right time. I got a lot of stick from my mates. It was going to be a lousy job, shepherding a bunch of old duffers around as their peon for the day. My outlook on the duties I'd been given improved immeasurably when I met my VIP group on the morning of the show. It was 'Hot Gossip', the exotic dance troupe from the Kenny Everett TV show. I was the most enthusiastic gofer the Air Force had ever produced.

After completing my 'Trade Training' my first posting was to RAF Coningsby, where I was working in the 'Aircraft Servicing Flight' hangar. This was a very steady job, interspersed with moments of high drama. For the most part though, steady. As a section we were responsible for carrying out routine servicing on McDonnell Douglas F-4 Phantom II aircraft, operated by 228 Operational Conversion Unit and 29 Squadron. It would take about a month to service each aircraft and there were several teams working full time. Normally, there would be three or four aeroplanes at various stages of being dismantled or reassembled in the hangar.

Although I had completed my trade training, I was still heavily dependent on the more experienced guys for guidance on how to do the job properly. There is no substitute for experience and that takes time to acquire. Technicians that worked on the Phantom were commonly known as 'Phantom Phixers'. Replacing F's with PH's was a common thread throughout the Phantom world. Sneaking it onto the job sheets was a game we all played, a typical entry would look something like; 'Component inspected and found to be phuqued'. Sometimes they got past the 'tech records' guys, but mostly not.

One sound nobody wanted to hear on an RAF station is the crash alarm. The first time I heard it I didn't know what it was, I did know something serious was happening. The guys in the hangar moved very quickly. Armed with all the safety equipment we could muster, fire extinguishers, tractor, towing arm, trolleys and jacking equipment we all made our way out onto the dispersal, ready to give whatever assistance the station fire and medical sections needed.

The stricken aircraft was one of our stations Phantom's. It was flying around the circuit with the nose undercarriage leg clearly stuck in the retracted state, both main wheels were down. This situation was going to give the pilot plenty to think about. He had quite a lot of externally mounted stores to consider. The most significant was the SUU cannon (a huge machine gun) under the forward fuselage. After a few circuits this was jettisoned onto the airfield in a cloud of dirt and turf. Rather closer to the ATC tower than the controllers would have been comfortable with.

After some practice approaches, the pilot made a lovely landing and gently lowered the nosecone of the aircraft onto the tarmac. They slid to a halt on the runway. The pilot and the navigator very coolly stepped out of the cockpit, climbed into a waiting minibus, and rode back to the squadron for a debrief. We were left to recover the wreckage back to the hangar for an engineering investigation and repair.

At first, I lived in the barrack block on base as a single airman. During the weekday evenings, I would enjoy running in the local lanes, or working out in the gym. At weekends I had a lively social life out with my mates or visiting my then girlfriend at home in Scarborough.

At the time I only had a motorcycle driving licence and was starting to realise that travelling around the country on my bike in all weathers was not very convenient. Arriving everywhere wet and cold is not ideal. I resolved this issue by buying a Reliant Robin three-wheeler which I could drive on my bike licence. My 'Tupperware Tricycle', equipped with a loud stereo, spotlights and a fluffy pig hanging from the mirror was conspicuous. Once the piss-taking died down, I had loads of fun in this little car.

Friday lunchtime was regularly spent in a local pub, nobody wanted to drive, so even my plastic pig had its attraction. Four or five inebriated mates, squeezed in and rocking the car as we drove back to base, wasn't an unusual sight in that part of Lincolnshire at the time.

Socializing was a big part of my life, being in the Air Force sometimes it's easy to isolate yourself within the camp perimeter fence. My sister lived in Mansfield with her coalminer partner, Tony. I would regularly drive over to their place for weekends. Tony was about the same age as me and from a large and very boisterous family, totally different to my own. He was also physically large, hairy, and loud, especially with a few pints in him. Tony was a good singer and talented guitar player, he was also a bit of a lad, occasionally with a short fuse. We often sought out bars around Mansfield that had folk nights or live music playing.

On this Saturday night, we were drifting from pub to pub, occasionally bumping into people Tony knew. A pint and a laugh was all we were looking for. As the evening drew on, we were getting drunker, and louder. I'm not sure who said what to who, but we managed to attract the attention of another group of drinkers, and they had taken a real disliking to me and Tony. There was four of them and two of us. They caught Tony's eye and in predictable fashion he was straight in the biggest guy's face. Nose to nose, F'in' and blindin'.

It wasn't the first time Tony had done this to me, and by the time he shouted, "You ha' that twat and I'll sort out these three." I had already worked out the odds were heavily against a good outcome. I grabbed Tony's collar and dragged him backwards a couple of steps, then I made short work of clearing the bar, and heading out of the pub into the back yard. A look over my shoulder, confirmed that Tony had rethought the idea of battering the guys in the bar, and was hot on my heals.

As I leapt from a pile of crates and barrels, over the yard wall, I could see the broken glass embedded in the mortar on top of the brickwork. Passing dangerously close to castrating me. I looked to my left and saw Tony jump onto an iron double gate with a spiky top, as he clung to it, it swung open and he sprawled headlong onto the wasteland at the back of the pub. We both ran flat out from a losing situation (Thirty odd years later Tony still reckons we could have won.) and laughed all the way to the next pub.

One freezing winters weekend I had driven home to Scarborough to visit my parents and girlfriend. One of the lads in the hangar asked for a lift as far as Hull. The weather forecast was horrible, so we arranged a lunchtime pickup on the Sunday, to allow plenty of time to get back to work. As I left my parents' house, with my bag of freshly laundered kit in the boot of 'The Pig', it started snowing, on the way to Hull it snowed harder.

Doug emerged from his house with his kit bag and a shovel. As we travelled south across the Humber bridge the roads got worse. Trying to find a passable route took us miles out of our way, until finally further progress, even with Doug's shovel became impossible. There were cars strewn everywhere in the deep snowdrifts.

We'd been driving all afternoon and into the evening. As luck would have it, we had ground to a standstill in a pub car park, just outside Lincoln. The landlord was a star. He sorted us out with something to eat and a beer. He even allowed us to use his spare room for the night rather than sleeping in the car. In the morning we thanked our hospitable host and followed the snowplough into Lincoln. From there we made our way back to the airbase.

We strolled into the hangar about an hour late for work, but otherwise none the worse for our extended journey. The Flight Sergeant (hangar manager) saw us wander in late and asked where we had been. After listening to our explanation, he looked flabbergasted and all he could say was, " You did that in a plastic pig!!".

The following spring, I married Tracy and we moved into the station married quarters near to the camp. We were young, broke and had no idea how to set up home. Our neighbours Dick and Lynn were a bit older than us and had been married for several years. They gave us a lot of good advice in the early days. Dick worked in the station armoury, and like most people I have met who work with high explosives, he was completely potty. He loved nothing better than a good night out with the boys talking about aeroplanes, beer, and bombs.

We arrived home from work at the same time one evening. As we walked to our respective front doors, Dick invited me along on a brewery trip, arranged by the guys that he worked with in the bomb dump. Batemans at Wainfleet have some very good beer he explained with a broad grin.

The coach was soon filled with a happy crowd of blokes with one thing on their collective mind, getting out of their collective minds. The bus ride to Wainfleet lasted a couple of pints, then we headed for the nearest pub. As was traditional the guys decided to stick a squadron zap (self-adhesive sticker) somewhere conspicuous and difficult to remove in the bar. The favoured place was in the middle of the ceiling. After a couple of subtle, quiet, and unsuccessful tries, a more team-oriented method had to be adopted. A human pyramid was the answer. We got three people high, not a bad effort considering the amount of 'Triple XB' we had consumed. The zap was applied to the ceiling and signed with a size ten boot print.

The Icarus Game

The whole mass of bodies then collapsed in a giggling heap in the middle of the pub. By this time the landlord had lost his sense of humour, and we were invited to drink elsewhere. This was not the first or the last time I've been turfed out of a pub. We took our bruises and headed for the brewery. I like breweries and Batemans is a good one. Educational, informative, and of course, it has a well-stocked bar. What more could you want.

By the time we got back on the coach, our collective mission had been accomplished. A couple more pints, a bit of team singing, some dirty jokes and we were back home. I staggered off the coach, and followed the chap in front of me who was wearing a flat cap. As he walked past the bus, an arm was thrust out of the window, and the hand at the end of it snatched the cap from the man's head. He reacted immediately by grabbing the offending wrist and hauling himself off the ground, planting his feet on the side of the coach. As the bus drove off the chaos grew louder. I watched as I continued to walk towards home. I was drunk, distracted by the acrobatics being performed on the side of the coach, and in hysterics, I walked face first straight into a lamp post. Dick picked me up and helped me home. I woke up the next day with a pounding hangover, assorted cuts and bruises and a cracking shiner. Her Ladyship was not impressed. Altogether a good night out with the boys.

A less pleasant duty of being an Air Force aircraft technician comes around from time to time. If an aeroplane crashes, the personnel at the nearest airbase are called out to secure the crash site and collect up the wreckage. This is a painstaking job, and usually done in filthy weather and mud. It is made a lot less pleasant, if the remains of the crew are known to be intermingled with the scrap metal. All aircraft and body parts must be collected and sorted. It can be grizzly.

Reluctantly, I was involved in a number of these jobs during my time in the RAF. I found the best distraction, against the fear of finding something meaty in the search for bits, was to be callous and take the piss as much as possible. Some people find this approach offensive, but it works for me. I spent more time than I like to think about trudging around muddy fields in wellies and rubber gloves, carrying a bin bag.

After a couple of years at Coningsby I was starting to get itchy feet. The guys that I worked with came and went. They all had one thing in common, they had been around a bit. Stories of adventures in different parts of the country or even far-flung exotic places around the world percolated the crew room. I was starting to feel there was a big world out there waiting to be discovered, so it was time for a change. The Phantom was a phantastic but old aircraft, that was reaching the end of its service life. In 1983 the Panavia Tornado GR 1 was fresh off the BAE (British Aerospace) production line and was cutting edge technology.

The first time that I saw one in the flesh, it was a lot less than impressive. A new trainer variant arrived in the circuit at Coningsby. Those of us who were interested went outside to watch it being thrown around the skies above the base. Wings forward, wings back. Right way up, upside down. A couple of touch 'n goes, and it was time for the pilots to land for a brew and to swap heroic stories in the mess.

The Icarus Game

The aircraft was on 'short finals when the ATC officer lent out of the window and fired a red flare, presumably augmented with instructions on the radio. He was on the ball, but the pilots weren't. We found out later that they were a German and an Italian. One an instructor, one a student. They had forgotten to lower the undercarriage. By the time they realised, the aircraft had landed on its underside and was grinding away its belly on the tarmac.

The remedy they decided upon was to pull back on the stick and apply maximum power in reheat. This livened things up, digging the leading edges of the tailerons into the surface of the tarmac and accelerating down the runway. Other than breaking the land speed ploughing record, this strategy did little useful. They ground to a halt in a cloud of dust and gravel at the end of the runway. Red faces all round. The station engineering officer had some head scratching to do. He needed to work out how he could remove this very expensive asset, that was blocking the runway, without further damage to the aircraft and in as short a time as possible.

Chapter 6

Marham.

After submitting my application, I was lucky to be accepted for a position on this shiny new wonder jet. Our next posting was going to be RAF Marham in Norfolk. A six-week course at RAF Cottesmore, explained the witchcraft involved in making this machine work. Then me and Tracy moved to our new base.

Working in the Tornado Aircraft Servicing Flight, (TASF). I was on semi-familiar ground. The learning started again. The organisation was similar, with several teams of riggers carrying out various levels of routine servicing around the hangar. The big difference I hadn't expected was in the social life. Coningsby had been good but Marham took it up a notch. We had a very active social committee who organised all kinds of events. Leaving drinks, family BBQ's, treasure hunts and the like. It was really positive to get everybody socialising together. A feeling of community is a particularly important part of service life, where separation is frequently par for the course.

We soon settled into our new environment and got to know our neighbours, and colleagues at work. Living next door, was a couple who had just returned from a three year long overseas tour at RAF Bruggen in Germany. Tommy and Pam had clearly enjoyed their time out there and talked about it a lot. This started me thinking about what I would like for our next move.

Although this wasn't going to happen for a couple of years, it does no harm to work on a plan.

Chatting on the doorstep with Tommy, he asked a favour. He owned a small river boat that he had brought back with him from Germany. It was moored on the River Great Ouse locally. He wanted a hand to get the boat out of the water and onto its trailer. Tommy had sold it and needed to arrange delivery to its new owner. That sounded fun so of course I jumped at the chance to help him.

Saturday lunchtime we set off in Tommy's car, with the trailer to where the boat was moored. I would navigate the boat a couple of miles down the river to a slipway just outside Ely, where we would meet up, get the boat out of the river and onto the trailer. The boat was a two-berth cabin cruiser with an oversized outboard motor. A very tidy outfit. After a brief explanation of the controls, I set off down the river with the engine just ticking over. Tommy set off with his car and trailer. A few miles outside Ely I saw Tommy standing on a bridge waving, so I pulled into the riverbank and picked him up. He wanted one last drive of his boat before he parted with it. He had parked his car on the Quayside in Ely a short distance from the slipway.

With Tommy at the controls, we cruised into Ely city centre. We needed to moor up, so that Tommy could take his car to the slipway. I stood on the front of the boat with the mooring rope in my hand. We looked cool, I thought. I was just about to leap ashore and secure the boat when Tommy hit a partially submerged wooden mooring post. The boat stopped immediately. I didn't.

I shot forwards off the front of the boat and in finest 'Looney Tunes' fashion gravity kicked in and I dropped feet first into deep water, just a few feet from a large crowd of onlookers. I was completely submerged in the freezing river. Spluttering as I surfaced, I swam around to the rear of the boat, and climbed back aboard. Tommy was in fits of laughter and my cursing at him just made him laugh louder. The crowd on the Quayside joined in. I retook my position on the front of the boat and took a dripping, soggy bow towards my adoring audience.

We arrived home, with me travelling in the boat on the trailer. I wasn't allowed in the car because I was still soaked, and Tommy valued his upholstery. Tracy took one look at me, and yet again rolled her eyes.

Although the work in TASF was steady, there were occasions when there was nothing much to do. In one corner of the hangar was the 'station Christmas tree'. This was how we referred to one of the prototype Tornado's that had been stripped for spare parts and was in a very sorry state. I was sat on the tailplane idling away a bit of time, either refitting or removing some component, and was in no hurry to finish the job.

From where I was sitting, I had a clear view of the hydraulic services pit in the hangar floor just to the side of the aircraft nose. These pits contained large reels with rubber hoses, through which hydraulic oil was pumped at very high pressure, around four thousand PSI (270 bar). The hoses would be pulled out and connected to a control rig, which in turn was connected to the aircraft's hydraulic systems, to allow testing of the various aircraft controls that they powered.

One of these hoses had been leaking and the pit was flooded in about a foot of hydraulic fluid. The man from the PSA (Property

Services Agency) was in the pit trying to stop the leak. I was watching out of the corner of my eye as he winched the cable drums out of the pit, then carried on working with a large stilson. Suddenly there was a loud, sharp crack and a cast-brass pipework fitting, weighing a couple of kilograms, shot out of the pit and went straight through the corrugated steel roof of the hangar. This was immediately followed by a plume of purple hydraulic fluid (OM15). This plume turned into a large cloud in the corner of the hangar and started raining down on me and the plane I was sitting on.

Slithering down from my perch on the tailplane, I skidded across the floor towards the pit. I genuinely thought I was going to find a decapitated corpse in the bottom of it. Instead, a very pale workman was staring up at me through oil-soaked eyeballs. By the time I'd grabbed him and started hauling him out, some of the other guys had dashed to the scene and were helping. He was very lucky to survive unscathed, just a moments carelessness was to blame. He hadn't depressurised the pipework before he started working on it.

Most of the time maintaining Tornado's was a routine matter, very much an eight 'til five business. Just occasionally an opportunity arose to break the routine. A notice came around the hangar, offering places for some of us to join 617 Squadron on their next operational detachment to RAF Bruggen in Germany. My name went straight on the list.

Squadron technicians are divided into two basic groups, liney's and rect's. Liney's or more accurately 'Flight Line Mechanics' are the guys who prepare the aircraft for flight, check the oils and gasses. Make sure there's a ground-power-set connected, stand on the end of the headset during start up and shutdown, marshal aircraft on and off stand, all that sort of thing. The rect's teams or 'Flight Line Rectifications' Teams are constituted of the various tradesmen, who carry out routine maintenance and repairs as they are needed. Typically, there are airframes, engines, electrical, avionics and weapons teams.

Although there is some interchange these labels basically define your role on the squadron.

I was assigned to one of the airframes rect's teams. We met up on the 617 Squadron site at Marham, early in the morning. The first job was to load the tools, spares, and equipment we were going to need into the waiting trucks and vans. I was travelling in a minibus, with some of the guys I would be working with over the next couple of weeks. We had plenty of time to get acquainted, the drive from Norfolk to Monchengladbach was a long one. We arrived with the rest of the ground crew at Bruggen a day or two before the aircraft and set up the site. At this time RAFG was a tax-free haven, and once the work was done, we soon found a bar to quench our thirst in. With beer and cigarettes at a fraction of UK prices there was no excuse not to indulge.

We were young and equipped with fully functioning livers. Hangovers lasted until the fried breakfast and mug of tea at first light. That cured all known ills. After a week of work, things had gone well. We had kept the aircraft serviceable, and the flight crew had hit all their targets. Saturday night came, and we went out in a series of small groups to paint the town. The centre of Monchengladbach was known as the street of a thousand bars.

The Icarus Game

This was quite an exaggeration, there couldn't have been more than two or three hundred. We tried all the loudest ones.

By the small hours of the morning, we had drunk our way back to the local town, Elmpt. Just a short walk from the camp gates and settled into the only bar still open that welcomed inebriated servicemen. Piggalle, was the local brothel, not something I had experienced before. I was amazed at the brazenness of the girls, they sat at the bar and were very direct in offering their services. The price list was always to hand and graphic, detailed explanations of the attractions on offer were intended to clinch the deal.

This was my first time in a brothel, so I grabbed a beer and let the old hands lead the way. The bar was a comfortable relaxed place, with sofas and comfy chairs arranged around a TV, playing porn movies. There was no doubt what the business of this establishment was.

One of the younger lads in our group was fresh faced, full of alcohol fired bravado and happy to 'give it a go'. The Chief 'our boss' went to work. His German was passable, and he convinced the hostess he was talking to, that our man was a virgin, therefore he was not going to take too much effort to sort out. Better grounds for a discount had never been put to the woman.

She was a sporting girl, so instead of arguing over the price, she fetched the ice bucket off the bar and suggested a whip round. We all chipped in. When the ice bucket returned to our madam, she emptied it on the table. A few coins some nuts and bolts and a stick of chewing gum were apparently not considered sufficiently legal tender for her services. Not for the last time I was faced with a furious group of deeply offended women, howling like Germanic banshees.

We gulped down our drinks and tumbled, giggling from the bar into the street. A couple of the boys had the presence of mind to help themselves to the ice bucket and the ornate wooden coat stand by the door on their way out. This didn't go down at all well, and we were chased through the town by a group of noisy, scantily clad women and an irate Turkish barman. On Monday morning our hard-won trophies were taking pride of place in the crew room.

Ours was not the only story doing the rounds of the squadron that Monday morning. Another group of our squadron revellers had crossed the border into the Dutch town of Roermond. After a similarly boozy night, one of their number had climbed to the top of a construction crane, and then made his way out to the end of the boom. Standing a hundred feet above the ground, waving his t-shirt above his head, and calling to the passers-by in Welsh, Bry was having a great time. When his mates eventually convinced him to return to earth, the waiting Dutch police picked them all up. The Politie were typically cool and returned Bry and his friends to the camp gates.

Squadron detachments embodied the work hard, play hard attitude of the time. The days were long. The pressure was constant. The play intense. Great fun if you're young and can keep up the pace.

As well as doing the job you are trained for, the Air Force has other tasks it requires its servicemen to do. One of these is 'The Section Duty Airman'. This came around once a year or so, and meant that you were the hangar runner, and odd job person for the week. It generally involved early starts, opening the hangar

The Icarus Game

and late finishes, locking up on a night. During the day you manned the front desk, answering the phone and did any fetching and carrying that was needed. On this occasion the duty airman was my mate, Andy.

'The Boss' had given him a bin bag full of restricted waste documents to dispose of. This was a tedious job and meant going to the station incinerator. Feeding endless sheets of paper into the flames, one at a time to ensure they were thoroughly destroyed. It regularly took an hour or two to do the task properly. Andy had a brainwave, he set off with the bag of A4 wastepaper and a couple of pints of MEK (methyl ethyl ketone), a volatile degreasing spirit, in common use at the time. Andy emptied the sack of paper into the incinerator and poured the MEK over it, he then lit a match and tossed it into the furnace.

WWWWHHHHOOOOMMMPPHH. The paper shot out of the chimney like a giant party popper, it spread far and wide in the wind. Andy was engulfed in a ball of flames from the open incinerator door. After spending an eternity collecting his precipitating paper storm, he returned to the hangar severely scorched. Of course, sympathy was in very short supply, and the sight of Andy with his singed moustache, eyebrows and fringe was fuel for a lot of piss taking.

The Air Force is an incredibly safety conscious organisation, and we were all constantly reminded of the risks that are involved working around fighter aircraft. One incident in the hangar brought the dangers home probably more than any other. A couple of armourers were working a night shift preparing an aircraft for flight testing. This involved fitting initiator cartridges (detonators), and connecting a lot of cables, arming the explosive cockpit escape systems.

This complex and intricate set of installations when complete, arms the ejection seats, canopy jettison and canopy MDC (miniature detonating cord). It is a fiddly job and the consequences of mistakes are loud and painful. During the job one armourer was inside the cockpit and one on the staging alongside the aircraft. The tradesman inside the cockpit arming the canopy made a single slip, and half a second later the canopy high explosive cord detonated. The thick canopy material is designed to fragment and explode outwards away from the pilot while he is ejecting. The hangar was filled with a ferocious maelstrom of razor-sharp fragments of Perspex traveling at about the speed of sound.

The two men knew that they were in mortal danger and covered themselves up as best they could. They both received serious injuries including plastic embedded all over their arms, faces and backs, ruptured eardrums, and damaged eyes. Fortunately, these sorts of accidents are infrequent, but they do happen.

After a couple of very happy years at Marham, my time to move on had come again. This was bittersweet. I was excited about the adventures the future held, but I would undoubtedly miss my friends and colleagues. In typical fashion a leaving drink was arranged. Proceedings began in the gliding club with a few beers. The traditional sinking a pint down in one went without a hitch, and I was presented an engraved hip flask from my workmates.

The Gliding club was the social venue of choice for a lot of functions at Marham, it remains one of those bars that I reminisce about. I don't even know if it still exists, and this was my last drink in there. It's strange the memories that endure.

For the person moving on from a unit, leaving drinks are usually messy affairs. Mine was to be no different. As the party broke up and people drifted away to enjoy the weekend, a smaller group of us headed for the bowling alley. I was already 'slurring my worms' and my knees weren't working at all well. This just encouraged my mates to pour more beer into me.

Retiring to the gents, a comfort break was my focus, when the other Steve in the group wobbled in, announcing that everybody else had wimped out and gone home. 'We, however, are not done.' What we really needed was a game of snooker and some more beer in the corporal's club. There was a problem, I was clearly not a corporal and therefore not allowed in the members only club. Steve's bright idea was a stroke of drunken genius. "We'll swap clothes". Everybody in the club new Steve, he was on the committee and a regular. If I was with him dressed in his uniform, as a corporal, nobody would challenge us.

To the amusement of the other users of the gents, we stripped down to our socks and pants and exchanged our clothes. I am about five foot ten with size eight feet. Steve was six feet with size ten feet. His uniform engulfed me, and my jeans bulged in a very unsightly way on him. Not deterred by such a minor inconvenience, we strolled into the corporal's club looking a most unlikely pair of friends. I don't recall how the snooker went; we may have potted a ball between us. We certainly had a good deal more to drink.

The night ended on my doorstep. There was something wrong with my front door handle, there must have been, because I couldn't make it work. Our whispering and chuckling had got loud enough to bring Tracy out of bed and downstairs to see what the fuss was. She opened the door to see me on my knees with the door key clutched in my fingers and Steve holding my wrist trying to steer my hand towards the lock. Steve's clothes had all shrunk massively and I looked like one of Snow Whites' dwarves in a giant's air force uniform. Inane grins from me and Steve were met with eye rolling and laughter from Tracy.

Steve was a very sociable and generous man. He was always the first to offer help in any way he could. Held in very high regard by everybody who met him he was a real gentleman. He passed on recently and I was very sad to attend the funeral of a friend who I knew as the life and soul of any party. I'll always remember him as a fun-loving comrade.

This time I was going to RAF Laarbruch in Germany. The move was complicated by the fact that Tracy was expecting. Our baby was due shortly after we would arrive. We spoke to the Medical Officer and the Station Families Officer; it was decided Tracy would remain at Marham, looked after by friends and family. I was to go to Germany as planned. She would then join me once she and baby were fit to travel.

I was sat in the airman's mess at RAF Laarbruch, tucking into sausages, having finished my days' work, when Andy (of singed hair fame) walked in, in his overalls. 'Congratulations dad, you had a little girl half an hour ago, mum and baby are fine.' I didn't know what to make of this earth-shattering news. All I could manage was. 'The sergeant will have your guts for garters, wearing your oily overalls in his mess.'

Finish sausages, grab kit bag, jump into Andy's car, get next ferry from the Hoek van Holland to the UK. By the following morning I was sat in the maternity ward of the RAF hospital at Ely with my new-born daughter in my hands. She was tiny. Six weeks later Tracy and Vicky joined me in Germany.

Chapter 7

Laarbruch.

When we first moved to Germany, we were concerned that we would miss our friends and family. Could we cope with a new life and a new baby. These doubts were very quickly dispelled. Beer, Bacardi, and barbeques were the order of the day. We lived on the married quarters site within the camp perimeter, in a very secure environment. The kids all played around the married quarters estate without a care.

Our first Christmas set the tone for the next few years. We were staying on camp, and it was going to be our first family Christmas. We had no special plans, so I had volunteered to be on standby duty over the holiday. This was no hardship for me, as a bonus it bought a few smarty points at work. We had some very close friends by now, particularly Simon and Sally. They adored Vicky, and pretty much adopted her. We planned for us all to spend Christmas day together unwrapping presents.

Germany really goes to town during the festive season, with markets and street fairs. In contrast to the dull austerity of England, with all the industrial unrest at the beginning of the eighties this was wonderland. At work everybody was making plans, dinners, parties, travelling home. There was one unfortunate group who were set to have a very subdued time though. An unlucky squad of single lads had been ordered onto the station guard for the holiday week, as crap duties go this was a biggie.

They needed some friendly support to get through the holidays. "You're all coming to my house for Christmas dinner, how many of you are there. Eight or ten. I'll let the missus know. Of course, she won't mind".

Initially when I broke the news to Tracy, she was a bit stunned, but after a chat with Sally they soon had it sorted out. Two lots of tables and chairs, two cookers, easy. That dinner was probably one of the best we had. The hallway was full of guns and respirators, and the table was groaning under the weight of turkey's and roast spuds. Most of the diners were wearing combat kit and party hats. It was a great atmosphere. The guys on duty couldn't drink, so it was a booze free dinner. Not a problem, we caught up later that evening.

It was a cold winter that year, so our Boxing-day morning walk with Sally and Simon in the local woods was going to need quilted coats and fur lined moon boots. Tracy had Vicky strapped in a papoose on her front, as we set out to walk off the previous days excess. We were well into the woods and chatting away as we walked, not paying much attention to our surroundings. Ahead of us on the path was what looked like a big hairy arse, protruding from the bushes. The girls took one look and ran off, jumping over a fence into the adjoining field. Leaving me and Simon to investigate the huge rump in more detail.

Armed with a stick, we couldn't resist a closer look. As we approached the animal, we could see it was a very large adult wild boar sow. Rooting through the undergrowth looking for her next snack. She hadn't notice us intruding on her dinner, we were stood right behind her. Simon poked the hairy arse with his stick, thinking the animal would be startled, not a bit. A very pissed off wild boar reversed out of the bushes, taking a good look at the pair of us. We now got a clear view of the size of this beast, our bravado instantly evaporated. We turned and ran as fast as our moon boots would carry us.

I didn't look to see if the monster was chasing us, I just focused on staying ahead of Simon and clearing the fence in front of me. We re-joined the girls, who had been watching us in disbelief from the other side of the fence. Simon was half a pace behind me. That gave us plenty to talk about for the rest of the holidays.

Weekends at Laarbruch were always fun, either staying on camp or exploring the area. This Saturday night was nothing out of the ordinary, just a walking tour of the bars on camp. There were lots to choose from, they were all popular and well frequented. German drink driving rules were very tight, so nobody would even consider taking their car to a bar, there was really no need.

Although groups of drunken revellers were commonplace around camp at weekends, I don't ever recall any aggression. Everybody was just out for a good time. We were heading home after a good night out. Simon, Sally, Tracy, and me, we were chatting and wobbling well, but making progress. A lone bloke was heading towards us and going to the bar we had just left.

The Icarus Game

For no reason we could think of, he stopped right in front of us and dropped his trousers and pants. "Get a look at that, girls." he hollered. Me and Simon were quietly impressed. Anybody prepared to get their tackle out in the early hours of a Sunday morning, during January when the mercury was down well below minus ten, was ok by us. He had clearly overdone the anti-freeze.

The girls both cracked up and burst into a fit of the giggles. Sally pointed at his rapidly retreating knob and squealed at the top of her voice, "Look at that, it's just like a willy but smaller". I think Simon's ego inflated quite a bit that night.

One of Tracy's friends was going back to the UK for a visit. Because of the anti-rabies rules at the time, they couldn't take their dog with them. We offered to look after him for a week. Bugsy was a young Border-Collie, and as mad as a box of frogs. He was by far the daftest dog you could imagine. Vicky by now two or three years old, had taken Bugsy into the garden to play. We could hear her laughing and gurgling, so we looked out of the kitchen door to check on the two of them.

What we saw was comical. Vicky was sat in the middle of the lawn, egging Bugsy on, and the dog was racing around her. Running flat out and completely blind. It couldn't see a thing because his head and snout was stuck in Vicky's plastic sandcastle bucket, the handle stuck behind its ears holding the bucket firmly in place.

During a quieter moment, Vicky and Bugsy were sat on the sofa together watching 'Button Moon'. Tracy looked in on them and found the dog with his head on Vicky's lap, Vicky's fore finger was pushed up to the second knuckle in the dog's nostril. "What are you doing to that dog." Is a question any mum would ask? "Bugsy's got a bogey nose" came the totally innocent sounding reply. I'm not sure which are the most disgusting, dogs or kids.

On 20 squadron the work was constant and well organised. Carrying out regular, running repairs and maintenance on the Tornado GR1's we operated. There was always time for a little horseplay though. Bondhu bashing was a favourite game. Jump in a Land Rover, fill it with your mates, then take it over the roughest terrain you can find on the site. There were always new, slightly tougher routes to challenge each other with. Outside every HAS, was a round concrete apron, big enough to park a couple of aircraft on, surrounding this apron was a blast wall or revetment. The revetments were about fifteen feet high and faced with concrete blocks, the face sloped up at about forty-five degrees.

Billy was a popular character on the squadron, he reckoned that it should be possible to drive a Landy around the sloping side of a revetment without rolling it over. If you could go fast enough, centrifugal force would do the rest. What you needed was a good run up. He started checking out all the HAS's on the squadron site to see which one had the best access for his daring stunt. The one he chose was right opposite the operations office window.

He rounded up half a dozen cohorts and set off to prove it could be done. With the tarpaulin roof off, the back of the Land Rover filled with excited, chattering lads, Billy and his crew mounted the revetment flat out in third gear. They roared around the top of this improvised wall of death, as fast as the Landy would go, returning to flat ground completely unscathed. We were all immensely impressed with the originality of this stunt, its planning and execution. The 'Boss', who had witnessed the spectacle from his office window, was less convinced of its merit. Billy got a right royal roasting; he was immediately elevated to legendary status by the boys on the squadron.

The second weekend in August was always a great excuse for an 'away barbeque'. It was the Rhine in Flames festival at Koblenz. The festival follows the grape harvest northwards along the Rhine and Mosel rivers. When the harvest is complete in an area, the towns have a party of some sort. Koblenz is the city where the two rivers meet, and their festivities, funfairs and fireworks display were a highpoint of the summer. There was always a good group of RAFG servicemen and their families there. The contingent from Laarbruch would drift down to the city, in cars towing caravans, or loaded up with tents, beer and barbeque essentials to enjoy the weekend.

We would normally all gather in one area of the campsite, opposite the Deutsches Eck. The first people arriving there would hoist the union flag, to act as a rallying point. It was a chance to meet other service families from the various RAF stations around Germany, an opportunity to swap stories. The German army put on a good display, up and down the river during the afternoon, it would always involve lots of pyrotechnics and parachutists. The night was rounded off with a firework display from the Ehrenbreitstein fortress, high on the cliff tops opposite.

A feature of the campsite which caused constant hilarity for the Britishchen Luftwaffe contingent, was the 'Camp Commandants' regular announcements over the PA system. They were always prefixed with, "Achtung, Achtung." and met with cries of "Achtung, spitfire" from the British ghetto. Naturally we christened him Adolf. In truth Adolf did a good job bicycling around the campsite on his rounds checking everything was spick and span, it usually was.

We had a minor fallout with him on the Sunday night though. A group of lads from RAF Bruggen were enjoying the party right up until the last minute, before leaving for home. Unfortunately for them, the campsite rules said that after ten o'clock in the evening, no cars could enter or exit the site, so sleeping campers would not be disturbed. This was enforced by lowering the barrier at the site entrance.

Our little group had missed this kerfew by about half an hour, they were stuck on the wrong side of the barrier. We could see there was a problem, so we went to help out, if we could. Adolf soon appeared and quoted the rules in his best Pigeon English. We explained in Pigeon German that this car must leave, now. His answer was an emphatic "Nein". In fairness he stood his ground right up to the point we threatened to throw him and his barrier into the river. Then he retreated to his office.

We still had to get the car and our colleagues off the site. So, a large group of our fellow servicemen was gathered together. We then bodily picked up the ford fiesta, it was being lifted over the barrier, when Adolf reappeared. He had finally conceded defeat and raised up his barrier. The Bruggen team were on their way.

We had friends visiting from Marham, one evening we decided to have a takeaway from the local town Weeze (pron, veetsa).

The Icarus Game

Steve, (previously featured swapping clothes at my leaving drinks.) decided he'd like to order his supper in German, so I gave him a crash course in pigeon German outside the schnelly (slang, takeaway). "Ich mochte zwei portionen hunchen mit pommes bitte". Chicken and chips twice please. Steve went up to the counter and in his newly acquired German said "Ich mochte zwei hundchen mit pommes bitte." The woman serving him fell about laughing, making doggie barks at Steve's tiny slip of the tongue. He had asked for puppy with chips!!

Chapter 8

Decimomannu.

As if serving in Germany wasn't enough fun already, the squadron was sent away periodically on detachments. These sojourns were essentially for the advanced training of flight crews in specific skills. Sneaking up on the baddies, bombing accuracy, that sort of thing. One regular detachment was an annual visit to Decimomannu (Deci [pron, Dechy]), in Sardinia during each July and August. This was manned on a voluntary basis and there was no shortage of enthusiastic candidates.

Deci during the 1980's was a multinational airbase, run by the Italian Air Force. It was used by us, alongside the German and American Air Forces, for practicing air to air combat skills. Using what at the time was high-tech navigational electronics, aircraft were sent up against each other in air-to-air combat situations, and their three-dimensional flight paths and projected weapons trajectories recorded precisely. These could then be tracked in real time, then replayed on the ground and debriefed by the crews. All done in the blue skies over the Mediterranean. It's a tough job, but somebody had to do it.

This was a time when the AIDS epidemic was at its height, and southern Europe was suffering badly. The gap in living standards between the wealthy and the poor was very stark. Drug abuse was commonplace, and a major contributing factor in this dismal social inequality. It didn't affect us particularly in our isolated world, but when we arrived in Sardinia, we got a few words of advice from the medics. "There's a box of condoms on the desk at the back, help yourselves. If you go on the beach, keep your boots on, and look out for used hypodermics". Nuff said. We all left the room with inflated condoms on our heads. It was the only use most of us had for them.

With very little to do around the isolated base, everybody on the squadron had to make their own entertainment. Some of the guys were more imaginative than others. Inevitably, this led to us creating our own brand of mischief. Work was the same as usual, the aircraft had to be serviced, repaired, and kept ready for flight. We worked in shifts from early morning until late evening in the arid Sardinian heat. During the day the temperature on the flight line regularly exceeded 40 degrees Celsius in constant, direct sunlight. There was no shade, and everything metal that you touched, burnt any skin it came into contact with.

The Nuraghi, was the British bar and the one we mostly frequented. It was one of several drinking venues around the base. Cheap and cheerful in typical NAAFI style. Most of the time this was an unspectacular place with the guys relaxing and chatting over a few beers. Occasionally it would liven up, usually for no better reason than somebody had got bored.

One stunt to vent excess energy, was to 'run the wall'. Attached to main bar area was a small outside courtyard, with a few tables and chairs. Surrounding this yard was a brick wall about six or eight feet high. The challenge was, to climb onto the wall at one end and run around the top for the full perimeter of the courtyard. Anybody in the yard at the time was obliged to buy a drink for a successful runner. Obviously, the people drinking, would try their best to ensure any attempt was unsuccessful. By throwing whatever came to hand at the contestant.

Timing was the key to this challenge. An empty courtyard made for an easy run, but no reward. A full courtyard meant certain injury and failure, but the potential of a large reward. I never saw anybody succeed in collecting their prize, but there were lots of cuts and bruises during the increasingly reckless, and imaginative attempts. One particularly infamous event featured a naked runner wearing a black bandanna on his head declaring at the top of his voice "I am the naked ninja". He lost but entered Deci folk law.

Making your way back to bed at the end of the night could be problematic. There were footpaths and roads, but the most direct route was across the bondhu. This scrubland was typically surrounded by very deep concrete storm ditches. One unfortunate soul from the squadron miscalculated his attempt to cross one such ditch, finding himself laid in the bottom of it looking up at the steep, shoulder high, grey walls either side of him. Being three sheets to the wind, he decided that this was not a bad place to spend the night. He reached out and found a soft pillow, then dozed off. Early in the morning he awoke with the sunrise only to discover that his soft and comfortable pillow was in fact a dead cat.

There was quite a lot of feral life around the airbase, most noticeable were the packs of sun-bleached wild dogs, referred to by us as 'bondhu dogs'. For the most part we didn't bother them, and they ignored us. Jimmy however befriended and adopted one. Jimmy was a stocky Glaswegian and liked nothing more than drinking and arm wrestling. He was unbeaten, and would relish making short work of opponents twice his size. He had the attitude and physique that made it clear he was taking 'nae nonsense fra' anycunt'.

His new best friend 'Dog' followed him everywhere, and it stank. The flea ridden mutt even took to sleeping on the end of his bed. After much pleading from his room-mates Jimmy agreed to sort his dog out. He took it in the shower, scrubbing it down with Brut 33 shampoo. Now he had a fluffy, fragrant mongrel, that followed him everywhere. His roommates still weren't happy, but they stopped complaining. Until the fleas started biting.

Midway through the detachment, we were press ganged into a squadron sports afternoon. This took the form of a five-a-side football tournament. It was to be played on the station five-a-side pitch. A hard gravel covered playing surface, surrounded by a waist high breeze block wall was to be our arena. The Boss rounded up a selection of teams, Riggers, Fairies, Leckie's, Sootie's, Plumbers, Rodnie's, and The Management. If you weren't playing, you were supporting very vocally. Attendance was compulsory.

It was a knockout competition with a case of beer to the winners. The matches turned into a vicious war of attrition, hard tackles, bouncing opponents off the ground and walls. All very abrasive surfaces, which took their toll in flesh and blood. Halfway through proceedings the Wing Commander had to call a 'time out', reading the riot act to the players and supporters. This was a sporting event, not an opportunity to settle every old grudge in the squadron's history. Only moderate abuse would be tolerated and no more gratuitous bloodshed on the pitch. I don't recall who won, but winning wasn't really the point.

The Italian Air Force still had conscription during the eighties, and this was an alien concept to us. Now and again, we had dealings with these drafted men, they were all young and seemed to be a very cheerful collection. Convinced the whole military thing was just one big temporary joke. Like military bases all around the world, one of the daily parades was raising the national flag. A sombre ritual, involving marching, bugles, whistles and lots of saluting, any serviceman will be familiar with the routine.

A couple of us found ourselves approaching the guardroom at the main entrance to the base one morning, just as this ceremony was about to start. So, like polite and respectful airmen, we kept a sensible distance from the action and stood quietly watching the parade unfold. It started with an NCO herding a group of conscripts into a straight line opposite the flagpole. He was barking orders at them in fine style, and they milled about as best they could. The only way he could get them into a regimental looking straight line, was to stand them with their heals against the kerbstone of the footpath outside the guard room.

Once the parade was orderly and at attention, the duty officer appeared, holding the flag that was to be raised. We were standing to attention facing the flag, the presiding officer was saluting very smartly. At half-mast the flag stopped. There was a bit of looking around and shoulder shrugging, then a conscript was despatched to shimmy up the pole and untangled the cords. We howled with laughter and applauded at the 'carry on' style parade. As the Officer retired to his office, the conscripts turned to us and grinned. One of them removed his beret to reveal a mass of green, white, and red hair, that perfectly matched the Tricolore they had just raised. I was amazed. I can only assume the guy was on guard duty as punishment for his radical hairstyle.

The detachment was nearing its end, and everybody was starting to wind down. It was going to be our last weekend in Deci, so a final blow-out was needed to close the chapter. We left the base as a group of around fifteen, walking the half a mile up the road to a local pizzeria. After a good meal, and plenty of Chianti we were on our way back to the base, when one of our number decided to liven things up. Billy ran down the road towards the airbase entrance, screaming blue murder. Pointing back at his bemused group of colleagues, he shouted at the armed conscript on guard that we were going to kill him. Fortunately, the guard didn't speak English, and despite Billy's encouragement to put a round or two over our heads, kept his cool.

After we finished apologising to the guards for our prat of a mate, we were allowed back on camp. We headed for the German bar, to say auf wiedersehen to our continental friends. Then on to the American Bar, then via the Nuraghi to the Tri-National Bar. When we arrived, it was closing time, but we figured they wouldn't turn away our friendly wit and banter, or our cash. The barman was a very effeminate Italian gentleman. He took one look at the rabble, who had just crashed through his bar room doors, promptly slamming down the metal shutters onto the bar. "Thissa bar issa close-ed. Go away".

If it had been possible to drag the guy through the steel barrier separating us from the beer, I'm sure we would have. Instead, we tried playing nicely, offering to buy him a drink. "No, go away". How about sex, is there anyone here you fancy? This resulted in a chorus of. "Fuck off we're not that thirsty" from our group, and another "No, go away. I'ma calla the Carabinieri", from the increasingly impatient barman as he turned the lights out.

We drifted away from the now dark bar, and most of us called it a night. One member of our group did comment on a lonely Fiat 500 parked outside, and assumed it belonged to the 'Grumpy Little Bar-steward'. I thought no more about it and went to bed. Sunday morning arrived several hours too soon, I was feeling very delicate as I walked across the bondhu to the airmen's mess. With my sights set on a full, fat boy fry-up and a bucket of tea, I arrived at the airman's mess entrance, where there was quite a stir going on outside. Jammed firmly in the doorway, stood up on end, was the Fiat 500 from outside the Tri National Bar. The haze started to clear, and I quietly used the side door to get to my fry-up.

All in all, the detachment had been a success, we returned home to Laarbruch, knowing 20 Squadron had done itself proud, upholding all the standards that were expected of us. Back on the squadrons' home site it was business as usual, and we all had a good tally of stories from our six weeks in the Mediterranean.

Chapter 9

20 Squadron.

Our unit had a long, proud history, the Tornado GR1's were just the latest in a varied list of aircraft operated by 20 Squadron. It was one of the regiments originally formed as part of the Royal Flying Corps, in September 1915, three years before the Royal Air Force was formed.

1985 was its seventieth anniversary. This was a landmark in our squadrons history that could not go unrecognised. A reunion party was organised on the squadron site. People who had served with 20 Sqn over the years, were tracked down and invited. It was going to be a big event, with some big characters attending. Guests were bussed in from as far afield as the north of Scotland. Being held in a HAS (hardened aircraft shelter) on the squadron site, meant we had total control of the party, and as HAS's are bomb proof we could be as noisy and rowdy as we liked.

There was a well-stocked bar, courtesy of the squadron funds and it was run by us, the serving airmen. The squadron also put on a barbeque and disco. A fleet of busses were laid on from the domestic areas. One thing the services excel at, is organising a good old fashioned pissup. Everybody was to get a free drink on arrival, this was managed by issuing each guest with a raffle ticket that was handed over at the bar. As we were running the bar these raffle tickets were recycled throughout the party all night. By the end of the mayhem, they were as dog eared as the guests.

With virtually free drinks, free food a very loud disco, and several hundred revellers from all kinds of backgrounds and all corners of the empire, the evening went fantastically well. When a group of exuberant aircrew, decided to see how many people they could get on a moped, and ride around the dance floor, they were met with enthusiastic cheers. Receiving a soaking in beer as they flamboyantly circumnavigated the event.

We turned up the following lunch time to clear up the wreckage, and the hazy recollections of the previous night started to emerge. One question that baffled most of us was. How the hell did all the squadron vehicles, end up parked in a very orderly straight line, on top of one of the bomb shelters ('J' buildings)? Twenty feet above the roads. Up near vertical grassy walls. More to the point how do we get them down?

At home we were planning a family holiday, I had been away a lot and we needed some time together. We knew my parents were going to join us, so it had to be reasonably sensible. I wanted to go to Berlin, but this was vetoed by the rest of my family. At the time Berlin was an enclave in East Germany and needed a lot of planning, and even more paperwork to visit. A pity because during the cold war it was the place to party. Instead, we decided to hitch up the caravan, fill it with beer, and head south, for some more Mediterranean sun.

We tried to explore as much of Europe, as often as we could, while we were there. Away barbeques at weekends were great fun, and occasionally we ventured further afield. We had bought a small caravan and were determined to get as far as we could with it. This was not without incident, as you might expect. On this holiday, I decided that if Hannibal could get his elephants over the Alps; we could get our caravan over them.

A big ask when it was being towed by a 1.6 litre Ford Escort. We packed up as much as we could fit in the car, with the three of us and my parents. The caravan was rammed full too. As we headed south the weather improved and we were having a lovely time. Pulling into an autobahn rest area for a leg stretch, we parked up behind a very smart, brand-new BMW M5.

This was a stunning car, me and Chris, my stepdad, were admiring it when the driver returned. He was an American serviceman, and we struck up a conversation with him, 'Hi, that's a smart car you've got there'. 'It's a rental' he explained, 'and you guys should look at the other side'. We did, holy cow, it was absolutely knackered. The bodywork was caved in over the whole length of the car, and the shiny metallic paintwork totally scraped off.

'What have you done to it!?' He went on to explain, he'd been pushing his luck a bit too hard on the Nürburgring racetrack, coming to grief against the Armco barriers. He was now on his way to return it to the hire company. 'I plan to post the keys through the letterbox, run like hell, and get on the next flight to the States.' We agreed, this was probably the best plan available to him. The alternative was going to cost a fortune.

Continuing our journey south, we looked ahead of us at the massive granite barrier that was the Alps. These mountains erupt steeply from the horizon, they are clearly visible hours before you reach them. Driving up the steep hairpins, to over two miles above sea level on the north side, dragging our home behind us, made the clutch smell and water temperature rise alarmingly. Coming down the south side, had the brakes smoking and begging for mercy. We had passed through Aosta in Italy, heading for the French border.

When we got there it was closed, an iron gate was padlocked across the entrance to the tunnel that was the road crossing. We had to pitch camp in a restaurant car park, whiling away the evening, until the border opened again in the morning. We were rudely awoken the following day by a lot of heavy machinery, we discovered that we had camped under a cement works cable car. At least we got an early start.

As I drove through the tunnel, I got my second surprise of the morning. The Italian sides' road, was nicely tarmacked, as was the French side, however there was a stretch of about twenty meters of rubble about six inches below the paved surface between the two countries. That short section was distinctly unloved. I didn't expect that. At thirty miles an hour, I got the car and caravan airborne, just before we crashed and bounced through the rocky, gravelly no-mans-land into France and headed for Monaco and the Mediterranean.

As well as maximizing the fun and games, we were stationed in Germany to do a job. Our group of squadrons formed part of Britain's nuclear response commitment to NATO, with the forty-year-old 'Cold War', raging at full throttle. Part of this capability took the form of fully serviced, fuelled, and armed aircraft, in a secure compound at the end of the runway. Crewed and ready to go twenty-four, seven.

If the much talked about 'four-minute warning' went off, we had to be able to get our plane airborne, immediately. Less than two minutes from siren to take off was the goal. As far as we were concerned, this ability represented our last kick at Gorbachev's nuts, before we all died in a nuclear apocalypse. The facility was known as the QRA (Quick Reaction Alert) and this duty was taken extremely seriously by all of us. The rules we operated under for the week on 'Q' were very precise.

We practiced endlessly, run like hell, strap them (the crew) in, light the fires and wave them goodbye. Each aircraft had two ground crew shifts, consisting of an airman and a JNCO. There were also two flight crews, each with a pilot and a navigator (Weapon Systems Operator). Each set of crews was on QRA duty for six or seven days. The work period was twenty-four hours on duty, followed by twenty-four hours off. The crews stuck together for the week, and at shift changes the whole crew had to be swapped out.

The accommodation was simple, but ok. We had a communal lounge, bunks and kitchen with endless bread, bacon, and tea. The flight crew had a similar setup on the other side of the corridor. Other than the daily check of the aircraft and practice callouts, the ground crew and flight crew had no cause to mix, so we didn't.

My airman was a pleasant enough chap called Ian. Having occasionally worked together on 20 Sqn, we knew each other and got along just fine. We familiarised ourselves with the surroundings, routines, and checklists of this slightly alien environment quickly.

Towards the end of the week, I arrived to start my shift, waiting for the early morning crew transport to the QRA compound on my own. This was unusual, Ian should have been at the pickup point as well. The crew bus was driven by an RAF Police NCO, it took us directly into the secure site. When the minibus arrived, the driver asked where the other crewman was. I had no idea. A radio call dispatched another policeman to Ian's barrack block to find him. I walked into the crew room at the QRA site, explaining the situation to the ground crew who were going off shift. We all knew the rules, until my absent man made an appearance, the other crew were stuck in the compound and on duty.

My flight crew pilot stuck his head around the door, expecting to find his ground crew ready to go out to the aircraft. Instead, it was the off going shift that got up and went with him, to do the daily checks. He didn't look at all impressed but carried on with his job. I hoped that Ian had a good reason not to be here.

The crews finished their daily checks on the aircraft and returned to the crew room. At the same time, Ian strolled through the door. "Sorry I'm late guys. It was my birthday yesterday, so I went into Nijmegen last night, had a few to many and slept in". The other crews all turned and looked directly at me. What was I going to do about this blatant dereliction of duty? This was the question on everybody's mind.

"Ian, give me your ID card. I am charging you with failing to report for QRA duty on time, in contravention to Station Standing Orders". I was put on the spot, and this was the only course of action I could follow. Everybody else seemed happy with the decision, going about their own business leaving me to sort out my errant airman. I knew that this was going to make me unpopular around the squadron. Nobody likes it when their mate is put on a charge, and I cursed Ian for putting me in such an awkward position.

I've always been an absolute lightweight when it comes to drinking. No matter how hard I try, or how much I practice. I'm always the first to collapse in the corner or end up with my head in a toilet somewhere. This is a real shame because I like beer. Simon also liked beer, and used me as his drinking guide, allowing him to judge how much beer he should be consuming. His method was to keep drinking until I threw up, then just have a couple more. Safe in the knowledge, he would be fine. That's friends for you.

Not all drinking is just for fun, this bar crawl had a specific purpose. Simons parents Bill and Liz were over for Christmas, and the men folk were out looking for a bar that would be open Christmas day, or as we referred to it that night. Tomorrow. Yes, we had gone out on the lash unencumbered by sensible females on Christmas eve.

This was very risky territory, and warnings had been issued by our respective wives. "Don't you dare come home late, or drunk. "No dear, of course not." I was feeling a little mischievous and started quite early on to get rid of excess beer down the toilet bulimia style. Simon's beer meter was getting recalibrated tonight. It was mean I know, but I stayed on my feet long enough to see Simon the worse for wear for the first time in a couple of years.

When the last bar closed, we set off home. It was the early hours of Christmas morning, and this pair of 'Santa's' were undoubtedly rat arsed. We both agreed, we were in so much trouble. On the way home, we cooked up our cover story. I fell through the front door, crashed around the hallway, getting my shoes off I tumbled up the stairs. Sitting on the end of the bed I was on the receiving end of Tracy's' best icy glare.

My story began. "It's no use being angry darling. I'm amazingly lucky to be home at all. We left the bar hours ago, and totally sober. You'll never believe it, but, on the way home, we were beamed up by Martians. They injected us with drugs to make us wobbly and interrogated us for days. They were going to send us back in the year 2050, but we convinced them to return us today. Cosh itsh Chrishsmash, they were just a couple of hours late". I then passed out on the bed.

Christmas morning, I was woken bright and early by my excited three-year-old daughter, I was feeling far from festive. "Mummy, daddy needs a doctor he's not well". "No darling, Daddy doesn't need a doctor. He's just a prat."

Tracy and Sally compared notes over breakfast, when Sally and Simon arrived to help Vicky unwrap her presents. Simon had performed the same routine as me, in his 'time traveller' induced state of delirium. To rub salt in, neither of us could remember which bars were going to be open later that day.

Boxing day passed by with a resumption of festive eating and drinking. Various friends drifted in and out, wishing each other the season's greetings. Most of the front doors were left open, and people just wandered the quarters site, popping in and out for drinks and nibbles. I went into the kitchen to make yet another plate of sandwiches, mostly turkey. I found a pot of my home-made turkey liver pate; Smearing it on some crackers I re-joined the melee in the living room with a couple of plates of food.

Circulating around the room with my plates of refreshments, extolling the virtues of my home-made pate, I got to Simon. He looked at the turkey sandwiches, then at me. "You've gotta be kidding, I've had enough turkey to last a lifetime". "No bother mate, try the liver pate." As I said this, I lifted the plate to his nose level. The result was spectacular. His eyes bulged, his mouth closed, and his cheeks inflated, distended by a mouthful of high-pressure vomit.

He clamped a hand over his mouth and dashed for the door. I dropped the plates, rugby tackling him in the middle of the living room. No way was he getting any privacy for this multi coloured yawn. Tracy saw what was coming and grabbed the waste bin, getting it under his head, just after vomit sprayed out of his mouth and nose, through his fingers and all over the carpet. I had a firm grip on Simon's ankles, he was going nowhere. "Gotcha, you bugger". This was the first time he had thrown up before me, ever, and I was going to enjoy it. He was kicking like mad, achieving nothing and going nowhere. Tracy and Sally were yelling at me to let go of him, but I was simply having too much fun to pay them any attention.

The next ten minutes was spent on my hands and knees, scrubbing the carpet. Simon got cleaned up, then after a couple of beers we were back on speaking terms. Thirty years on, Simon still reminds me that I'm a lightweight who can't drink, whenever he gets the opportunity.

Chapter 10

Changing Times.

Initially, we had been posted to Laarbruch for three years, but were having such a good time I applied to extend our tour by a year. Approaching the three-year point, the extension of our tour was confirmed. Around this time many of the people I had enjoyed working with, socializing with, and playing alongside, were being posted back to the UK. The mood of RAFG seemed to be changing, it was perceptible, but hard to explain exactly why. For me it seemed to be losing its sparkle.

On the 1 May 1988, things changed for all servicemen in BAOR/RAFG, instantly and radically. In one night, the IRA carried out two attacks on British servicemen. The first was the shooting dead of a serving airman, he was based at RAF Wildenwrath, another serviceman was also injured. The two of them were sat in their car at Roermond, in the Netherlands.

Thirty minutes later a bomb planted under a car in a discotheque car park, in Nieuwbergen just over the Dutch border from Laarbruch, exploded. This device took the lives of two airmen, injuring another two, all these men were serving at RAF Laarbruch.

The victims of these attacks were very easy targets for the terrorists to identify. All cars in BFG displayed distinctive number plates, the drivers had short hair, and British accents. Anywhere in Europe, or even at home, in the UK, we would stand out.

The Icarus Game

Although there had been IRA attacks in Europe before these killings, these latest ones were very close to home. This was the continuation of a long history of IRA attacks on British servicemen, it was not to be the last.

The level of awareness regarding our personal vulnerability to attack rose very sharply. The security personnel on the base invited families to attend specially tailored security courses, explaining what IED's (improvised explosive devices) consisted of. What they looked like, how they were planted. The syllabus included searching cars, and personal security advice for wives and children. These courses were voluntary and well attended. Everybody took it seriously; British servicemen and their families could be seen all over Europe, checking around their cars, before getting in and starting the engine. Nobody complained when they were searched going on and off the base.

None of this stopped us enjoying what was left of our tour in Germany, but constantly suspecting the loyalties and motives of the people in towns we visited, took the edge off the jollities a little.

As well as socialising, I was keen on racing my motocross bike. I was a member of the station enduro team, also racing with the local Dutch motocross club. Enduro races were organised by the army, they took place on their tank training ranges, and were very competitive. For the army, training dispatch riders was the most important reason for these competitions, for us it was pure fun. The events would last up to twelve hours, racing over the toughest terrain the course builders could find. They wrecked bikes and riders; I was always absolutely knackered at the end of them. As a team we did well, no thanks to me. We had a couple of very good riders, although I tried hard, I was there to make up the numbers.

We would usually arrive at the course the evening before a race and set ourselves up. Those that could be bothered might put up a tent, I usually slept in my car. The night before the race the competitors would congregate and enjoy some healthy rivalry, over a beer and a burger. At this event things got a bit more entertaining than usual. We had gathered around a large bonfire with our drinks and supper. One of the lads was bragging about his brand new, fresh out of the crate KTM, that in his view was clearly going to win the next day. One of his mates asked for a go, to put it through its paces. We could all see a flaw in this idea, but foolishly the owner agreed.

The rider was a lot better than average, filled with Bavaria's finest beer, he made tearing around the bonfire, on this very shiny machine look spectacular. Pretty soon he was up on the back wheel, getting carried away with his own skills. Encouraged into trying more daring tricks by his appreciative audience. Attempting to ground out the rear mudguard on the dirt during a wheelie, he over balanced a bit. The bike flipped over backwards, bounced, and came to rest, having cartwheeled, and ploughed through the bonfire.

The owner was dumb struck, as he recovered his battered and slightly scorched, brand-new scrambler. We were just glad we hadn't been bragging about our bikes, which were safely strapped on our trailers.

In typical army style, these events started at six in the morning, after a heavy night socialising, the scrutineers' compound was full of hangovers. I got sorted out, spinning the back wheel off the start line, I set off in a cloud of dust and gravel into the course. Soon catching up with the first casualty of the race, it was one of my teammates.

He and his bike were leant against a tree, he was trying to keep the chin guard of his crash helmet out of the stream of vomit leaving his mouth. Of course, I was full of sympathy and covered him in dust as I skidded past. Later, during the same lap, my teammate got his own back, going down the steep side of a quarry. He even managed a one fingered salute, as he literally flew past me, landing at the base of the cliff that I was struggling down.

Back on the squadron, I had been detailed onto a temporary job, running the squadron work party. This was an obscure task that was a six-month chore. Around the site, maintenance work always had to be carried out. This ranged from painting anything that didn't move, to building sandbag defensive emplacements, along with anything else the boss wanted done. Anybody who had stepped out of line at work, would be assigned to the squadron work party for a day or two, as punishment for their misdemeanour. I saw a lot of some guys, others only got caught out the once.

One of my regulars was particularly uninterested in all things Air Force, he was counting down the days to demob. One morning, me and the rest of my motley crew were having a brew before starting out, waiting for the unpredictable absentee to show up. We finished our tea and went in search of him. I found him sleeping off his hangover on top of the lockers in the changing room. "Oi you, get down off those lockers and put that fuckin' axe down" was a phrase attributed to me for a while. We bundled our comatose, depressive drunk into the Land Rover, and found somewhere quiet to fill sandbags. We entertained ourselves by depriving him the luxury of sleeping off his headache.

Friday afternoons were regularly a time for 'leaving do's', or other work-related drinking. This session was held in the rugby club, it differed from other parties, because there was no beer to be had. Instead, a dustbin had been filled with 'Pink Polar Bear'. The ingredients, I think, were milk, vodka, and grenadine. Bearing in mind that the vodka was duty free and nearly as cheap as the milk, it was a volatile cocktail. You just dipped your pint glass in the bin, and away you go. The creamy mixture was sweet and delicious, but deceptively potent. After a few hours of drinking this, I decided I'd better go home and eat something, so I said my goodbyes and left the rugby club.

By the time I was halfway home on my pushbike, the vodka was swimming about in my skull. Navigating my bicycle was severely problematic. Ending when I rounded a sharp bend in an alleyway and hit a fence still peddling like mad. I flew over the handlebars, cleared the fence, and landed, sprawled out in somebody's garden. I scrambled back over the fence whilst apologising to the lady of the house, she had appeared at her kitchen door, to check I wasn't dead in her garden. I arrived home covered in mud and bruises, filled with vodka. Not for the first or the last time.

Having completed my temporary duty on the squadron work party, I had another move, this time to the ASF hangar. This job was mostly routine maintenance and modification of the aircraft's weapons pylons, these were mounted under the wings and fuselage of the plane and carried an assortment of stores, ranging from fuel tanks to bombs and missiles.

One afternoon I had wandered into the Visiting Aircraft Section's crew room for a brew. I was sat chatting with the other guys when an American flight crew came in. They were taking their 'Black Hawk' out on a training flight; did anybody fancy a ride? A couple of us jumped at the chance. I'd flown in helicopters in the past, but nothing like this. It was a far more battle-hardened machine than anything the Air Force had at the time. The Black Hawk was a virtual spaceship, loads of power, and built for low level tactical flying. One feature that set it apart from other helicopters, was the large elevator below the tail rotor. This made the plane extraordinarily manoeuvrable, as we were about to find out.

Sitting on the sill of the open side door, I was occupying the machine gunners' post as we took off. We cleared the boundary fence by a couple of feet, then dropped into a fire break through the woods. Even wearing goggles my eyes streamed tears, giving me a fuzzy view of the world passing by in a blur. For the next hour, we hurtled around the German countryside, barely coming above the treetops. It was absolutely fantastic, watching the trees and fields race by over the machine gun, that I was hanging onto like a limpet. I've never been in such an adrenaline pumping machine since.

We continued with the round of drinks parties and barbeques to the end of our tour. I still miss carrying tables, chairs, cool boxes of food and crates of beer around to various neighbours on Saturday afternoons. One barbeque stood out from the haze of parties, if only because the hosts, Tony and Sandy had a pet pig called Jasmine. We spent the afternoon eating sausages and spareribs, laughing at the potbellied pig. It was chasing four-year-old Vicky around the garden, she was laughing and squealing while jasmine tried to catch the tassels on her wellies.

Our time in Germany was coming to an end. We had all thoroughly enjoyed every minute of it. A change was due, and I started looking forward to my next posting. We were going to RAF Abingdon, in Oxfordshire, where I would be working on the Repair and Salvage Squadron, R&SS. I was to work on one of the teams of airframe fitters, carrying out large complex structural repairs on the Air Forces fixed wing aircraft. These were the long jobs that operational units didn't have the manpower, or resources to do. Teams of technicians were sent all over the country to work for weeks or months on a single project. It generally involved a lot of sheet metalwork, pawing over blueprints and flattening rivets.

The Icarus Game

Me skiing in Winterberg, Germany, around 1964

Air Cadet camp, RAF Linton-on-Ouse, 1976

739 Scarborough Squadron.

I always loved bikes. Not so big on the health and safety thing in my youth.

CTCRM Lympstone, 131 Troop mid-course, 1979.

The Icarus Game

RAF early days, Basic training, 1980

Some of the Tornado artwork 16 & 20 sqn's Tabuk

The 'Happy HAS 4' crew.

Our first day shift in months.

(There's always one.)

RAF Detachment Tabuk.

Op Granby.

Nobody's stealing this Tornado.

She's ready to go with laser guided 1000 pounders.

Chapter 11

Coming Home.

Tracy and me, had a lot to think about when we returned to the UK. I only had a couple of years to serve until my twelve-year fixed term engagement with the RAF was complete. I needed to start thinking about what I would do when I left. We also needed to consider where we were going to live. Signing on for longer was not something I was interested in. The world was changing. The Soviet Union was collapsing, military bases were threatened with closure. Redundancy was a real prospect and the opportunities for promotion, and career development offered by all the armed forces looked to be declining rapidly.

For now, we were living in married quarters on the station at RAF Abingdon. Initially I spent time on base training for my new job. Once that induction was completed, I was away, a lot, working. I really didn't like the weeks on end I spent away from my family. It made me feel very isolated. I'm sure Tracy felt the same way. We had come from 'party central' to what felt like a cultural and social wasteland.

A lot of the people I was working with, had been stationed at Abingdon for years and thought it was great. As an outsider stepping in, I was less convinced. Listening to my workmates comparing the over inflated value of their Oxfordshire houses bored me to tears. I only had to sweat out the last couple of years, in the rapidly shrinking RAF. Then I could look for something more interesting, and better suited to my aspirations. What those aspirations might be I had no idea, but I've always been good at taking advantage of opportunities.

One Saturday morning, we had gone to the local supermarket to do the weekly shop. As we walked out of the supermarket and across the car park, Vicky ran ahead of us to the car as she always did. She started checking around the wheel arches, then she got down on all fours and peered under the rear bumper at the underside of the car. A rather bemused woman passer by watching this, couldn't contain her curiosity and asked her what she was doing. My gloriously innocent four-year-old daughter, looking totally cherubic in her gingham summer dress and blonde pig tails turned to the lady and smiled. "I'm checking our car for bombs". By the stunned expression on the woman's face, I don't think that answer had entered her head as a possibility.

As I was going to be away from home a lot over the foreseeable future, we felt moving Tracy and Vicky closer to family would be a good idea. My father-in-law lived in Scotland, so that's where we focused our search for a new home. We bought a flat on the foreshore in Troon. It was near to family support for Tracy with spectacular views of the isle of Arran. We were surrounded by long flat beaches and countryside. The weather could be wild though. On a nice day it was glorious. When the storms blew in off the Atlantic, it was ferocious. Walking along the sea front at Troon, gives you a clue what to expect from the forces of nature. Because of the constant battering from the wind, all of the trees lean away from the sea at forty-five degrees, and not much grows above head height.

Shortly after we moved in, I put up a shed in the garden. I stepped back to admire my creation. Drew, the lovely old boy from the flat above us, leaned on the fence and cast a critical eye over my work. "You'll no be leavin' it like that will ye. It's nae steaked doon". He went on to explain that I needed to hammer fence posts into the ground at each corner and bolt the shed to them. "Otherwise, it'll end up blown onto the railway embankment in the next good storm". That winter during a wild night, at least one other shed did exactly that. I was pleased I took his advice.

It didn't take long for me to realise, that Scotland was a very different country to England, and it went well beyond accents and wearing kilts. Standing on the pavement in Irvine, watching an Orange Order parade marching by with their sashes, pipes and drums was not something I had seen anything remotely like in England.

The viciousness of the nation's reaction, when Maurice Johnston, having left Celtic, returned to Glasgow to play for Rangers, was something I couldn't comprehend. I'd never seen openly hostile religious bigotry like it. I was working on the east coast at RAF Leuchars, near Dundee, and even the relatively sensible RAF engineers in the hangar that I worked with, were being more abusive towards each other than normal. It was all 'Blue nosed fuckers and Fenian bastats'. I'd never heard either of these terms used in such a venomous manner before.

Once I'd got my head around the cultural differences, I really enjoyed living in Scotland, Tracy and Vicky were preoccupied with a pony that Tracy's' dad had bought for Vicky. I developed a love of fishing, either off the local harbour wall, or on one of the many Lochs and rivers in the area. Occasionally I got the chance to go into the countryside shooting. I always enjoyed these outings; they were very sociable events.

Tracy and Vicky, spent a lot of time at the stable yard her dad ran. It was teaming with animals of all sorts, mostly dogs and horses. One dog in particular caught their eye. She was a young border terrier called Ellie. Ellie, lived in a stable on her own because she was a bad tempered and anti-social little dog, she absolutely hated other dogs and would snarl and snap at them whenever she got a chance. Guy and Lorna were happy for us rehouse her, so Tracy adopted her and brought her home. We renamed her Smellie, because she stank. If she wasn't wet and mouldy, rolling in fox shit or something else repulsive, she was farting.

It was Christmas time, and we had gone for a walk along the foreshore. When we returned home, the sight that met us was hilarious. The dog had got into the living room and unwrapped all the presents that contained chocolate. She had devoured a couple of selection boxes, and a tin of Quality Street. Basically, her own body weight in confectionary. She was sat in the corner, like a little hairy Buddha, with a massively distended stomach. I picked the very heavy little dog up, and put her in the garden, so she could vomit and shit to her hearts content.

During the week I stayed on the base at Leuchars. The other guys I worked with all lived locally, and in the evenings, went home to their families. I spent most nights after work on my own. I idled away a lot of the evenings in the gym or doing drawings and oil paintings in my room, not that I was any good, but I had a lot of time to pass. Although I had my own room, the showers and toilets were communal and at the end of the corridor.

After a shower one evening, during a momentary lapse of concentration, I applied a liberal measure of what I though was haemorrhoid cream to my backside. The area warmed up, and carried on warming up, until the heat was verging on painful, I realised my mistake. I had used 'Deep Heat' instead of 'Preparation H' on my delicate rusty sheriffs-badge. OOOh yaa. After an eyewatering sprint back to the showers, and some frantic scrubbing, the pain slowly subsided, eventually I carefully waddled back to my room. Next time I'll read the label, what a mistake to make.

Keeping a shotgun at the time, I had a permit to shoot on the local estuary during the duck and goose seasons. As the estuary was tidal, it could be a scary place to be alone, especially at twilight. One evening after dinner, I set out to shoot on what was a small island at high tide, but just a clump of trees in the middle of the mud flats at low water. As I walked across the flat silt towards the trees, I took a step forward and immediately realised I was in trouble.

My foot quickly sank deeper than normal below the silty surface, then continued to sink and slip away from me. I didn't know it at the time, but I'd stepped into a silted-up river bed, and the soft mud below the riverbank was very deep. I tried to backtrack, but couldn't get any grip on the steep, slippery, hidden river bank.

By now, I was thigh deep in the soft clingy sediment, and still sinking, as I slipped further into the invisible riverbed. I turned as best as I could to face back the way I'd come. With all the strength I could muster, I rammed the barrels of my gun into the more solid mud behind me. The only part of the gun that protruded above the clawing muck, was a small piece of the wooden stock which I hung onto. By now the mud was waist deep, and I started the very slow process of hauling myself back out of the slime. By laying as flat as I could on the surface, pulling on my gun stock and wriggling my legs, I eventually started to make headway. It felt like an eternity just to move a few feet.

By the time I got off the estuary, I was thanking my lucky stars, it was pitch dark and the tide was coming back in, covering the mud flats, and hiding all the dangers that lay below them. I got back to my room, went into the communal shower fully clothed and carrying my mud encased gun. I then spent about an hour washing the stinking, sticky silt off everything that had sunk with me into the mire. I was back on the estuary again the following night, nervous, wary and a bit wiser.

RAF Abingdon hosted an annual air show, a major event for the airbase, and the local town. This was one of the few times the whole of R&SS got together at our home base. We were all recalled to Abingdon for a couple of weeks each year, and heavily involved in preparing for the show. Doing whatever was needed to help the station get ready, roping off car parks, putting up signs, painting anything that looked a bit tatty, that sort of thing. We also dusted off our own squadron side show stands that we would be manning during the show. It was quite a busy and fun week.

For us, it was also the only chance in the year to enjoy a squadron social event. So, it was time, in mid-September for the 'works' Christmas party. Me and my mate John were walking across the airfield towards the corporal's club, where the squadron dinner was to be held. It was beginning to get dark, at about seven in the evening, we were not too far from the runway. We heard the roar of jet engines behind us, stopping to watch an RAF Tornado take off in the late summer twilight. Being close to a fast jet in full reheat, is a set of sensations you get nowhere else. It's truly awe inspiring. You don't hear it, so much as feel it. The roar from the afterburners pulsates through your whole body. It's like the world around you is shaking.

We watched, as the aircraft rotated, then lifted above the horizon. The unthinkable began unfolding, right there, in front of us. The undercarriage had barely retracted, when there was a thump, thump noise. The plane could only have been a few hundred feet above the airfield when things started to go awry. The left-hand engine afterburner started to fail. It went out, came back and then extinguished. The right-hand engine followed suit shortly after. The aircraft then started to sink towards the earth. There were two clear pops and we saw the crew eject clear of their stricken plane.

Me and John, looked on in disbelief, as two parachutes opened, and the crew drifted down. The aircraft sank slowly below the horizon, a huge fireball signalling that it had hit the ground. Then a plume of smoke climbed high above the Oxfordshire skyline. We both knew what was coming next. Turning back towards the barrack block we had to get out of our Hawaiian shirts, and into something more suitable for a night collecting aircraft wreckage. The crash alarm sounded, and that was the end of our squadron Christmas party for 1989.

It turned out, the aircraft involved was a 14 Sqn Tornado GR1. It had flown into a very large flock of birds, shortly after take-off.

Steve Woodhouse

The explanation that circulated the station after the crash, was highly entertaining to us mere plebs. The pilot was apparently the 14 Squadron Boss and he and his crewmate, were returning to RAF Bruggen having just received a roasting at the MOD in London. It was for the actions of one of their squadrons over exuberant crews, who had flown a bit too close to a hang-gliding competition, getting themselves filmed doing it by some news reporters. If this version was correct, then the Boss had just experienced a truly lousy day. He had received a bollocking for somebody else's rash flying and collected a Martin Baker tie pin.

Having lived in Troon for about eighteen months, it was becoming clear that jobs which appealed to me, and paid a decent wage, were few and far between in Scotland. So, I started looking farther afield. I had a little over a year left in the RAF and was looking more seriously for a new line of work. At this time, rising interest rates were crippling us, the mortgage repayments on our flat had more than doubled. I spotted an advert in 'The Sun' job section. 'AF fitters wanted, good rates'. I applied. I then took my entire years leave allocation from the RAF, then headed south for Luton airport.

Outside the hangar, I met the agent who I had spoken to briefly on the phone a couple of weeks earlier. He gave me a quick, don't say that, say this, kind of briefing, he knew what the company wanted, and I was close enough. After a short walk around a Boeing 737, with the company's maintenance supervisor, he was happy I knew how the machine worked, and more importantly how to dismantle and reassemble it. This was the first time I'd been close to a 737, but aeroplanes have a lot of mechanical similarities with each other, finding the important bits was relatively straight forward. I was staying with our friends' parents in their spare room, which was a huge benefit. Familiar, friendly faces when I got in on a night was a real bonus.

In all I spent about three weeks as a 'connie' servicing and repairing an assortment of airliners. I met a few decent guys and enjoyed the work. Just as well, because I worked solidly for as long as I could stay awake. At the end of my time there, I had a quick chat with the contract's manager. As he was recovering his companies' consumables from my tool kit, he asked if I was looking for a more permanent job. Until then, he didn't know about my RAF background. I told him why I had to leave Luton and return home and he promptly offered me a job for when I finished with the Air Force. I went home with a job offer, along with what amounted to a couple of months Air Force wages in my pocket. I was feeling pretty pleased with myself.

It was clear to me that to earn a decent wage, with my skill set at the time, we needed to be in a prosperous, industrial area of England. We sold our Scottish flat, packed up our home again and moved back into married quarters at Abingdon, ready to start our search for a new place to live. We had decided to settle around the home counties. Eventually finding a house we could just about afford in Leighton Buzzard, and immediately started the process of buying it.

One of the advantages of serving in the Air Force, is that you receive first class medical and dental treatment. For the previous few years during routine dental check-ups, various dentists had commented on my wisdom teeth. "Are these giving you any trouble" was a regular question. My wisdom teeth were emerging horizontally, instead of vertically, impacting on my rear molars. I decided to bite the bullet, excuse the pun, and have them removed before I left the mob. The station dentist referred me to a dental consultant at the RAF hospital at Wroughton.

On my arrival, I was met by a very relaxed and cheerful squadron leader in a white coat, he was the consultant performing the extraction. He lost no time in getting me into the reclined examination chair, had a look in my mouth, then a quick look at the x-rays, and said, " yup they need to come out". "I'll do one side today, when the holes heal up you can come back, and I'll pop out the other side."

It all sounded very straight forward. The operation started with a local aesthetic, injected into my gums via a normal dentist type syringe. Then he produced what looked like a small version of a plumber's mastic gun, pumping in more anaesthetic through the side of my face into my jaw and cheek. "We'll just give that a minute to work." He said as he headed out of the treatment room and into the corridor.

Half an hour later, a nurse appeared at my side and asked where the surgeon had gone. Unable to speak I indicated to the door. "He's ever such a good dentist, but very infuriating." she said, as she briskly headed out of the door to find the wayward dental surgeon. A couple of minutes later, the nurse reappeared leading the dentist back to his patient, without a word he set about my defective rear teeth with a series of scalpels, pry bars and pliers, none of which would have looked out of place in my rigger's toolkit.

It was a brute force, mechanical job, to get the teeth extracted. As I was numb from the neck up, I just laid back as the surgeon cut, levered, and contorted his way through the procedure. I left the hospital with fibre wadding filling the craters in my mouth, chuckling to myself, aware that I was missing a couple of wisdom teeth but feeling no pain.

Chapter 12

My War.

August 1990 saw global media coverage of the beginning of the Gulf War. Iraq had invaded and annexed Kuwait. They were systematically destroying the country, burning oil wells, killing civilians. Doing whatever they could to destabilise the region. The American led response would take the world by storm. It started with Operation Desert Shield. A massive mobilisation of troops, ships, and military hardware into the eastern Mediterranean and Middle East. The military build-up, alongside the diplomatic efforts, lasted until the end of the year.

As a member of R&SS, specializing in structural repairs to all types of fixed wing aircraft flown by the RAF, I felt sure I would be involved. If the predictions were to be believed, our level of expertise was about to be in high demand in the Gulf. I was one of the technicians who had developed a wide range of skills and experience, working on and around fighter aircraft. I had also spent a couple of years doing a lot of sheet metalwork, specializing in aircraft structural repairs. Having already completed ABDR (aircraft battle damage repair) training, including some practice during station exercises, this put my name firmly in the frame to join the coalition war effort. There were a lot of guys with experience like mine in the Air Force. We were all going to play our part.

The Icarus Game

Being put on twenty-four hours standby, in readiness to deploy to the theatre of operations was not a surprise. At that time, I was getting towards the end of my RAF service, having completed eleven of the twelve years I'd signed up for. This was a strange situation for us. On one hand we were preparing for me to leave the RAF and return to civvy street. On the other, I was preparing to go to war. The idea of seeing active service, left me with a mixture of feelings. I was now married with a five-year-old daughter, the thought of being separated for an indeterminate length of time from my family, the destabilising effect this would have on us was a worry. The thought of not returning at all, was one I didn't want to contemplate. However, this is what I'd signed up for, actual modern warfare. To participate, would be the most challenging and exciting thing I had ever done.

Inevitably, the call came as we knew it would. By now, the news coverage of the developing conflict was virtually constant. I thought I knew what I was heading into. Really, I had no idea. I left home very early in the morning and headed into work. There was a group of six of us, forming an ABDR team. Although we all worked on R&SS we had never worked together before. There was an air of nervous anticipation within the group, we were all excited to be going. Very quickly we started swapping stories, comparing backgrounds and experiences. There was a buzz in the minibus as it took us to Brize Norton. We walked into the departure building and started the pre-deployment preparation process.

Being the Air Force, it was all well organised. First desk, paperwork. Name, rank, number. Sign here. Then it was the medical screening. Roll up your sleeves. Sharp scratch. Fresh issues of Nerve Agent Pre-treatment (NAP's) tablets, and autojects (Atropine/Valium) for use in the event of a nerve agent attack. "Next!". Then personal gear, a new NBC suit, new canisters for your respirator. Collect your personal weapon and magazines, mine was a very familiar 7.62mm SLR. The hall was packed with a mixture of servicemen, mostly Army and Air Force. It was incredibly busy. All these people heading off to fight in the Gulf.

I was just one of over 53,000 British servicemen, who were eventually deployed into action during 'Operation Granby'.

The Abingdon BDR team as we referred to ourselves, congregated near the tea urn and waited for our next instructions. Our names were called, and we set off for the departure gate. At this point, we had no idea whereabouts in the conflict we were destined for. At the gate, we were told the Tri-Star outside was for us, it would be landing at Riyadh in Saudi Arabia. We were consigned to cattle class on this flight. The front two thirds of the plane was packed with equipment and munitions. We joined about a hundred other battle-ready servicemen, with their kit, all packed into the back third. It was a sweaty crush, and a long flight.

We had been airborne for what felt like an eternity, when the captain made an announcement on the PA. It was only ever going to be bad news. Up until that day, it was thought that Riyadh was out of range of Iraqi scud missiles. Apparently, this was no longer the case. As we approached the city, an attack was in full swing. The airport personnel had turned off the lights and taken cover. Literally.

It was about ten o'clock in the evening, we approached the blacked-out airfield and the Tri-Star crew was trying to contact the air traffic controllers, without any luck. We flew around in circles for a while, but the clock was ticking. We had to either land or go elsewhere. Landing on a runway that was unlit, in the dark, with no ATC was going to be a neat trick. As we approached the airfield, we got a running commentary from the guys sat by the windows. Explosions were going off all around the city. From my seat in the middle of the cabin, all I could see was flashes of light across the aircraft's windows.

For the first time, dying in a smoking hole full of twisted metal seemed like an unpleasant possibility. What a poor show, I might not even make it onto the battlefield.

The landing turned out to be uneventful, for us passengers at least. I'm sure the flight crew would have a different view. Scud missiles were still falling around the airfield, explosions flashed across the city as we taxied onto a large dispersal. The aircraft doors were opened, and a lone figure stood on the tarmac below the door. The little twat shouted up that he couldn't help us disembark, because there was an air raid going on and he was supposed to be in the shelter. He then shrugged his shoulders and tried to walk off. He changed his mind, when he was told very bluntly that there were a hundred blokes on the plane, they all had guns, and at that moment he was the only target. He dragged a set of steps to the door, then hastily led the way to the hardened shelter.

A hundred blokes, all aching from a long-cramped flight, loaded down with their kit, wearing new NBC suits freshly extracted from impenetrable, super thick vacuum-packed bags. Wheezing heavily through respirators, whilst trying to run the couple of hundred meters to the air raid shelter, must have been a comical site. When we were stopped at the entrance and asked for ID, a line had clearly been crossed. "Get out of the fucking way

Dickhead" followed by a stampede of squaddies seemed to convey the message very clearly.

The air-conditioned tranquillity of the concrete bunker was a respite that didn't last long. Behind his desk in a corner, an admin NCO had set up shop. He had lists of names and he alone knew where each one of us was going.

As soon as the missile attack had finished, our team was to board a RAF Hercules transport aircraft destined for Tabuk, in north western Saudi Arabia. That was ok, at least we had time for a brew.

The westbound flight, back across Saudi was only three or four hours, there was plenty of room on the Hercybird to stretch our legs. This was the first proper look I'd had at the Saudi Arabian desert; it is vast. Hour after hour of rocks and sand, the only feature that stood out, was the occasional isolated patch of green. Because of the rotating arm making up the irrigation system, these green fields were round. This novel feature of the landscape kept my interest for a few minutes, then it was back to my mates inside the Herc.

Our team was back together again, doing what all groups of servicemen do when they are not productively occupied. Taking the piss out of the organisation that dumped us where we were at that very point in time. Our escapade had begun in great style. We then started to consider what lay ahead of us. Whatever we thought was in store for us, would never come remotely close to the reality. Not in our lifetime anyway.

The Icarus Game

We walked down the loading ramp at the rear of the Hercules, onto the Airfield at Tabuk. The first thing for the smokers to do, was light up a cigarette. There was a lot of open space here, absolutely acres of sod all. We found a particularly barren piece of nothing, and a couple of the boys lit up. The first chance for a smoke in nearly twenty-four hours, I felt the relief for them, even though I didn't smoke. It was one of those Aaaaaahhhhhh moments.

Within seconds, a huge fuel tanker skidded to a halt on the gravel next to us. A purple faced, ranting Yank, with a gun slung around his neck jumped out of the cab. "What are you guys doing" the driver screamed. Pointing at his freshly abandoned truck. "That tanker is full of gas, you can't fucking smoke here". We looked around us at the absolute wilderness that stretched for miles. "What are you talking about you imbecile, park your tanker somewhere else", we had six guns, he only had one. Our little group finished their smoke, then sauntered back towards the aircraft we had arrived on. This guy was obviously taking his war way to seriously.

We made our way to the 16 Sqn line control building, to announce our arrival. There didn't seem to be much happening, which was quite surprising, given there was a war on. Everybody was really laid back. Our chief stepped forward when he saw the Squadron Warrant Officer. "Good morning, sir", he said. With a sweeping gesture of his arm towards the rest of us. "We are your battle damage repair team just arrived from Abingdon".

"Battle Damage? I've already got ABDR guys. You lot might as well fuck off; I don't need you". Shot down in flames we retired for a brew. A less dramatic approach was obviously needed, to integrate ourselves with our new workmates. After revising our plan, me and one of the other airframe's corporals went back to the control room. As we walked in I spotted a familiar face. Sat behind a desk chewing the butt end of a fat cigar, looking up at a chinagraph board, was a Sergeant I had worked with at Marham.

"Hi Mark, you bump into the weirdest people in the middle of a desert". "Woodhouse, what rock did you crawl out from under". Pleasantries out of the way, we had a quick catch up. Then we began to consider the uses our BDR team could be put to. Mark was one of the line ops controllers, he had spent most of his war growing a splendid set of whiskers.

He rounded up the squadron SNCO's and they had a short chat. It was decided that we would take on some of the none trade specific work. Releasing the squadron tradesmen to carry out engineering maintenance and repair work.

What a result, I was given a tractor, a towing arm, and a radio. As far as I was concerned, I had just bagged the best job of the war. Moving aircraft and equipment around the site, put me in contact with just about everybody on the squadron. I was never more than a few minutes from a brew and a chat. Collecting and spreading news, rumours and gossip was an integral part of my new job.

Our shift ran from 7pm 'til 7am, with half an hour travel each way to and from the accommodation compound. This gave us a thirteen-hour working night, seven days a week. Swapping shifts from nights to days was very problematic. So, nights it was for the foreseeable future. The temperature gradient between day and night in the desert is huge, in January it is in the high twenties and thirties (C) during the day, and close to zero at night. We would leave the accommodation compound in shirt sleeves at teatime, and by midnight we'd be wearing everything we owned. We'd still be freezing until the sun came back up.

This shift pattern had gone on for a few months without too many grumbles. However, the physical differences between the day and night shifts were becoming obvious, even the medics had noticed, so it must have been glaring. The day shift consisted of wide-awake, sun bronzed Adonis's. The nightshift was manned by semi-conscious, pale-yellow creatures, that cowered in the shadows avoiding any glimmer of daylight. Acute vitamin 'D' deficiency was the diagnosis, we needed some sunshine.

To change from days to nights, meant that both groups had to work a shift extended by an extra six hours. At first the day shift was reluctant to give up their tanning time, but eventually they conceded. After this we changed shifts once a fortnight or so.

Chapter 13

Tabuk.

When we first arrived in the operational theatre, the weaponry on the aircraft was very much standard issue equipment. Some of it was hand me downs, from older aircraft types that were no longer in service. The weapons designator system, for instance, was inherited from Buccaneer, it was twenty-year-old technology. Ok in its day but now virtually obsolete. It didn't take long, before the major weapons companies were beating a path to our corner of the desert, asking us to test their latest offerings. Some of it was junk, but some of the new weaponry available to us was phenomenal. Getting new bombs and missiles to play with, really focused the whole squadron in the most positive way imaginable.

Air raid warnings were a frequent event at Tabuk. Not that we were the intended target. The Iraqi missile batteries would launch scud attacks towards the major Israeli cities, and they would fly over us en route. The routine will be familiar to anybody who has served with the military. The sirens go off. You turn your back to the wind, fit your respirator and shout "Gas. Gas. Gas". Then run for shelter. Once under cover you put the rest of your NBC kit on, then wait for the 'All Clear', or for the earth to start moving.

After a while, it became obvious that taking cover for hours on end was hindering our ability to work, so immediately taking cover became less of a priority. We just put on our respirators and carried on working, making sure we knew where the nearest shelter was. Even if we were the intended target, scud missiles proved to be inaccurate, given the size of the dessert, the odds of being hit were slim.

During one air raid warning I was not especially busy, or to be honest, terribly concerned about the outcome of the attack. I parked my tractor out of harm's way and climbed up the side of a HAS (hardened aircraft shelter). From my vantage point high above the desert, I had a spectacular view of the panorama laid out in front of me. It hadn't changed noticeably since the crusades. Even after we found oil under it. This is just something else for us to fight over.

Revelling in my contribution to this fight, as far as I could see, I was the only soul above ground in this whole wilderness. No missiles streaking across the sky above me. No bombs dropping around me. Just solitude and tranquillity. It can be found in the most surreal of circumstances. I took off my shirt, rolled it into a pillow, laid on my back looking up at the clearest of blue skies, soaking up the sun's rays, waiting for the 'All Clear'.

There were occasions, when simply nothing was happening, these times were filled with all kinds of pastimes. We had built a volleyball court at the side of our HAS, and this was the team game of choice around the squadron. We played most days, and by the end of our war we could keep a decent rally going. I found an old 9 iron lying about on the site, spending quite lot of time wandering across the bondhu, looking for something to use as a ball. Dung beetles worked the best, they are the right size and shape, they sorted my slice out a treat.

There was always a lot of excitement when red cross parcels arrived. People, and groups from all over Britain were putting together boxes of treats, sending them out to the servicemen in the Gulf. Chocolate, toiletries, and magazines were all favourites. They would soon be devoured, stashed away, or read until they fell apart. We also received a lot of 'bluies', airmail letters from friends and family. these were particularly treasured. Sometimes they would arrive from school kids. 'To a soldier in the Gulf'. We made a point of picking these up and answering them. I must have written dozens of letters to people I didn't know and would never meet.

During any war there are herds of bureaucrats milling about in the offices of the MOD, trying desperately to demonstrate their own indispensability, trying to create themselves a little empire. Dreaming up schemes to justify their own existence. One such scheme had dramatic and predictable consequences in Tabuk. It was decided by the 'powers that be' in SW1, that because of Saddam Hussein's history of human rights abuses, there was a credible risk of him using biological or chemical weapons against us.

Obviously, we all needed protecting from such an attack. We were rounded up, and the medics set about implementing an inoculation program. I remember that anthrax was prominent on the list of biological agents we were 'protected' against. With true military efficiency the whole squadron, ground crew and aircrew were injected with a cocktail of biological agent, tolerance enhancing drugs within a few hours, all on the same day.

The result was catastrophic. The combination of medication that was administered, completely wiped us out for a couple of days. It felt like the worst case of man flu you could imagine. Hot and cold sweats, weak aching muscles, total loss of concentration. The entire squadron was decimated, in a near catatonic state. This was far more devastating to our ability to wage war, than anything the Iraqi's did. I still haven't contracted anthrax though, so that's a bonus.

Whilst we were in the war zone, our regular wages continued to go into the bank at home. Keeping a roof over our family's heads as you might expect. We received the equivalent of a couple of pounds a day in riyals, the local Saudi currency. This payment was made in lieu of missing a hot meal in the middle of our shift. Cash in local notes was very welcome, it paid for cigarettes and toothpaste mostly. A field post office was set up, and you just went along with your 'posbee' (post office account) book to collect your pocket money as you needed it.

Towards the end of the conflict, the bean counters at home were scouring the books to find penny pinching ways of saving their own salaries. Mostly by making our lives just a bit more uncomfortable. They homed in on our missed meal allowance.

The method the mandarins decided upon to deprive us of our pocket money, was to provide a hot meal on site. Imagine a typical airport with a single canteen for all the staff. A room to which everybody must be transported to at mealtimes. Not a practical proposition. Add to that, the cost of flying a purpose-built facility, to cater for several hundred people. Its equipment, its staff, nearly halfway around the world. You could put a Michelin starred restaurant in Kensington for less.

Nobody at Tabuk wanted this to happen. The system we had, worked to everybody's benefit. A cooked meal in the mess, before you left the accommodation compound on the bus for work. A sandwich during your shift, and another cooked meal when you returned to the compound at the end of your day, or night. Simple.

The Hercules transport arrived with the new field kitchen on board, a collective groan went up around the base. Aircraft came and went frequently at Tabuk, as you would expect at an air base. So, when we heard that a particularly quick-thinking loader, had offloaded the field kitchen from the inbound Herc, then transferred it directly onto another outbound Herc destined for the UK, we were jubilant. What an absolute star. I would love to have seen the faces in Whitehall, when they discovered their precious field kitchen had re-appeared, without warning at Brize Norton. The airmen's mess on the domestic site was by now overrun with spare cooks.

The business of war rumbled on, and we continued to do our day-to-day job, preparing aircraft for their missions. We were very successful in fulfilling our commitment to the allied effort.

The days were long, and there were lengthy periods when there was absolutely nothing to do. I needed a project. We drank a lot of tea during working days and nights. The usual method of recycling the waste was to take a leak on the side of the HAS. I decided to build a bespoke urinal, to improve sanitation and alleviate any confusion as to where this function should be conducted. It started with a deep hole full of rocks to act as a soak away and developed from there. It was a work of engineering genius, as far as I was concerned, conceiving the idea, and building It, kept me amused for a couple of days. The area around the HAS started to smell better almost immediately.

Some of the guys were talented artists, they entertained themselves painting insignia on the side of the aircraft. Some of these works were astonishingly good. Particularly bearing in mind the materials used, were just what was laying around the squadron at the time.

Sending 'Saddamagrams' was another popular pastime. This involved painting an emblem or message on the bombs that were to be dropped on enemy targets. Sometimes, these messages were sent on behalf of friends back home. The promise of a pint when I got back was enough to get you a photo of your message applied to a laser guided thousand-pounder. For me, it added a little levity to the war I was engaged in.

The fight was going very much in our favour, this was made apparent when we had a morale boosting visit from General Sir Peter De La Billiere. He was the Commander of the British Forces in the Gulf, a long-standing senior officer, with a solid track record. When he arrived at Tabuk, he made a point of visiting every corner of the base, talking to everybody he met. You couldn't help but be impressed by his very focused approach to the task in hand.

It was obvious to everyone that the conflict was coming to an end. CNN was showing footage of assorted dignitaries, celebs and politicians poking around with film crews. We saw them on the TV news reports but never in the flesh, what celebrity would come to Tabuk voluntarily?

Our targets had all been obliterated during the relentless bombing campaign. Saddam's Air force was annihilated, and his armies were in total disarray. We all wanted to march down Baghdad's Main Street, but this was ruled out. It was now just a matter of waiting for the senior military figures and politicians to sort out the surrender terms. For Iraq this was the start of a long period of unrest and misery. For us it was the end of an adventure. Well almost.

We heard that the field kitchen was on its way back. For those of us on the receiving end, this thing had come to symbolise everything that was wrong with our armed forces. Petty bureaucracy, trying to muscle in on genuine hard work and commitment. We were ready for it this time. On the base was a crew of engineers, equipped with a mass of earth moving machinery. Their role was to repair runways and roads after any attack. They took their heavy-duty digging gear to a quiet corner of the airfield, there they excavated a very large hole. As soon as the field kitchen arrived, it was taken away and buried for eternity beneath the desert sands. What field kitchen?

That should be the end of the silly field kitchen saga, but no. Somebody really had a bee in their bonnet over this one. During our last weeks at Tabuk, another even bigger, better field kitchen arrived, along with a Military Police detachment. They were taking no chances this time. It took ages to assemble, and with a fanfare it was operational. Ta-Dah. We had one meal in it. Then the Abingdon contingent collected our belongings, said our goodbyes, and climbed aboard the VC10 waiting to return us to Brize Norton. Our war was over. Thank you and goodnight.

Chapter 14

Civvy Street.

I was delighted to be back home, and when I walked into our RAF married quarter at Abingdon I was greeted by a very happy and relieved wife. Vicky however was less sure. After months of being away, I'm not certain that my six-year-old child knew quite who I was, or understood why I'd been absent from her life for so long. I had just walked in the front door and behaved like I lived there.

We all had a lot of catching up to do. Most of our possessions were still in boxes from the move down from Scotland. Tracy had only unpacked the basics, so when we got the keys for our new home in Leighton Buzzard, a few days after I got home from the Gulf, packing was minimal. The move was done in a weekend, and it was just a matter of settling back into the old routine, for the last few months of my Air Force service.

My final job with the RAF, was at Wittering, repairing Harriers. These vertical take-off aeroplanes were unique but starting to show their age. The latest generation were just about to come off the production line, but for now the RAF still operated GR1's. These needed regular structural repairs to their very highly stressed airframes. Although they were capable of manoeuvres that defied belief, using their vectored thrust power plant, this came at a cost. They vibrated, and shook about far more than a conventional aeroplane, consequently they developed a lot of cracks. That was my job, I was part of the team that repaired all those cracks.

The work at Wittering turned out to be much more enjoyable than I had expected, the job was steady. I could travel home every night and knew a lot of the guys I was teamed up with. It wasn't without its distractions either. One afternoon in September we were busy riveting a patch onto the side of a fractured Harrier, when the station crash alarm sounded. We went outside to watch the unfolding events. As we weren't part of the station crew we stayed out of the way. The Battle of Britain Memorial Flight was approaching the airfield.

Hurricane LF363 was en route to Jersey from Coningsby, along with the Lancaster and a Spitfire, within sight of Wittering its engine suffered a camshaft failure. The report says that 'There was a loud bang, it started to run very rough, with smoke pouring from the exhausts. The pilot, Squadron Leader Allan Martin, attempted to force land the aircraft at RAF Wittering, where emergency assistance would be available. Unfortunately, the engine failed completely at a late stage of the approach; the Hurricane stalled and crashed onto the airfield with the undercarriage still retracted. It slid backwards down the runway, as it came to a halt, it was engulfed in flames. Luckily, the cockpit escape door had fallen off in the impact, and the pilot was able to scramble out, and in his own words, "leg it". It was pure good fortune that he escaped with a broken ankle and minor burns.

From our vantage point, this looked like a scene from a wartime movie, it was hard to believe it was happening, right in front of us. We were relieved to hear the pilot had escaped with relatively minor injuries, but the near total loss of a valuable historic aircraft was a shock.

The armed forces employment contract is an unusual one, from the day you enlist, you know when you'll be leaving. I joined up on the twelfth of August 1980 and signed on for nine years, I later extended my service to twelve years. So, I knew for a long time that on the thirteenth of August 1992 I would be leaving the mob. Tracy liked being married to the Air Force, it offered a high degree of financial security, but by the time we left Germany, I'd had enough, and I wasn't going to sign up for any more time.

This desire for continuity, was possibly the single biggest factor in Tracy's decision to leave me. That, and me being around the house, generally getting in the way, being an inconvenience. I'm sure the only thing that had kept us together over the previous year or two, was living in separate counties, or on different continents. Things had been steadily deteriorating between us for a long while. I just hadn't wanted to accept it. When I came home from work one day to an empty house, I realised that things must have been worse than I'd thought.

Looking into my daughter's bedroom, as I went up the stairs to get changed out of my uniform was upsetting, her bed had been stripped off and the room was empty. No clothes scattered on the floor, no toys, or giggling friends, just silence. My bedroom was equally sterile. I showered and went downstairs, making a mental inventory of what was left in my house, it didn't amount to much. Sat in the living room, with my evening meal on my lap in an empty house was very gloomy. I didn't like it at all. Tracy had taken Vicky and returned to her mums in Scarborough. That meant an eight hour round trip, for me to spend just a few precious hours with her.

On the upside though, I was effectively single again. Thirty years old, own house, own car, not too atrocious to look at, and happy to be as affable and outgoing as I needed to be. I made the most of the attributes I'd been given. In short, I was like a kid in a sweet shop, making up for lost time. I've never seen the point in moping about, feeling sorry for myself.

There was also the minor matter of finding another job. I spent quite a few of my evenings writing application letters to potential employers. I did still have a mortgage to pay, and a daughter to support if the letters from Tracy's solicitor were to be taken at face value.

August 1992 saw the end of twelve years' service in the Air Force. It had been a great experience for me, I'd had a lot of memorable times and made a lot of good friends. I now had to decide what I was going to do next. I felt a change of direction was what I needed, so I'd applied for a range of different jobs. Anything but mending aeroplanes for a while would be fine by me. I eventually took a job as a 'Sales Rep' for a large chemical company based in Middlesex.

During a trip up to Scarborough to visit my parents and spend a little time with Vicky, Tracy said she wanted 'to talk'. Not something we had done much of during the preceding months. Over a couple of drinks, she convinced me to give our marriage another-go. It happened out of the blue, but I was happy to reunite our family, after nearly twelve months of separation.

Tracy and Vicky were settled back home in Leighton Buzzard by the following weekend.

Things at work had started slowly, endeavouring to find my feet in this new environment was a steep learning curve. Once I'd got my head around the products I was selling, and the people I was selling them to, business started to pick up. I began by selling a huge range of chemical products to general industrial customers. Soon after I started, some internal changes were made within the company. After a brief spell of being made redundant, I was reinstated and selling to the transport and aerospace industries. I was back on familiar turf but in a totally different role.

When I started on my patch, the annual turnover was below ten thousand pounds a year. After two years I was turning over more than two hundred thousand pounds. I'd worked hard at it. This rate of growth was not without the obligatory moments of stupidity on my part though. Selling to the transport world included dealing with several large local bus and haulage companies. They had hundreds of busses and trucks on the road every day, they all had to be washed, scrubbed, and serviced.

This took a bewildering volume and range of products. One of my favourite add-ons to sell, (because it was easy), was water and detergent pumped out through a pre-mixed dispenser. A simple box attached to the wall. Mains water was piped into it along with a metered detergent supply, and with the press of a button out came soapy water, mixed at a pre-determined ratio. Transport managers loved this, it saved them money and kept the concentrated detergent away from the eyes and hands of the cleaners. 'Elf an' safety innit'.

Whilst installing one of these marvellous little commission generators in High Wycombe bus station one afternoon, I came unstuck. It was a straightforward job that should have taken about half an hour. The customer had picked a suitable spot with a water supply, all I had to do was connect my box. Unfortunately, the stop valve on the end of the copper water supply pipe was so badly corroded that it wouldn't budge. I checked with the manager and was assured the water to this pipe was turned off, so I cut off the corroded valve. Bollocks. Water sprayed out of the severed pipe under mains pressure and soaked the floor and my feet. Shit and bollocks. I stood in the middle of a rapidly expanding lake of water in my suit trousers, smart brogues and a clean shirt and tie.

Knowing that I needed to remedy this cock up, which was relentlessly flooding the bus station floor, I took a new stop valve out of the boot of my car. Loosely assembling it, I tried to force it onto the open end of the pipe. The result was spectacular, a huge plume of water sprayed for three hundred and sixty degrees from my hands, soaking everything within fifteen feet of me. I was drenched. Fortunately, on that afternoon in High Wycombe, the bus station only had a couple of hundred people milling about. A bloke in a suit taking a cold shower, in the middle of the crowd of shoppers was not going to attract too much attention. Of course not, I'd brought the place to a virtual standstill.

After a brief thought about what I was doing, I worked out that if I opened the new valve first, tightened it onto the pipe, and then closed it, a lot less water would be sprayed in my face and around Buckinghamshire. Success, I finished the installation, jumped into my car and left. I was soaked, and reminded myself all the way home, that on occasions I could be a proper prat.

Vicky was playing upstairs with her friend, there was lots of laughing and giggling coming from her room. This suddenly turned to screaming and crying. We shot upstairs to see what was wrong. The two girls were inconsolable. Having built an obstacle course out of books and toys, they were racing Vicky's gerbils, PJ, and Duncan around it. In their excitement, whilst cheering on their respective gerbil, Duncan had been trodden on. I don't know how much blood a gerbil contains, but most of Duncan's had come out of his nose and mouth, it was now staining Vicky's carpet. 'Mummy, Duncan needs to go to the doctors.' Duncan was pronounced dead at the scene.

I'd received a rather cryptic message from the office to contact a potential new customer, a chap called Gary at Air Atlantique. This was a little odd because, I was already dealing with their engineering department. I gave him a call and arranged a meeting at his local McDonalds. When we met up, he was keen to arrange a supply of some products that his company already bought from us. I was confused, but one division of a large company, not knowing what the other department is doing, is not unheard of. I said nothing, breezed through the meeting, handed over some safety documents on the products we had discussed, then made a note to have a chat with Air Atlantiques engineering manager. We continued our discussion about aeroplanes and life in general over another coffee.

It turned out that Gary was a Flight Engineer with the airline, and like me, an ex-Air Force technician. We got to swapping stories, and the meeting ended with an invitation to meet Air Atlantiques 'Chief Pilot', who at that time was on the lookout for Flight Engineer candidates. I was mildly curious about possibly flying aeroplanes for a living. My previous experience had been repairing them.

Resistance was futile, I knew that. And I knew that being mildly curious has got me into plenty of trouble in the past. If the truth be told I was not too keen to get back on the spanners, but at this point I knew nothing of the role played by Flight Engineers. A few days later the meeting was confirmed and before I knew it, I was sat outside the Chief Pilot's office.

Gavin, it turned out was a very relaxed and competent manager, with an air of total self-confidence. I on the other hand, was trying to fathom out the series of events that led to me being sat across the desk from him. We talked about the company, about my background. Why did Atlantique need more Flight Engineers on their Lockheed Electra's? Because these old aeroplanes were designed in the nineteen fifties and sixties and had to have three crew members. The company were using First Officers in the FE roll, (Systems Panel Operator's, SPO's), and neither the company nor the First Officers liked it one bit, for lots of reasons.

The job would mostly be night work. The idea of never having to get out of bed at six thirty in the morning again to go to work really appealed. While I was there, I did a few psychometric, personality and general maths and English type tests. Apparently, I was just the chap for the job. All I needed to do was pop down to Gatwick, get a medical certificate and sit the ATPL tech group exams. Pass all that lot, and the job was in the bag. I left Coventry Airport with a pile of manuals to study.

This was a very exciting development, and completely unforeseen, I decided immediately, that it was an opportunity I would pursue until it concluded, one way or the other. Success or failure were the possible outcomes at this point, which makes things simple.

The ball was started rolling by booking a class one medical with the CAA, without this certificate any further effort would be pointless.

Meanwhile my day job continued. This time I was following up on a random query, relating to cleaning hard set mortar from cement mixers. Armed with a couple of gallons of hydrochloric acid based cleaner, I set about a concrete encrusted cement truck, somewhere in Hertfordshire with a bucket and a brush. Using the product neat the cement just dissolved away, and if you ignored the cloud of pungent yellow smoke that was forming around me, this cleaning compound could be considered ideal for the job.

Freshly emboldened by my initial success, I climbed about on the truck, scrubbing madly at the heaviest areas of filth I could reach. All the time giving a running commentary to the transport manager, extolling the benefits of this highly acidic, corrosive product. Cockiness, once again got the better of me and I took my eye of the ball, or rather I took my eye off the cloud of yellow smoke. I inhaled a good lungful, coughed, and spluttered, lost my footing, and fell off the truck.

The Icarus Game

The ignominy of bouncing arse first from the rear mudguard of the cement mixer, was only surpassed by landing face down in the biggest puddle of cement slurry in the yard. The pin striped suit I'd worn the previous day, to introduce myself to the world of aerial freight transport, was now soaked in muddy water, and covered in cement. I needed that new job.

Chapter 15

Flog It.

Sales jobs have ups, as well as downs, and distractions from the daily grind could be found, if you were open in your outlook. Christmas can be a fun time for sales reps, blowing the expenses budget on wine and chocolate for your favourite customers, spreading the season's cheer. This time I was in Leicester, at a bus depot chatting to the ladies that spent their working days cleaning bus interiors. Tea break interrupted my product effectiveness brainwashing session, so armed with a box of Quality Street, I walked to the tea cabin with the cleaners.

'How do you like it' came the question as soon as I walked in. 'Anyhow I can get it.' I grinned. 'But white, no sugar works best'. 'Read us a story Steve, you've got a proper posh voice.' Said one of the girls, as she passed me a dog-eared copy of Rustler. 'Ok, what's your favourite'. I then spent the next twenty minutes reading an erotic account of a hunky fireman, saving a horny damsel in distress, from being stuck in a lift. Drinking tea and eating chocolates with half a dozen cleaning ladies.

Not unsurprisingly, our hero even found the time and energy to give the fair maiden a good seeing to, before throwing her over his shoulder and descending his enormous extending ladder. The word 'Shaft' seemed to be used a lot more than necessary, and always elicited a leery oooh, and a giggle, from my audience, so I emphasised it more than was decent. It was a clean bit of naughty festive fun. The ladies went back to work a bit happier, and I had sold another tanker full of detergent before I drove back down the M1 chuckling to myself.

Behind the easy-going exterior, things at work were going through another state of change. As far as I was concerned it was for the worse. I had always been on a 'commission only' contract, and the rapid growth in the turnover of my territory, had led to an equally rapid growth in my earnings.

The company wanted me to hand over some of the accounts that I had won, giving them to more experienced sales managers to handle on a day-to-day basis. They also wanted to welcome me into the fold as a salaried salesman. I wasn't happy with either of these proposals. If your experienced sales managers want some prize companies on their books, they'll have to get off their backsides and work for them. And no, I won't accept a pay cut, even if it will give me some financial stability. My boss dug in his heals, so I tossed the company car keys across the desk to him and left. That was that.

By the end of the following week, I was working again. This time selling aluminium tubing and television aerials. What's more I was earning more than the chemical company wanted to pay me and had a better company car. Happy days.

Overcoming the hurdles set by the CAA proved to be a slow and painful grind. As a government agency, their rules are set in stone, there is no room for wheeling and dealing. You simply must tick all the boxes. I'd passed the medical, I'd also spent months, ploughing through the study material for the exams I had to sit.

It was now the moment of truth. Two days of exam papers to sit in the strictest of environments, all adjudicated over by a ministry official. A couple of airframes papers, structure and pressurization, hydraulics mixed with pneumatics, engines, theory of flight, electrics, avionics, Flight Engineers general paper. A total of seven long exams, if memory serves. To pass each paper, you need to score better than seventy five percent.

Succeeding in more than half the papers gets you a partial pass, you can then re-sit the remaining papers. A maximum of three attempts was allowed at the tech group of papers. If you don't pass them all by your third sitting that's it for the attempt. You then get to wait twelve months, for another-go at the exams, from the beginning.

As well as passing these exams, I had to amass one hundred hours of flight training time, under the supervision of a Flight Engineer Type Rated Instructor (TRI). To this end I was encouraged to join as many flights on the Electra as possible. I really loved this sudden and unexpected change in my lifestyle. As often as I could, I'd work all day as a salesman and fly all night as a trainee Flight Engineer. This was a chance for me to meet and talk to all the other flight crew at the airline. I drove them nuts, with a million questions and soaked up the experience I was gaining.

My first close-up experience of the Lockheed L188 Electra was when I arrived at East Midlands Airport with Gary and the rest of our crew. I was there for an introduction ride, so would be tagging along for a couple of days. As we climbed out of the crew bus and walked towards the aircraft, I was amazed by the sheer size of the machine in front of me. Dominating the wings were four huge propellers.

Boarding an aircraft as a passenger, you take it for granted that it's going to be big with lots of seats. Climbing the ladder into an aeroplane that you hope to be a crewmember of soon, gives things a whole different perspective. The freight deck seemed enormous to me; my viewpoint of aeroplanes came mostly from fighter jets with two seats. This was totally different, and more reminiscent of my flights around Arabia in a Hercules during the Gulf conflict.

That night we were going from East Midlands to Madrid, then onwards to Oporto in Portugal. We were operating just one flight schedule, for a typical and very busy night on the DHL network. I had never been in such close proximity to a hugely complex set of routines, operating in real time before. Everything is done against the clock. Getting my head around this was going to take some doing. Give or take a splash of fuel the Electra can carry fourteen tonnes of freight.

The freight arrives at the aircraft along with a team of loaders. The security screened, weighed, pre-packed aluminium containers filled with parcels, known as ULD's, are loaded onto the aircraft and secured in around fifteen or twenty minutes. The whole process is extremely physical, with lots of pushing and shoving. Each bin can weigh around one and a half tonnes, and there are eight of them, with a half bin in the rearmost position. Propelled by four or five hefty lads, pushing them across rollers they move around very quickly.

Once the loading is complete, the load team and all their mechanical equipment move on to the next aircraft. Things had been so hectic since we arrived at the aeroplane, I had barely noticed that other planes were taxiing past us and taking off. While the loading was going on, Gary had fuelled the aeroplane, whilst the other crew members completed the pre-flight checks. The doors were closing as the first officer called air traffic on the radio for our start clearance. I was strapped into the jump seat behind the captain with a headset on, watching and listening to the whole start up and taxi routines. It was bewildering. By the time we got airborne my brain had turned to mush, so I sat back and enjoyed the flight. My only useful contribution to this whole process, was making the coffee's during the cruise.

As I was to discover, the actual flight is the quietest time of the working night, and that is only relative, it's still busy. Coordinating all the processes, checks and drills that happen on the ground and during the flight, along with keeping on top of the paperwork before, between and after flights, seemed to be the toughest part of the job. As for the actual flying and navigation, at this point, that was all a total mystery to me. We landed in Madrid and the chaos resumed. Freight off, fuel on, freight on, checks, drills, airborne again.

It was an absolute blur of activity. By the time we arrived in Oporto, I was shattered, but the night was not yet finished. The freight was off, and we had to secure the aeroplane for the day's layover, before getting into the crew bus, leaving the airport, and getting a taxi to the hotel. The first time I had a chance to talk to the captain and first officer, was about twelve hours after we first met in Coventry, over the hotel breakfast in Oporto.

After a day's sleep and a bite to eat, we were back in the taxi, heading for the airport, to do it all again in reverse. A couple of rotations of this route later we ended our trip in Brussels. Then it was a matter of hitching a jump seat ride, back to East Midlands in the early hours of the morning. It felt like a very long night shift. Eventually we got into a car driven by a cadet pilot back to Coventry. By the time I'd left Atlantiques ops office and driven home, I was absolutely knackered. The previous couple of days had been a real eye opener.

These sorts of flights became more frequent and was clocking up a few hours here and there, towards my hundred-hour goal. Then I received a phone call from Atlantique. Could I spare a week? To go and collect an aeroplane that the company was in the process of buying. It needed to be test flown and delivered back to Coventry. A week sounded a long time, "Where was the plane". "Opa Locka, Miami". This would rack up a lot of hours, and flying around Florida doing the testing would be a blast.

It was the first time I'd be on the operating crew of a trans-Atlantic flight too. I wasn't to be paid for any of these training flights, but the company would pick up the tab for everything. Too right I could spare a week.

At the hotel in Miami, we met up with our companies' engineers, financial director and the agent brokering the sale. It was going to be a couple of days before we could test fly the aeroplane. The company preparing it for us was still working on it. Could we entertain ourselves in Miami for a while?

The first test flight was done over the Everglades, but in truth there was so much wrong with the aeroplane, we could have been anywhere. The fabulous views across Florida were of little interest to us, as we concentrated on the none-existent cabin pressurisation, non-functioning generators, and erratic engine temperatures and prop RPM's. By the time we landed, the snag list was extensive. The engineers looked glum when we handed the plane back to them. The week the company had scheduled to collect this aeroplane was clearly going to stretch out a bit.

By now my mentor, Gary was taking more of a back seat during the routine flying, and just gave the occasional word of encouragement, or an explanation on a procedure I was uncertain about. This trip was going to be different though. The prime business in Florida was to carry out test flights prior to purchasing this aeroplane. This is a very detailed process that involves a lot of system testing.

The most taxing of these routines is shutting down and restarting all four engines, one at a time during a single flight. If it's done incorrectly, it can be catastrophic. Gas turbine engines work at much higher temperatures than other motors. To complicate things a little more, some parts of the engine get a lot hotter than others. So, you can only start an engine if it's at operating temperature, or entirely cooled. On the Alison's fitted to the Electra, that means if you want to shut down and then relight an engine, it must be running again within ninety seconds of shutdown, or not started until it has thoroughly cooled down, and that takes fifteen minutes.

This can be a very expensive thing to get wrong. It's quite possible to do a massive amount of damage to the engine, the propeller, or the airframe, if you make a mistake. Failing to get the engines restarted within the ninety seconds can add up to an hour onto the test flight. At a couple of thousand pounds an hour to fly an Electra, the pressure is on. This is one of the drills that keeps the Flight Engineer, and the rest of the crew concentrating very hard. During the test flight Gary did the first two shutdowns, while I watched. We then swapped seats, and I did the second two. It went fine which was a huge relief.

The next test flight uncovered a few snags with the aircraft, which we handed back to the engineers to fix. A couple of days later we were airborne again, checking the work that had been done. The following morning, once everybody was happy, we departed Miami and flew up the Eastern Seaboard of the United States, with a night stop at Goose Bay in Newfoundland.

Goose Bay is a regular stopover point for trans-Atlantic traffic. It was a place I'd heard a lot about whilst I was in the Air Force. This was my first visit though. It's incredibly isolated, even by Canadian standards. A single road ran through the town, with a set of traffic lights in the middle of the settlement. Our hotel was at one end of the road, the only bar in town was at the other end.

We had a pleasant stay, and the following day we prepared to leave. There was one snag though, we had filled the Electra with fuel, only to discover that neither our fuelling account nor Amex card worked here. We all emptied our wallets of cash and cards, waiting an age, while the bowser driver started the long job of swiping them through his payment machine. Eventually, the huge bill was settled, and we continued our journey home to Coventry.

This little glimpse into another aspect of flying, outside of the routine freighting for the big parcel distributers was great fun. It certainly motivated me and made me concentrate a lot harder on my upcoming licensing exams.

I did make rather hard work of these crucial technical theory tests; despite a lot of study, I could only manage a partial pass on the first sitting. On the second sitting I bagged another two papers. That left the flight engineer's general paper, between me and my new job. The problem was that no study material was available for this paper, unlike the other papers, which were for pilots as well as F.E.'s and so were familiar around the company. When I'd sat this exam paper on previous attempts, I would come out of the hall and write down as many questions and answers as I could remember.

Then when I got home, I'd dig through the manuals, trying to find the correct answers for the questions I was uncertain of. By the third sitting I was much better equipped than previously.

After about a year of study and exams, I waited by the front door for my results. I was cock-a-hoop when my pass certificate came out of the envelope. It was late Thursday morning, and I got straight on the phone to Air Atlantiques Chief Pilot. "Hi Gavin, it's me again, I've got my 'Tech Group' results and I've passed".

"That's great Steve, well done. I've got an Electra type rating course leaving Heathrow this weekend. Be here at eight o'clock on Sunday morning. You'll be away for three weeks". "You'll need to sign your employment contract and training bond before you go. They'll be here, waiting in Op's for you". After a short pause, "You did want the job, didn't you?".

YYEESS. After investing more effort than I'd put into anything before, I'd cracked it. Then I remembered, I already had a job. I jumped into the company car and drove to Aylesbury. I needed to explain to my boss, Richard, why I was leaving my second job inside a year with no notice. He took it very well and wished me all the best. I left the offices, walked around the corner, and caught the bus home. Now I needed a car.

Chapter 16

In at The Deep End.

On Sunday morning, I arrived bursting with enthusiasm at the operations office of Air Atlantique. Before anything else could happen, I had to sign my contracts. The training bond, and employment contract meant I would be working for the company for the next two years, as a flight engineer. These contracts were to cover the costs involved getting me qualified as a crew member. It was a surreal couple of hours. I met up with the other trainees who would be on the L188 Lockheed Electra type rating course with me. Four first officers and me as the token flight engineer.

We were a mixed bunch, two of whom were already working for the company. Ken had built his hours as a flying instructor, with Highland Airways in Inverness, Paul had been flying a reconnaissance plane, doing topographical surveys, and shipping lane patrols, with Atlantic Reconnaissance. Jake had been working as a flying instructor at Southend, Tim was seconded to us from British Airways. I was the only non-pilot and had no idea what to expect over the next three weeks.

Before we had even got into the minibus, the plan changed. Gavin, who was going to accompany us to Seattle, as one of our instructors, had been called upon to fly a charter for the company.

So, we were given our airline tickets, a few dollars each, a photocopy of the Chief Pilot's credit card, and sent on our way. We were all chattering like excited schoolboys in the bus to Heathrow, except Jake. He was having difficulty breathing and remembering his name. After a night out with Gavin, celebrating getting his new job, he had yet to wake up enough to realise that he had the mother of all hangovers. The only thing keeping him alive during the drive to Heathrow was a regular supply of nicotine.

Most of the talk revolved around piloting interests. Licencing is always a hot topic among new flight crew, it's an absolute minefield of rules and requirements. In 1995, we were still operating under BCAR's (British Civil Airworthiness Requirements) and had yet to join the European system. Under these old rules having passed the medical, navigation group and technical exams, flight tests and instrument rating, pilots would be issued a BCPL. The 'Basic Commercial Pilots Licence' allowed them to fly light aircraft for hire and reward, but not air transport. That meant flying instruction, parachute dropping, glider towing, aircraft delivery, and aerial survey work was about the limit.

After the BCPL holder had completed seven hundred flying hours, they could apply for a CPL. This 'Commercial Pilots Licence' allowed the holder to act as first officer/ co-pilot, for the air transport of passengers and freight on an airliner. Upon amassing one thousand five hundred flying hours, you qualified to apply for an ATPL. The 'Air Transport Pilots Licence' allows you to be the commander of a public transport airliner.

The ATPL is the goal for all commercial pilots. This signifies a level of experience beyond question, opening-up a lot of opportunities. Gaining this experience was the tricky bit.

Companies knew the rules, and would often exploit young enthusiastic pilots, on the premise that they were providing experience for them. Particularly in the conversion of a BCPL to a CPL. This often involved a lack of any tangible payment, and in the worst cases, pilots were expected to pay for the privilege of gaining experience.

This became more complicated, when it was explained that flight time recorded in your logbook was further subdivided into 'Handling Pilot' and 'Non-handling Pilot'. If, as the first officer, you had control of the aircraft during take-off and landing, you were deemed to be 'Handling', and could log a full hour for each hour flown. If, however, you were operating the radio and completing the flight log, then you were considered to be 'Non-handling' and could only claim thirty minutes in the hour. Worse still, if you drew the short straw and were operating as the 'Systems Panel Operator' (SPO/ Middle seat), you could only log twenty minutes for each hour flown.

For this reason, the more flight engineers there were in the company, the better the young pilots liked it. My job was to occupy the middle seat and operate the systems panel during the flight, carry out pre-flight inspections, refuel the plane, occasionally top up engine and gearbox oils, help diagnose engineering problems and join in with the loading and strapping down of freight. A duff job if you were a pilot, a great job if you were a flight engineer.

The day's travelling went by very quickly, and before we knew it, we were checking into the hotel in Seattle. The companies account took care of the room bills, and our dodgy photocopied credit card amazingly secured the extras, meals, and bar bills, on the promise that our boss would be arriving imminently, with the genuine plastic.

We dumped our gear, and made for the bar to meet our ground school instructor, Ed. Or to give him his full title, Captain Edgar J. Lamb Jnr 3rd. A grand moniker for a large character.

Ed was a retired Eastern Airlines training captain, who had been flying Electra's since their introduction in the late 1950's and early sixties. He had a lifetimes worth of experience and anecdotes to pass on. A big man in all senses, over six feet tall and as he called himself 'a full-sized guy'. He was not a presence that could be overlooked, loud and confident with a style that suited an ebullient American, complete with broad red suspenders (braces) holding up oversized jeans.

Ed's job was to teach us the technicalities of the Electra. It's history and development, as well as detailed explanations and demonstrations of the assorted systems onboard the aircraft. Upon our return to the UK, we would have to pass the CAA's Electra ARB (Airworthiness Review Board) exam. This is a technical written paper, conducted under the usual examination conditions at Gatwick.

This was an intense couple of weeks in the classroom, working through the various systems in detail. As well as the classroom and aircraft manuals, we also had access to a variety of aircraft components, training rigs and the flight simulator. With Ed's precise explanations, handling the aircraft parts for ourselves. Seeing the system in operation on the training rig, and seeing it working in the simulator. We were very well equipped to discuss the technicalities of the aircraft during flying training sessions. It made the checks and drills we had to learn later a lot easier to digest.

During a break in the lessons, we were sat having a coffee and trying to unscramble our brains. Attempting as best we could to get our heads around the operation of the Electra's massive propeller. How it converts four thousand shaft-horsepower into controllable thrust. We could not help but overhear Ed's loud southern drawl on the telephone to his wife, who was at home in Miami. "Just sweep the sucker out with a broom" was the snippet that caught our attention.

"Everything ok Ed?" we enquired when he re-joined us. "Oh, sure. It's just my wife being a drama queen. She's found a 'gator in the garage and doesn't know what to do with it.". We spluttered on our coffee's. "How big is this 'gator?". "Around six or seven feet, I think. Normally I take care of this kind o' thing.". Well, if Mrs. E. J. Lamb 3rd Jnr. can deal with Ed, ejecting a six-foot alligator from the garage with a broom should be no problem. They breed them tough in the Southern States.

The course was going well for all of us, concepts that we thought would be difficult to understand were starting to make perfect sense. During the evenings we spent a lot of time as a group learning the limitations of the plane, all the numbers that we needed to know, and be able to recall instantly. It's important not to break the aeroplane through ignorance, and 'limitations' is a section of the type rating exam. There's a lot of numbers to learn, maximum speeds, oil quantities and pressures, engine turbine temperatures, RPM's, cabin pressure differentials, altitude limits and a hundred others. All of which must be applied, all the time you are in the aircraft. It's like learning your times tables, lots of repetition until it sinks in.

Me and Jake were stood on my room balcony with a beer, looking out over SeaTac Airport. Watching the aircraft landing and taking off. Simply admiring the industrialised, Northwest Pacific coast sunset. We were discussing how surreal it was that we had been able to work ourselves into this position in our lives. It was a glorious evening and one of the few occasions I've taken the time to reflect on what a fulfilling life I lead.

Neither of us could believe our good fortune, Jake had worked long and hard to reach this point, I had also put in a lot of effort and been helped massively by being in the right place at the right time. I've always considered myself to be luckier than most. Our reflections didn't last long, a summons to the bar brought us back to reality. More beer, more Alka-Seltzer and ibuprofen. It's a tough job they say, but somebody had to do it.

Both Jake and Ken, had come through the flying instructor route into the airline, they were passionate about flying. During our drinks they went into detail about the thrill of learning to fly and how it had opened up so many avenues for them, both socially and professionally. I now had access to a variety of aeroplanes and was very keen to learn. Jake offered to teach me, at mates' rates.

Our time in the classroom with Ed was at an end, and he had done a pretty good job with us. After ground school on the Friday, we drove him up to the airport for his flight back to Florida. We had the following day exploring Seattle, then on the

Sunday Gavin arrived for the next phase of our ground school training.

Nobody was more pleased to see him than the hotel manager. We had run up a respectable tab in the bar on our photocopied credit card, and the manager was getting impatient to have his bill settled. Gavin's actual credit card was immediately maxed out. Of course, we blamed the excesses on Ed.

The next part of our training was a week in the flight simulator, learning and practicing the 'Normal', 'Abnormal' and 'Emergency checklists'. For the Electra and there are a lot of these. We had prepared in part for this by learning all the checklist 'Memory Items', and reading through the checklists as often as we could. The 'Memory Items', are usually the first couple of actions on the checklist, that are intended to keep you alive long enough to carry out the rest of the checks. Typically, it's actions like; 'Don oxygen mask-100%'. 'Shut down engine'. 'Discharge fire extinguisher'. The type of response to a situation that makes a potentially disastrous event survivable. The rest of the checklist should then lead the crew through stabilising the situation, then recovering as much functionality from the aircraft as possible.

The simulator was a relic from the fifties, an amazing piece of electrical wizardry. The front of an Electra fuselage containing a full working cockpit, was mounted on a platform, and set in a room about half the size of a tennis court. This room had rows of wardrobe sized, steel cabinets, filled with valves, relays and capacitors, the cabinets were crammed into every inch of available space. Each array of circuitry was connected to the controls and instruments on the flight deck. The whole thing was a marvel of space age engineering. It was also August, the outside ambient temperature was in the thirties, add to this the heat generated by the mass of electrics controlling the sim, and the temperature inside the cockpit soared into the forties. We didn't call it the sweat box for nothing.

The sessions in the sim were incredibly busy, the workload on any flight crew during normal operation of the aircraft is high, during abnormal or emergency operations, it becomes a high-pressure exercise in managing priorities.

The first few sessions were tough, and they were just reinforcing regular routines, cockpit setup and checking emergency equipment. Engine starting was focused on very thoroughly. With turbines at around $150,000 a pop, you don't want to cook them too frequently. In a modern airliner any parameter that is exceeded during engine start, will result in the onboard computer (FADEC or similar) cancelling the start process. In the nineteen fifties such things were science fiction. If we didn't spot and react correctly to a malfunction, it was going to be expensive.

We were steadily working our way through the various exercises. With two crews to train, we were doing half a day in the sim, then swapping over to do the other half of the day in the classroom. This classroom time was used either to prepare for the next sim session, or to revise the previous work we had done with Ed.

Paul, Jake and me, were in the sim when Gavin had to nip out for a 'comfort break', leaving us with the aircraft at ten thousand feet. I sat back and put my feet up, waiting for him to return and the session to continue. Paul and Jake looked across me, at each other and were clearly hatching a plan. "What?" I asked. 'Do you think this thing will roll' they asked each other. I had no idea, but I knew I was about to find out.

They grinned and went for it. Jake called for more power, so I eased the power Levers forward. He lowered the nose to accelerate the plane, then pulled us into a gentle climb, simultaneously putting in aileron and rudder to roll the aircraft onto its back. As we started to go inverted, the simulator spat out its dummy.

Warning horns blared, lights were flashing and the gyro's toppled. All the instruments went crazy. We were now in an inverted spin, heading rapidly for the ground. Jake fought manfully with the controls throughout the chaos as we watched the altimeters unwind. But his effort was totally futile. We had clearly exceeded the machines capabilities. It took about two minutes of frantic wrestling and sweating before we hit the ground and the lights went out. Ooooohh. Bugger. It was now time to deny everything.

Gavin returned to the cockpit, and was totally perplexed, 'What have you lot done to my sim? I only left you alone for two minutes.' 'We don't know what happened, it just switched off' we protested. 'I'll get the engineer to take a look.' Gavin said, as he headed down the flight deck steps. We all skulked off into the rest area and made a jug of coffee. After half an hour or so Gavin reappeared with the bad news. The engineer was going to be working late to try and fix the sim, he had no idea what the problem might be, or if he had the spares he would need. We all returned crestfallen to the hotel.

The next morning at breakfast, Gavin appeared looking as stern as I've ever seen him. 'The sim is seriously damaged! The engineer has been working on it all night, he has had to wire a parts supplier in Russia for the spares he needs.' This could be the end of the course. It might even be the end of the sim altogether.' We were mortified, our dream jobs were evaporating right in front of us. Then Tim chimed in, 'It's no good Gavin' he wailed 'I can't lie any more, it was these three' he gestured towards Paul, Jake, and me. 'They were trying to roll the sim and crashed it.'

'YOU BASTARD WILLIS.' We all cried in unison.

At this point, Gavin couldn't hold it together any longer, he struggled to stifle his laughter. It took him a full minute to compose himself. 'It was just a blown fuse. Finish your breakfasts and get down to the sim, we've got a bit to catch up on.'

We had a little down time to do some sightseeing, so we all headed into town to do all the touristy attractions. Up the Space Needle, into Pike's Place Market, coffee in the original Starbucks. On the waterfront was an unusual gift shop that fascinated me, it was full of the strangest curiosities.

The two exhibits that I found the most morbidly attractive, were a couple of mummified corpses, picked up from the Oregon trail during the mass migrations west in the mid 1800's. One was a woman who had died of tuberculosis, the other was a man who had been shot in the abdomen. Both had just been discarded on the side of the road, at the height of the 'Gold Rush,' they had desiccated in the sand and sun. A hundred and fifty years later, they are on display in glass cases in a Seattle gift shop. Not what they expected when they set out for a new life in the promised land to the west.

The rest of our sim training went without a hitch. That is not to say it didn't involve a lot of sweat and concentration, it certainly needed its fair share of that. By the end of the course, we were picking up faults, failures, and emergencies within a split second of them occurring. Nothing slipped past any of us. The merest flicker of a warning light or twitch of a needle on any gauge, the distinctive sound of a popping circuit breaker or an out of place click of a relay, had us all scanning the instruments like hyper aware meercats.

These responses were the desired outcome of the course. This conditioning would follow us all for years to come, flying around in aeroplanes that pre-dated the jet age and were older than all of us. In these classic old aircraft, it's not a case of will it go wrong, more a case of when, followed by, what the fuck will it do next!

The last day in the sim ended traditionally, with us all dying in a heroic ball of flames. This is basically a scenario were, if it can go wrong, it will, until the aeroplane just physically can't fly any more. It goes something like; "Engine fire", dealt with. "Hydraulic leak", dealt with. "Engine failure" dealt with. "Electrical fire" dealt with. "Fuel leak" dealt with. "Propeller overspeed" dealt with. "Which of those engines we just shut down is the least knackered, let's try and get it relit". Give up trying to extricate yourself, your aircraft, and your crew from certain demise before you hit the ground, sea or mountain and your commitment to the job in hand is questioned seriously. None of us would come into that category. The course ended in the bar for a boozy debrief and medals.

Chapter 17

Opa Locka.

We were scheduled to return to Coventry the following day, then we were going to Gatwick for our ARB type rating exams, followed by base training on the aircraft. This plan dissolved when Gavin appeared in the bar, with news from 'Chaos Control'. 'Paul, Jake, and Ken, you're returning to the UK as planned. Tim, Steve, and me, we're not. We've got to go to Miami and pick up an Electra that has just had a major overhaul. It should take about a week.'

The undisguised envy on the faces of the guys that were returning home was obvious. They were missing out on an all-expenses paid, week of flying an old turbo prop around the Florida Everglades and Caribbean, again. Our mates were absolutely right, we were indeed, the jammiest of bastards. The flying would be interesting and varied, it would also count towards my hours tally and training. A week at Opa Locka was going to involve a lot of eating, drinking, and assorted other distractions. Another week away from my home and family, did give me a twinge of guilt, but only until the next pitcher of beer arrived at the table.

On Saturday morning we said our goodbyes, to our crewmates who had finished their time in Washington state and were returning to Coventry. We then drifted into town for a stroll around. We had already seen a lot of the sights, so we decided to find some 'boy's stuff' to entertain us. As we were wandering around Seattle's beautiful waterfront, Gavin spotted speed boats for hire, perfect. These were proper American machines, with huge gas guzzling outboard engines.

We rumbled away from the jetty at a sensible speed and once we were in clear water opened the taps.

This thing really shifted, we tore across Puget Sound in front of a plume of water, skimming from wavetop to wavetop. It was a blast. After we had spent an hour exploring this gorgeous corner of the Pacific Ocean, we headed back to shore. We spotted a large canoe with an all-female crew of eight or ten.

The canoe was the type with an outrigger to stabilise it. We had to show off just a bit, so we whizzed by it, waving to its occupants. As the wake from our boat totally swamped the vessel, the ladies had to bail out their less than buoyant craft, in shark infested waters. Their screams of abuse towards us rang out clearly, even over our huge engine, leaving us in no doubt we had seriously pissed them off. Oooops.

We prepared to board an internal flight from Seattle to Miami. As we were arranging our seats, the girl at check in offered us the opportunity of a discounted upgrade. For just $100 each, you can upgrade to first class. I could see my colleagues were tempted; My inner council house kid was screaming in my ear. 'A hundred bucks, for a cup and saucer with your coffee and a plate for your sandwiches, are you completely soft in the head?' I pointed out that $100 each in a smart restaurant in Miami would buy a fat steak and lobster 'surf and turf,' and a lot of beer. That sounded much better value to me. We had a brief layover in Los Angeles on the way down the west coast. Standing on the viewing gallery at LAX with a beer in my hand, looking out over the airport, towards Venice beach, I couldn't help but reflect on the last few months.

I really had been incredibly lucky, everything I'd tried to do, had gone better than I could have dreamed.

The three of us arrived in the sweltering heat and humidity of Miami, heading directly for the hotel bar. We were part of the team from Air Atlantique, we were there to collect our aeroplane from the maintenance company at Opa Locka. It had just undergone a major overhaul. Being a sensible grown up, and the boss, Gavin insisted we spend our days at the airport, just in case we could do anything useful.

It turned out to be a good decision. We spent our time planning the test flights, familiarising ourselves with the aviation charts of that part of Florida. As a crew, we also had to familiarise ourselves with the test flight profile. As the captain, Gavin had to make certain that every scrap of mandatory paperwork relating to the aeroplane was in order. Testing all the new parts that had been fitted and needed flight checking, was going to give us a bit of additional work. This would be over and above the standard test flight items. The job had to be done thoroughly, the company certainly didn't want to pay out a small fortune for maintenance, then end up with an aeroplane that wasn't in good order.

The maintenance work was proving to be troublesome. The overhaul would be completed on the aircraft, then during ground testing and engine ground runs, faults would be found.

The Icarus Game

This meant the aircraft had to go back into the hangar for more repairs, then extra ground runs had to be done. As the aeroplane was over thirty years old, this was not surprising. A lot of the parts used were refurbished and of dubious provenance, the maintenance company insisted they were all top grade, but the failure rate during testing suggested otherwise.

The flight test could not be conducted until the aeroplane was signed off by the engineers as fully serviceable.

As the trainee flight engineer, I entertained myself by dividing my time between test flight planning and shadowing our engineers. They were preparing their report on the state of the aeroplane, and checking the work that was being done on it. This gave me a chance to see and get to know the components inside the machine close-up. There were times I got to assist with the work that was being done, I also helped set up some of the major parts.

Adjusting the massive propellers, involves the engineer climbing up a ladder behind the rotating blades. Adjusting the control linkages and hydraulic regulators while the engine is running to get the blade angles correct. Holding the ladder and watching the adjustment process carefully, put my left ear a couple of inches away from almost a tonne of rotating steel, traveling close to the speed of sound. This is one time you really need to focus on the job in hand. Something I had to get used to as it was a going to be a frequent position for me to be in.

Evenings were predictably spent in the local bars, getting to know my new work mates, they were excellent company, if slightly crazy. Just before I arrived in Miami, our short-sighted financial director had been pulled over by a disbelieving police officer, for driving one of the hotels' golf buggies on the freeway. He had no idea how he'd got there, and was lucky the officer didn't throw him straight in jail. Instead, he directed our wayward colleague back to the safety of the hotel, before he got squashed by a truck.

I was playing pool with Neil, when our other engineer appeared at the table. Phil was looking very pleased with himself. He had been telling us earlier in the evening, how he'd converted his garage into a party room for his teenage kids. This conversion included installing a urinal, just like a proper pub. He had just returned from the gent's restroom, proudly showing us the piss-soaked, plastic urinal filter he had acquired. It would be the perfect accessory for his kids' party room. The growing damp patch around his jeans pocket, didn't seem to concern him at all.

Our financial director hadn't been idle, while the maintenance work was going on, he was ferreting around in the hangar. He found a Maule MX7. It was a low hour's, single engined, workhorse of a plane that had four seats and could carry a payload of nearly half a tonne. Ideal for ferrying company personnel and parts around. He struck a deal with the owner, and announced to us that he had bought it.

Me, and another of our engineers were given the task of dismantling it, and getting it secured in the freight deck of the Electra. How hard could that be. The following morning, we took the wings off, commandeered a forklift truck, and…..it didn't fit through the freight door. Off came the propeller, it still didn't fit. We removed the undercarriage, dismantled the tail plane, and sat the fuselage on a pallet, with a lot of juggling and pushing, in she went.

Because our stay in Miami had dragged out longer than expected, our hotel reservations had run out, we were moved from the suburban country club we had been staying in, into the city. This was great as far as we were concerned, it gave us a whole new area to explore. The new hotel had a large lake surrounding it on two sides, I was diving into the hedges and long grass straight away, alligator spotting. The other guys weren't at all keen, but I thought finding huge carnivorous reptiles in the wilds of downtown Miami was a great idea. They are tricky to spot, but definitely there.

One evening we were all meeting, down in the hotel bar. As soon as we entered, the place erupted with cries of, "You gotta be fuckin' kidding man." The whole bar was yelling. This commotion went on for quite a while. The TV on the wall was showing OJ Simpson walking free from court. We had been following the case and knew who he was, but in truth it didn't mean that much to us. For the rest of the people in the bar though, it was life and death. This had been a very divisive trial, showing some of the worst aspects of Americas' legal system and social inequalities to the world. I had arrived in the USA in the middle of August, it was now the start of October.

After several aborted attempts, and a lot of unused planning, the flight test was finally satisfactory. The aeroplane was accepted as being fit to return to service. I was quietly disappointed that the air test had gone so smoothly. The faults we found were all minor, being repaired very quickly after we landed. With over a week of work and preparation behind us, we only got one test flight in Florida. We packed our cases and took off from Opa Locka for the last time, in Air Atlantiques' freshly rebuilt Electra. Heading off the coast turning northbound along America's Atlantic Seaboard. We studied the charts all the way up the coast, picking out places of interest as we passed them. Fort Lauderdale, Cape Canaveral, Daytona Beach. All the places I'd only ever seen on the television as a kid, were now stretched out in front of me.

We had a brief stop to make in Macon, GA. to collect a radio set for the companies DC6. Continuing north to Bangor, ME. for a stopover. The flights were long but uneventful, flying up Americas' Eastern Seaboard gave us some spectacular views. There is something quite special about flying a historic aircraft over iconic parts of the world. Looking down on Manhattan as we passed by was just brilliant.

The final leg of the journey was from Bangor, across the Atlantic Ocean to Coventry. We passed the time doing continuous fuel calculations and some fault diagnosis, on the parts of the plane that were clearly struggling to keep up. Our newly acquired Leatherman multitools were also given a thorough testing, by the time we landed at Coventry very few of the instruments on the flight deck were in their original positions.

We handed the plane over to the company's engineers with a fresh list of defects. As I was leaving the airport I bumped into Jake. I think we were suffering from a bit of mutual envy. He had missed out on a week's flying and exploring in Miami, but he had completed his ARB exams and 'base training'.

He was sporting the gold braid of a first officer on his sleeve, which he hung nonchalantly out of his car window. I'd had a great time in Florida, but I was now acutely aware that I had more exams to sit, and my 'base training' to go through. First, I had some making up to do at home. I had been away about six weeks, and Tracy had reminded me during every phone call that this trip was a lot longer than I had initially said.

During the next few weeks, I passed the ARB type rating exam at Gatwick, and completed my base training and 'Base Check' flight test. My flying hours total was climbing rapidly and after another month or so, my line training and line check were completed. All the boxes had now been ticked, and I took my licence application to Gatwick in person. I sat and waited while it was processed. Walking out of the front doors of the CAA offices, with my newly printed Flight Engineers Licence in my hand, was a great feeling.

Chapter 18

On Line.

Now I was on the roster, as a regular member of the companies' flight crew. One of only two flight engineers. Flying, scheduled and ad hoc charters on the Electra, alongside the airlines other flight crew members. The scheduled flights we did for the freight carriers was steady work. It formed about half of our overall flying. Ad hoc charters were more fun as far as we were concerned, you had no idea where they would take you, or what you'd be carrying. They were also much harder work. Loading and strapping down whatever turned up to be transported, it was often heavy going. Sometimes you would go into places where they'd never seen an Electra before.

Frequently I had to give the ground crew a crash course in Electra ground operations, the guys were familiar with other aircraft types. So, it was just the details that were specific to our aeroplane that they needed to know. This was usually done in loud pidgin English, with lots of hand signals. 'The air start goes in there. We start that engine first, OK'. 'This is the signal for air on, air off' I'd yell into the ground crews' ear whilst pointing at the appropriate bit of the aeroplane.

The standard equipment fitted to an aeroplane, is usually decided by the company that buys it new from the factory. Our aircraft were originally made for a variety of operators, so they all varied slightly, and had been around the block. In practical terms this meant that each of our aircraft had differences, in the equipment they were fitted with, and where those components had been positioned.

Unlike during training, our working schedule didn't usually give much spare time for relaxation. It was normally organised around legally permissible duty time, (Cap 371), so it was very much a matter of fly, eat, sleep, repeat. When the opportunity for relaxation and enjoying the place's we visited arose, we took it. The first charter I did, that allowed downtime in the scheduling was to Amsterdam.

It lasted a couple of weeks and required two crews and one aircraft. The first crew, flew from Amsterdam to Linz in Austria, waited for the return load then came back to Amsterdam. By this time, they were out of duty, so the other crew did the next rotation. Effectively you worked for twelve hours and then had around thirty-six hours 'rest' in Amsterdam. So, we did our best to get as rested as newts.

Because nobody wants to turn up for work, 'the worse for wear', we tended to let our hair down immediately after we'd finished a duty. That way you had time to get some sleep, sober up and get yourself fed, before you returned to work. Seven o'clock in the morning, may seem like an unusual time to be heading into town for a pint or two, but it made perfect sense to us. We had no problem finding bars open at that time of day.

We had been enjoying our social drink for most of the morning, the topics of conversation had been many and varied, as the beer flowed it inevitably returned to flying. We were discussing my flying lessons, which were going to start at the beginning of the summer. Jake was going into detail about the lesson on stalling, in particular the characteristics of a Cessna 152. He became more and more animated and expansive, as he enacted reducing the airspeed and increasing the wings angle of attack until the stall warning buzzer sounded.

"Then you enter the buffet phase and finally...." Jake had his chair balanced on its back legs as he demonstrated entering a full stall, arms outstretched. We watched in astonishment as his chair overbalanced backwards, and his feet disappeared from sight, he tumbled head-first down a cast iron spiral staircase. The crumpled heap, now in the basement, unravelled itself, regained its' composure and climbed the stairs back into the bar. Jakes' return was met with a round of applause. We had a quick medicinal brandy, before we returned to the hotel for some overdue sleep.

Over the next few weeks, the six crew members and the engineers that were working with us, managed to sample all the delights that Amsterdam had to offer. Amazingly only one crew fell victim to Dutch hospitality. A couple of the lads had been out for a beer and were in a taxi on their way back to the hotel. The driver was a friendly, chatty sort and they were passing the journey deep in conversation. The driver reached into the glove box, producing a small polythene bag containing an unknown sort of dope. 'A passenger left this in my car, would you guys like it.' Why not? Thought our intrepid pair. 'How much?' 'Oh, nothing it was just left in my cab.' This was an offer, way too good to refuse.

The Icarus Game

They sat on the wall outside the hotel, fashioning themselves a joint which they shared before heading back to their rooms. They had just got into the elevator, when the full effects of the dope hit them, with a vengeance. By the time the lift reached their floor, they fell out of it, neither of them had any idea who, or where they were. They could only manage to crawl aimlessly up the corridor on all fours, having to be deposited in their rooms by the hotel staff. Remarkably after a good day's sleep they suffered no long-term ill effects.

Amsterdam was great fun, but at the other end of the route was Linz, in Austria, and for one crew member this provided a pleasant distraction. In the very swanky hotel bar, was a grand piano which our first officer spotted straight away. Each evening before going to his room, he would sit at the piano and play whatever came into his head. His talent as a pianist did not go unnoticed, and a very attractive waitress soon spotted the handsome young man playing in his pilot's uniform.

She paid him a lot of complements, and attention. As we checked out in the early hours of the morning on our last day, the bar had just closed. His admirer had finished her work and was heading into the reception area when she spotted him. She smiled, and they started chatting together. Before we knew it, the two of them were in a passionate embrace in the passage that led to the toilets. He was wasting no time, and the girl's clothes were soon in a state of disarray, she didn't seem to mind at all, they were totally oblivious to us.

Our captain brought an end to his first officers' ardour by shouting across the hotel reception, 'Oi, put that girl down. The taxi's outside waiting for us.' Casanova, released his grip on the girl, gave her a peck on the cheek and picked up his suitcase. As we headed out of the door, the waitress was standing in the corner rearranging her blouse and skirt. All we heard her say was 'You English, you are always in such a hurry'.

My first real life emergency and engine shutdown happened a few weeks after my training was completed. We were over Spain, returning to Coventry from Valencia. Gavin had left me and the first officer, Nik on the flight deck while he went for a smoke and to make some coffees.

We were relaxed and putting the world to rights, when we both spotted a flicker of red light, somewhere on the instrument panel. We concentrated on the four low oil pressure warning lights above the bank of gauges, a few seconds later the No 3 warning light came back on, and stayed on. We scanned down the instruments to the oil contents gauge for the number three engine. As we watched, the needle dropped from eight gallons to near zero in a few seconds.

Nik called it, 'Engine failure No 3.' He then looked at my hand which was already on the 'No 3 'E' handle. 'Confirmed, shut down No 3.' I pulled the big red 'E' handle and the engine wound down. Nik confirmed the propeller had feathered and adjusted the trims.

Gavin poked his head into the flight deck. 'Are you two jokers trying to wind me up?' We explained we weren't, we had just shut down the engine because it had lost all its oil. We thought we were heroes. 'So why are we still at twenty thousand feet?' Asked Gavin. Me and Nik looked at each other, while we worked it out, dredging through what we had learned in the classroom.

The inboard engines, numbers two and three, drive the EDC's, engine driven compressors that provide the air to pressurize the cabin. By shutting down an inboard engine we had just lost half of the air for our cabin pressurisation. Ahhh, it eventually dawned on us. 'Request descent to fifteen thousand feet, I'll be with you when I've made the coffee.' Said our very patient Captain.

When we arrived at Coventry the aircraft was handed to the engineers. They changed the engine, then stripped down the broken one. They told us that the turbine labyrinth seal had failed, allowing all of the oil in the engine to be sucked into the turbine, burned, and blown out of the jet pipe.

The weather was improving as we drifted from winter into spring, it was time to start thinking about my flying lessons. Atlantique had a steady Electra contract running between Coventry and Edinburgh every night. Starting and finishing at home was very unusual for us, so me and Jake, got ourselves rostered together on this route as frequently as we could. We would typically arrive back at Coventry at 5:30 in the morning, get out of the Electra, brief, and take off in the Cessna 152 at around 6:30. This was a glorious time to go flying, we had the skies to ourselves.

Steve Woodhouse

The first obstacle for me to overcome, was getting the plane off the ground. This 152 had a tail wheel, instead of the usual tricycle arrangement. Having sat in the Electra for the previous six months, watching some very talented pilots' blast effortlessly down the runway centreline, then climb gracefully into the sky, my first efforts at taking off were embarrassing. I'd apply full power and the plane would veer violently off the centre line, I'd over correct, with a boot full of rudder and we'd screech across to the other side of the runway, zig zagging our way to getting airborne. It took a couple of goes and some severe tyre wear to get my feet connected to my brain, stopping these excessive corrections. Within a few hours of flying, I was feeling comfortable with the controls, the checklists and working the radio.

It was time to venture further away from the airfield, stretch the envelope a little. I was mastering the very basics, now we were going to do some stalling and spinning. The stall recovery exercise proved to be enjoyable, it all worked as advertised, so not too much of a challenge, and neither of us fell down the stairs. Spinning was a bit trickier. 'Reduce the airspeed until the point of stalling, then kick in full rudder.' Was the instruction I got from Jake. I tried several times and could only achieve a gentle spiral dive. Jake had a brainwave.

The aircrafts centre of gravity was clearly too far forward. He climbed over the back of his seat into the cargo space behind us, moving the C of G rearwards, and gave me the thumbs up. Great, we were spinning like a top, falling earthwards at quite a rate. All I had to do now was recover the aeroplane to straight and level flight, with my instructor in the space behind my seat. Apply opposite rudder, release the back pressure on the control column and hope the spinning stops, nose on the horizon, full power, then climb away, wait for your instructor to return to his seat. Bingo.

One flight that every pilot remembers forever, is their first solo, the time you are considered competent enough to be in total control of an aeroplane. It's an amazing feeling after a lot of preparation. You look around the cockpit and it's just you, a thousand feet above the ground. You move the controls and the aircraft responds. You make a decision and there's nobody to correct you if it's wrong. The sense of euphoria is absolute.

This maiden flight only lasts about five minutes. Long enough to take off, carry out your checks and drills, complete a circuit and land. I taxied back to my parking place, singing loudly and out of tune, with the biggest stupid grin on my face I've ever had. It took a bacon roll and a brew to stop my hands shaking. Jake was as relieved as I was that it had gone well. After all it was his decision to entrust me with the companies Cessna 152.

The next lesson started less well, we arrived back at Coventry in the Electra, the weather was gloomy. Heavy black clouds filled the sky. We studied the met reports carefully and decided the cloud base was high enough to allow me to fly a few circuits on my own. I was always looking for a chance to fly, not an excuse to avoid it. Jake settled down with a brew to watch, as I planned for my flights.

I taxied out and took off, I had reached about five hundred feet, just passing the end of the runway, when I flew into a snowstorm, disappearing totally from sight. By this time, Jake had been joined by one of the engineers and they both watched in dismay as I vanished into the blizzard. 'That's the last you've seen of him, has he paid you yet,' said Neil. Jake was thinking along similar lines.

My world disappeared in a whiteout. Cessna 152's are not equipped to fly in icing conditions, I was well aware of my predicament, even if I wasn't experienced enough to properly deal with it. I decided to do what I knew worked. Looking down at the instruments I continued my heading and climbed to a thousand feet, levelled off on the artificial horizon and turned right ninety degrees, counted to twenty then turned another ninety degrees right, I should now be on my downwind leg.

After what felt like an eternity I popped out of the snow, into dull, gloomy air. Looking down to my right, I could see half of the runway. Enough, I hoped, to land on. I completed my checks and turned the aeroplane onto finals. The wheels touched the ground and I'd just slowed down to taxi speed as I disappeared into the snow again. I slowly inched my way back to the hangar and shut down the engine. Fuckin' hell!! That was enough for one day.

Chapter 19

Ad Hoc-ing.

Still wet behind the ears, I joined Jake and Gavin for an ad hoc trip around Europe, none of us had any idea where it was going to take us. These types of charters were referred to as 'tramping'. The first legs of our little odyssey were from Coventry to Saarbrucken in Germany, then on to Valencia, in Spain. After that it was anybody's guess where we would end up.

We arrived in Valencia the following morning, in time for breakfast and spent most of the day sleeping. When we met up later that afternoon, there was no sign of us going anywhere. The three of us left the hotel reception to go into town and find some dinner, and a little entertainment. Gavin led us into a part of town with lots of restaurants and bars. The evening was fun, and after a good paella for dinner we drifted from bar to bar. Beer and cheap Spanish brandy were the drinks of choice.

We felt it would be rude to end the night without trying some of the local delicacies, so we three amigos went into the first lively Tapas bar we passed. The food looked very enticing, displayed behind the counter on small plates. I was already wobbly, when Jake insisted that I try another particularly rough brandy, along with a lump of very smelly Manchego cheese swimming in a saucer of olive oil. My constitution was by now at full stretch, and my stomach churned, I dashed outside, across the pavement and stuck my head into a rubbish bin. I'm still not keen on sheep's milk cheese, or fetid rubbish bins. Spanish brandy, I can manage just fine. Manchego cheese aside it was a good night.

Despite the strange colour I'd turned the night before, the following morning I felt great, we sat in the hotel restaurant enjoying a long slow breakfast. Interrupted only when the 'ships' mobile phone rang. We were to leave the hotel for the airport immediately, a charter from Valencia to Tunis had just dropped onto the commercial manager's desk. We sat on the plane drinking coffee whilst we waited for confirmation of the charter and the freight to arrive.

For these types of charters, Atlantique normally engaged the airport handlers to load the aircraft. The handling companies always promise a full load team, and all the necessary equipment, when they send their invoice. When the freight arrives, we would typically find, the load team consists of two blokes and a forklift truck. They were expected to transfer ten or more tonnes of goods onto the freight deck of the aeroplane and strap it down. It's pointless complaining, the schedule doesn't allow for it, we'd just help load the cargo ourselves.

Setting off from Spain across the azure blue of the Balearic Sea and across the Mediterranean towards north-eastern Africa, we were enjoying the stunning views. Leaving Spain, it was a beautiful winters day, cool and crystal clear. A couple of hours later we were greeted on the hot, sun-bleached concrete apron at Tunis, by a very cheerful handling agent. He had just pedalled his bicycle across the airport to meet us and couldn't have been more helpful.

While our freight was being offloaded, we were told that another consignment had been arranged for us, we were to take it to Frankfurt. He handed Gavin the paperwork, after a brief look at the flight plan, Gavin asked me to fuel the plane up to twenty-four thousand pounds, and he gave Jake the job of working out the load sheet. He then borrowed the agent's bike, to pedal a couple of miles around the airport in the heat of the midday sun to the handling agent's office, in order to settle the landing fees and other charges.

This is where my problem started. Put simply, the refuelling valves work from the aircraft batteries, the fuel gauges work from the aircraft generators. We had no ground power unit to provide the 115v/ac electricity, that would normally come from the generators. I connected the fuelling truck and opened all the fuelling valves using the planes batteries. Fuel was now flowing under pressure into the aircraft tanks.

My mistake was to look at the fuel gauges, expecting them to rise as the tanks filled up. The hours in the classroom discussing the differences between dc and ac power, which systems on the plane were powered by what type of current, didn't enter my head. As far as I was concerned the fuel system was 28v/dc and could work off the batteries. After a few minutes I tried to measure the amount of fuel in the tanks by using the sight sticks under the wings, but in the bright sunshine I couldn't get a reading. That's what I thought, looking back they were probably already completely submerged in fuel.

The fuel gauges still hadn't moved, so I asked the bowser driver if he was sure the fuel was flowing. He pointed to the truck's delivery gauge, which was spinning furiously. Then the inevitable happened, the fuelling valves started to shut off, one by one, as the tanks reached their capacity, the fuel shut off valves did their job.

Oh shit, instead of filling the tanks to about half full, I'd filled them right to the top. We had about ten tonnes more fuel than we wanted. What's more it was ten tonnes of very expensive fuel. As the driver disconnected his bowser, I sheepishly climbed the aircraft's ladder and went onto the flight deck. 'Hi Jake, have you finished the load sheet yet?' I knew I had royally screwed up.

When Gavin returned on his bicycle, I had to explain what I had done, meanwhile Jake tactfully found something important to do at the other end of the plane. Gavin groaned; he knew exactly how I'd cocked up. How he held back the desire to tell me exactly what he thought of me, I don't know. He left his instructions, climbed back on his bike, setting off around the airport in the African sun once again, to arrange the payment for the extra fuel. We taxied out in Tunis with the aeroplane undercarriage groaning under the weight it had to carry. Over the next couple of days, we went to Frankfurt then Cologne, Liverpool and finally returning to Coventry without having to refuel at all.

We had just landed at Coventry from the regular Edinburgh route, gone upstairs into the operations office and handed in our paperwork. The op's officer looked up at us and announced, 'I need you guys back in tonight for a week with DHL.' We were fine with that, scheduled flying for the large carriers is well organised, and the more we flew, the more we got paid.

The three of us met up in op's again that evening, collected our paperwork along with Andy, our engineer. A short hop to East

The Icarus Game

Midlands got us into the network. We were then going to spend the rest of the week flying between Berlins' Schönefeld Airport (SXF), E. Midlands and Cologne, day stopping in Berlin. Our captain was an absolute tightwad, coaxing him out of his hotel room was impossible, he would only eat when the food was free. Me, Jake, and Andy however wanted to explore this thrilling city. Over breakfast we decided the first thing we had to find was the Brandenburg Gate. Later in the day we met in the lobby and learned from the receptionist that it was in 'Potsdamsomething' or somewhere like that, so off we went.

We found the local railway station and jumped on the first train heading into the city. We didn't bother with a ticket for two reasons. First, we couldn't work the machine, it was all in German. Second, we were going to start and perpetuate the rumour that all public transport on the continent was free. If anybody on the train challenged us, we would simply offer them a handful of cash and play the dumb foreigner.

The train was an old East German model, it was very utilitarian, with hard wooden seats and lino floors. However, it was on time and going to the Hauptbahnhof. That must be a good place to start from, we thought. Studying the maps on the platform we found a place called Potsdam, that must be it. We boarded the next train, and an hour later arrived at our destination. We left the station and walked towards Potsdam Centrum. If there was going to be a huge granite monument, resplendent with warriors on chariots and flags, it would surely be there.

Eventually we were faced with a large flat, mud and gravel car park. In the middle was a concrete arch, was that it? Somehow it seemed much smaller than the pictures, totally devoid of any warlike chariots, or other heroic symbols of the Fatherland. It had also been painted magnolia. We walked over to it, walked around it, stroked it. Looking at each other we could see our shared feeling of disappointment.

Jake needed a fag, but he didn't have any, so we went into a nearby newsagents. While Jake bought his cigarettes, I asked in my best corrupted German 'Entschuldigung, wo ist das Brandenburger Gate bitte.' The shop keeper looked perplexed. 'It is in Berlin of course, That's fifty kilometres that way.' He gestured over his shoulder. Bollocks, we were in totally the wrong place.

We were starving by now, and Andy spotted a chicken and chip van as we headed back towards the railway station. Eating our dinner as we walked, we couldn't help but laugh at our total inability to find one of Europe's most iconic monuments. Joking about the naturally intrinsic sense of direction possessed by all pilots, we retraced our journey on the train, arriving at the hotel just as our taxi for work pulled up. We dashed past our captain; he was checking out and helping himself to a free apple from the reception desk fruit bowl. 'We'll be down in a minute,' we called as we took the stairs three at a time to our rooms.

The following afternoon we tried again. This time though, we went to Potsdamer Platz, finding ourselves in the heart of Berlin. A short walk alongside the Tiergarten park brought our quest to an end. It was just like the pictures and certainly worth every bit of effort, even if it was just for the fun of telling the story in the crew room.

Taxis feature quite regularly in the life of flight crew, and their quality varies across a wide spectrum. On this morning we had just arrived in Lisbon, walked out from the front of the airport onto the taxi rank. We put our cases into the open boot of the old Mercedes, climbing into the car at the front of the queue. The captain and first officer had occupied the back seat, leaving me in the suicide front seat. The Portuguese driver turned and looked at me expecting directions. I could barely see his eyes through the filth encrusted jam jar bottoms he used for spectacles.

Once I'd given him the name of the hotel, there was no hesitation. He clamped his foot hard on the accelerator, screeching away from the airport arrivals area. Hurtling down the spiral ramp, and without so much as a glance in his mirrors, we shot straight into the traffic on a packed dual carriageway. He kept his right boot buried firmly in the sticky, worn out carpet of his cab, as he weaved through the rush hour traffic. Before we had regained our balance or come to our senses, he stamped on the brakes and we had miraculously appeared outside our hotel. We were all stunned into silence by the experience. He turned to face us, and through his Mr Magoo grin, announced, 'Hey, Fittipaldi'.

Meanwhile my PPL training was coming on nicely, it was time for my NFT (navigation flight test). My examiner, Piers, gave me a triangular route to plan, Coventry to Fenland airfield, Sleaford then back to Coventry. All was going well, planning, checks, drills, radio, heading control and height keeping were all good. My problem came when Piers asked me to point out my first turning point, Fenland airfield. I had passed Spalding and crossed the A16. The airfield should be directly below me according to my calculations. 'It's right below us' I said as confidently as I could.

'Great, can you see the runway'. I looked down at the huge expanse of green. I circled around and identified every road, river and village for miles around on the chart. 'We are right over it.' I said again. 'But can you see the runway.' Piers persisted. 'No'. I had to admit I couldn't'. Ok take me to Sleaford. We carried on with the test, all the rest went well.

Jake listened to the debrief with me. Piers talked in detail about the test, generally how good my flying had been, then came the kicker, that I knew was coming. 'Pity you couldn't find Fenland'. I can do you a retest next month. This was disappointing but not the end of the world. When Piers had left, me and Jake got straight back in the 152 and headed for Fenland. Again, I looked down at the lush green Fens and again I couldn't see anything that looked like a runway.

We circled it while Jake found the field, pointing it out to me. That road there is this one on the map. Yes, I'd found that last time. Jake narrowed it down inch by inch. 'Can you see the scrap yard? 'Yes'. 'Great, the field is right next to it.' I'd spotted it at long last. Halleluiah. The only difference between the green airfield and the surrounding green countryside, was a shed in one corner with a small windsock. Next time I knew what I was looking for.

The following month I took Piers around the route flawlessly, this was soon followed with an uneventful 'solo qualifying cross-country flight', and a successful 'General Flight Test'. I now had my Private Pilot's Licence.

The Electra division of the company was still relatively small. We operated three Electra's, employing a couple of dozen flight crew members at the most. There was still a steady turnover of people though, as guys gained experience, they became more attractive to the bigger airlines, and our pilots were by nature always looking for a new challenge. That meant we had a steady flow of new first officers to train.

Training comes in many forms, the initial formal training gets you started on-line, then the real learning starts, as I had found out plenty of times to my embarrassment.

This day though, it was somebody else's turn to be brought down to earth with a thump. Mark was a new first officer, he had been online a few months and was very keen. We had arrived in Ostend to pick up an out of position load for one of the parcel carriers. Eight and a half ULD's, prepacked and ready to go. We should be loaded, refuelled and on our way in an hour.

The load details were given to the captain, in this case it was the long-suffering, Gavin. He handed the details of bin serial numbers, and weights to Mark, for him to prepare the load sheet. I had refuelled the aeroplane and done the walk around during the loading process.

Returning to the flight deck, just as the loading was finished, I saw that Mark was looking a bit worried. 'Gavin, the loading has been done wrong, this bin at the front should be at the back and the back one should be at the front.' Gavin turned to the loading supervisor and shrugged. 'Sorry, this lot will all have to come off and be reloaded correctly.' The loaders were not happy, but the bins were offloaded, shuffled around into the right order, then reloaded. About forty minutes later and behind schedule we were done. Mark checked his paperwork one last time, he turned to Gavin and the load team supervisor. 'Actually, I think it might have been right the first time.'

Steve Woodhouse

At this point his world imploded. The load supervisor ordered his team off the aeroplane. 'If you want that load turning around again, you will have to wait for the next shift, I've got other aircraft to deal with.' With that he and his crew left. Ooh bollocks. Try explaining the fourteen hours delay we were just about to incur to the customer. My contribution at this point was, 'I'll make some coffee's, shall I?'

Chapter 20

Guardian Angels.

Sometimes things just go wrong. Other times I am convinced there is a higher power at work. Entertaining herself, by knocking down your house of cards, just because she can. The week I have in mind was just such a time. Our guardian angel clearly didn't want us flying around Germany in the depths of winter.

The week began on a stormy night, approaching short finals into Cologne. There's no two ways about it, it was howling a gale and lashing it down with rain. The runway lights flared in the windshield as we approached the threshold. The windshield wipers were making little impact on the torrent of water racing up the screen. We were all ready to land, we could just make out the touchdown zone in the murk of darkness and water. The captain, Jim then called for full power and initiated a go-around. This came as a surprise to me, because during the landing, I generally had my head down watching the engine gauges. As I pushed the power levers forward, I glanced up from the instruments and saw the problem.

On the centreline of the runway, smack on our touchdown point, was a ULD. One of the large aluminium cargo containers used to speed up the loading of freight onto the aircraft. They are about the size of a garden shed, nine feet square and six feet high. As we called air traffic notifying the controller of our missed approach, he asked the reason why. 'There is a ULD on the threshold of one four left'.

'This is not possible' replied the controller, there was a short pause as he reached for his binoculars. 'Unbelievable', he sounded astonished. 'I'll have it removed, immediately'.

The following night our guardian angel spat out her dummy again. We were in the cruise returning to Cologne from Hamburg, the gale force winds from the night before had passed through. This time Pete was in the captains' seat. All was good in our insulated little world, until the aircraft yawed severely to the right. At first, we didn't know what had caused this un-commanded movement. Nobody had touched the rudder pedals. I was scanning the engine instruments. All the propeller RPMs were fine, but there was no torque coming from the number four engine. I retarded the number four power-lever, it made no difference. We looked down at the fuel flow gauges. As I pushed the power lever forward the torque (Shaft Horsepower) and prop RPM didn't change, but the fuel flow increased. That was weird, we didn't know what was wrong, but it definitely wasn't right, so we shut the engine down.

As soon as we parked on stand the engineer was up his ladder and had the cowls opened. He was inspecting the engine closely; I did my walk around and refuelled the plane for the next sector. As I finished, he came down his ladder and announced, 'That is the cleanest engine I've ever seen'. The fuel supply pipe from the fuel pump had fractured at the banjo connector. This resulted in gallons of fuel, pressurised by the fuel pumps, being sprayed over the outside of the engine. The potential risks this presented were obvious, spraying a mixture of liquid kerosene and kerosene vapour over a hot gas turbine engine and electrical generators is not to be recommended. A replacement part was tracked down by our engineers, and fitted in an hour, quite an achievement for our engineering department.

Our guardian angel hadn't finished tormenting us yet. Later in the week the same number four engine started using oil. During turn arounds I was having to put more and more oil in it before each flight, just a few more sectors and the week was finished. The engineers would have the weekend to find and fix the leak, or change the engine. The last sector of the week was from Basel to Brussels and it was a foggy and cold night. I'd just emptied the last can of oil from our on-board stock into the top of the engine. It was now full and only had to keep running for about an hour and fifteen minutes.

We pushed back off our stand and taxied to the runway. In the fog we were out of sight of everybody else on the airport. A last scan of the instruments was all good, we started our take off roll. V1, rotate, came the calls, positive rate, gear up. Then the oil contents disappeared out of the number four engine. I called. 'Low oil quantity, number four'. We shut the engine down just a few seconds into the flight. We all suspected this was likely to happen. 'If it can go wrong, it will, and at the worst possible moment'. This is the phrase that sums up flying perfectly. We continued climbing to our cleared altitude on three engines, carrying out the engine securing checks on the way to Brussels.

The spare parts, engineers and most importantly of all, our lift home were all at Brussels. There was no way we were landing anywhere else.

Jim, Jake, and me, had been flying between Edinburgh and Coventry all week. We were running out of things to do with our spare time in Edinburgh, that didn't involve drinking. Somebody came up with the bright idea of going to the swimming baths. We got on and off busses, until we finally arrived at the Royal Commonwealth Pool.

Me and Jake were particularly pleased to find that it had a separate diving pool, with a good selection of boards. Jim was rather less enthusiastic; he had been reticent about the idea all the way there. Now we were looking up at the ten-meter-high board, he had to come clean. He could barely swim. That's ok, it's a small pool, from where you land to the edge is only five meters at the most. He wasn't convinced, but he certainly wasn't going to let us get one over on him.

We started on the lowest springboard. I took a couple of steps, bounced off the board and entered the water headfirst without much of a ripple. Jake followed me and threw in a fancy pike manoeuvre for good measure. It was Jim's turn. He bounded down the board, bounced off the end, adopted a star jump shape and landed on the water horizontally, flat on his belly. Smack. Me and Jake winced for him. He floundered his way to the steps and climbed out. 'I think I know where I went wrong' he said as he tried again. Smack. Another star jump, belly flop combo. As he surfaced, me and Jake both called to him, 'Please don't do that again, we'll give you some lessons.'

The Icarus Game

We stood on the low board, while Jim walked to the end of the two-meter springboard. Ok, now sit down, put your arms out in front of you and allow yourself to roll forwards off the board. Perfect, he entered the water headfirst for the first time all day. While Jim took a breather on the side of the pool me and Jake mucked about a little on the springboards. Jake then said he was going for a dive off the high board. I knew my limits, and said I wasn't, but I was all for cheering him on. I sat with Jim as Jake went up the thirty odd feet of steps. He walked to the edge of the ten-meter board, did a handstand, then dropped vertically into the water. Me and Jim were highly impressed.

Newly invigorated, Jim got up and climbed the two-meter springboard, as Jake climbed out and sat next to me on the poolside. Jim ran, bounced, and had clearly remembered nothing from his lesson, as he over rotated, he landed flat on his back on the water surface. The slap echoed around the building. He climbed out of the pool looking like a boiled lobster. That was enough for me and Jake, we dragged Jim, who by this time could barely walk with us to the changing rooms.

Coming out of the swimming baths, Jake spotted a pet shop. He had promised his boys a pet, and now was the ideal time to get it. We wandered around the pet superstore, until he found what he was looking for. A rat.

The assistant came over and Jake pointed out the rodent he wanted. 'That one there, the one with the big bollocks.' The shop assistant reached into the cage and produced the rat of Jakes choice. 'What are you going to call him.' She asked smiling. 'Basil.' Said Jake.

We took Basil on the bus back into town. Then he came with us for a curry. The girls at the next table in the restaurant, thought the box on the chair making scratching noises was hilarious. The waiters pretended not to notice. The table of girls had immediately worked out what was in the box, and correctly guessed his name. There were lots of Faulty Tower's references made during our meal.

Basil may have enjoyed his curry, but he certainly did not like flying, he was very quiet on the way down to Coventry. At one point we thought he might have died. Jakes' boys were delighted when he appeared in the middle of the night and got everybody out of bed to meet their new housemate. Basil had the run of the house and lived a long and happy life in the Midlands.

Sitting on the apron at Glasgow we were looking closely at the weather reports. We only had to get the plane and the parcels in the cargo deck to Edinburgh, about a ten-minute flight away. The weather was shocking though. Thick fog was covering the whole country. We knew that getting off the ground could present us with huge problems. We spelled the risks out in minute detail to our Op's officer. Maybe he just didn't get it. 'The customer insists you get their parcels to Edinburgh'. Came the very assertive reply.

The problem we had was simple, the Electra is a Cat 1 aeroplane, this means to take off or land, we must have the minimum visibility specified by the Jeppesen or Aerad charts at any given airport. In this case we could depart Glasgow, providing we had a hundred and twenty-five meters of Runway Visual Range (RVR) and a suitable landing airfield.

To land at Edinburgh, we needed an RVR of five hundred and fifty meters. The visibility at both airports was around two hundred meters. So, we could take off, but we couldn't land at either place. Most people can see the flaw in this plan. And even the bolshiest manager isn't going to make me crash an aeroplane in a field out of stupidity. The answer was simple, the fog was forecast to clear by early morning, so we made sure we had the maximum amount of fuel on board that we could carry.

One last phone call to Op's, 'Are you absolutely sure you want us to take off'. 'YESSSS'. It was legal, this is a phrase I heard a lot as flight crew, mostly from people sat in warm, dry offices. So off we went. The visibility was down to a hundred and fifty meters in Glasgow. Sitting up as high as we were, we had difficulty seeing the painted white lines on the ground. The captain requested an airport 'follow me' vehicle, complete with flashing orange beacon to guide us out to the runway. Bright runway lighting made the take-off relatively straight forward. We turned and flew slowly towards Edinburgh. There was no hurry, we couldn't land when we got there, the visibility was still down at two hundred meters.

Arriving overhead Edinburgh airport, we took up the holding pattern. This had all the makings of a long night. We started collecting weather reports. To the north, Aberdeen was fogged out, heading south was no better, Newcastle foggy, Leeds foggy, Manchester foggy, Liverpool foggy, E. Midlands foggy, Coventry foggy, Luton foggy. The nearest airport that was open and within our limits to land, was Brussels!! That was going to be a fun phone call to make when we eventually landed.

'If we have to divert to Brussels, how long can we stay in the hold over Edinburgh?' Out came the calculator, 'A couple of hours, no problem,' came the answer from the first officer. 'But we'll be out of duty before we're out of fuel.' I went and made some coffees. The radio played met' reports the whole time we were in the hold, and it sounded monotonous. The air traffic controller tried to help as well; he couldn't come up with any better suggestions than the ones we had worked out. He asked how long we planned to stay in the hold for.

After forty-five minutes going around in circles above Edinburgh it was clear that things were not going to improve, so we requested a diversion to Brussels. The controller chuckled as he cleared us up to twenty thousand feet and sent us south. The first officer carried on collecting weather reports as we joined the airway. We were between Newcastle and Leeds when the first glimmer of hope came over the radio. Liverpool's ATIS was giving a slight improvement at four hundred and fifty meters.

We briefed for a landing at Liverpool and requested a diversion. It was a long shot; we still needed a further improvement to Five hundred and fifty meters.

As we descended, we were listening avidly to the weather report (ATIS). Providing we had the minimum required visibility at the final approach fix, we could continue the approach down the Instrument Landing System, (ILS), to our decision height of two hundred feet above the runway threshold. We established on the ILS and the controller gave us the news that the RVR was now five hundred and fifty meters. The Electra didn't have an autopilot capable of flying a precision approach, so it was down to the crew to follow the instruments and fly the aeroplane.

Our Captain, Jim, was sound, he nailed it. The needles didn't flinch from the glideslope or localiser all the way down the approach. As we neared our minimum descent height, dense fog still shrouded our world, the first officer called 'Deee---ssii----shun'. By the time he'd stopped saying it, the runway was still hidden in the mirk, 200 feet below us. 'Go around.'

The visibility was atrocious, it was now below our requirements for another go. We climbed away, back up to our cruising level and set course for Brussels. As we crossed the Channel, we could see mainland Europe lit up in front of us, as clear as a bell.

'We were taking bets where you guys would end up.' Said our Op's man. 'So, where are you?' 'Brussels' said Jim. The silence on the other end of the phone was deafening. 'You're kidding, right'. 'Nope, I'm not kidding, we're in Brussels. Book us a hotel.' Our decision makers had made an expensive misjudgement.

Chapter 21

Marseilles.

Above the first officers head on the Electra flight deck, were two rows of four small orange lights, one for each engine, and one for each gearbox. These were the CHIP lights. The chip lights were the visual warning part of the Oil Debris Detection System. Each engine, and each reduction gearbox, was fitted with a magnetic drain plug, equipped with a couple of electrodes. If metal particles were present in the oil, they would collect on these magnetic plugs. Eventually, enough would build up to complete the electrical circuit between the electrodes, illuminating the corresponding warning light on the flight deck. This told us that something was going seriously wrong with either the engine, or the gearbox.

We set out from Coventry to start our week down-route in the early evening, going to Brussels, joining the DHL network. On our descent into Brussels, the number one reduction gearbox chip light came on. Taking the only sensible response to this, we shut down the engine, landing as planned in Brussels.

Joining the engineer alongside the suspect engine, I made myself as useful as I could. Armed with a ladder and a spanner, he took the drain plug out of the gearbox, sticking his finger in the hole to stop the oil pouring out. I took a good look at the plug's electrodes; they were spotlessly clean. He took his finger, which was by now nicely boiled, out of the hole and refitted the plug.

After the cables were reconnected, we went back to the flight deck. The warning light was out, that was confusing.

We were running between Brussels, Lyon, Nice and Marseilles all week. This was a fabulous route as far as I was concerned. Spending my afternoons strolling aimlessly around picturesque Mediterranean towns, contemplating what was for dinner, cannot really be thought of as work. Looking back over my career, very little of what I've done can truly be considered work. I count myself as being incredibly fortunate.

We had been flying up and down Europe for a couple of nights, with no further repetition of the gearbox light issue. Then returning north, on it came again. We followed the same procedure, shut down the engine and landed at our planned stop on the route. This time I went out to the engine and removed the drain plug. Again, it was spotless, so I refitted it. The warning lights, were again, all out. We had no idea what was going on, maybe it was a spurious warning, or a fault in the wiring.

The following night we were heading into Marseilles, when the chip light came on again. It was like Groundhog Day. Lifting the engine covers after we'd landed, I didn't think I was going to find anything wrong. I was horrified when, as I withdrew the magnetic plug, a long thin piece of metal was attached to the magnet, wiggling its way out through the hole in the gearbox casing.

It was a large piece of a circlip. The sort that is used to retain bearings in place. It was about two inches long and a quarter of an inch wide. I guessed it was about a third of the whole thing. On the previous occasions, this piece of steel must have dropped back into the sump of gearbox when the plug was removed. I returned to the flight deck and showed my crewmates what I'd found. We were now staying in Marseilles, while our engineers flew down with another gearbox.

This is a major job to do at the best of times. The huge propeller must be lifted off, the gearbox separated from the engine, replaced, and the propeller refitted. Doing this so far from our engineering base was a serious undertaking. It took all night to get lifting slings and a crane organised. The replacement parts and personnel were flown down from Coventry and Brussels. It took all the following day to do the job. Amazingly we left Marseilles on schedule, with a fully functioning aeroplane and a flight deck full of tired, oily engineers.

When we returned to Coventry, our managing director never commented on the effort that had been put into keeping the charter going. He just grumbled about the cost of rebuilding the knackered gearbox.

A few months later, we were returning to Marseilles. This time, we had to get a scheduled flight to Brussels first, taking over from the crew that had been operating the route. There was four of us, three flight crew and an engineer. As we disembarked our scheduled flight, the cabin crew handed us each a carrier bag, containing a little refreshment for later. This was very well received by us. The handling agent collected us from the bottom of the aircraft steps, taking us straight to our waiting Electra.

We arrived in Marseilles before midnight, which was a very early finish by our standards. We weren't leaving until eight o'clock the next evening. Twenty hours to kill, this called for a bit of gentlemanly drinking. After all we had to keep our body clocks on nights, we also, already had some freebies. On the way to the airport hotel, we stopped at a petrol station and bought a slab of supplementary beer.

By four in the morning, we only had to stay up another hour or two before breakfast was served. It would be rude to miss it. The captain and first officer called it a night at that thought. Me and Mark, the engineer decided to take on the challenge. By the time we staggered down to breakfast, we were very much the worse for wear, we looked a proper state. The staff were great, they put us on a table out of the way of the other guests and fed us strong coffee.

Waking up at ten o'clock that morning after only three, or four-hours sleep, I was absolutely buzzing. Having no idea why my mind was racing and totally alert. I figured going for a run was the best way to burn off the excess sugar and alcohol in my body. Jogging at a brisk pace, I left the hotel and set off in the bright morning sunshine. Not paying any particular attention to my surroundings, I'd probably covered about three miles since leaving the hotel. Imagine my shock when I was rudely shaken out of my jogging stupor. Not realising that I had strayed onto the coastal A7 autoroute. This was very bad. I was running down the hard shoulder of one of the busiest motorways in Europe. Huge trucks were thundering by. Inches away from me, blasting their horns.

After running for about half an hour, I had no idea how I came to be on the motorway. The road was edged with high, wire mesh fences to keep idiots like me out of harm's way. I was thinking about retracing my steps, hoping to leave the motorway via the same route that I had joined it. Then I spotted a storm drainage pipe running under the road.

It was big enough for me to crawl through in my t-shirt and trainers. After several minutes scrambling through the concrete drainpipe under the carriageways, listening to the traffic noise above my head, I eventually came out on the other side of the motorway and outside the safety fence. It took another hour to pick my way back to the hotel. Collapsing back into my bed I slept solidly until it was time to leave my room and go to work. The worst part was, I'd slept through dinner. Note to self, washing down Jack Daniels and champagne cocktails with Stella Artois is not to be repeated.

Landing in Marseilles again, this time with a new first officer, 'Cocky'. In the few short months, he'd been with the company, he was making an impression. Not a good one. He was universally despised. This was the first time I'd flown with him.

Occasionally, being a twat myself, I felt it would be hypocritical of me not to give him the benefit of the doubt. Our captain, however, was showing all the signs of running out of patience with our new colleague. All his attempts to guide the chap the right way, were met with sarcasm and backchat. 'I know what I'm doing!!' Is not what you say to the training captain, when he points out some shortcoming in your performance that needs refinement.

Enjoying my hotel breakfast with Cocky, he casually asked if I'd had any problems when I arrived in my room. Perhaps getting changed? 'No. I've been able to dress myself for quite a while now.'

At that point our captain arrived at the table, still in his uniform. 'I don't know what's wrong with my suitcase, I can't get the thing opened.' I turned to face Cocky, he was looking as guilty as sin. The captain looked at him, 'Do you know something about my suitcase?' Cocky couldn't lie, 'I might have changed the combination on the lock, while I was making the coffees.' ''Why would you do that.' 'I thought it was his case.' He said, nodding towards me. 'Oh, that makes it ok then.' 'What number did you change the combination to?' 'I can't remember.'

The captain thought it through for a few minutes. 'After breakfast come to my room, collect my suitcase. Before we go for dinner tonight, you will have it opened. Ok.' Clicking the combination lock from zero to nine thousand, nine hundred and ninety-nine was going to take a while. Cocky wasn't going to get much sleep.

Later that afternoon we met in reception for dinner, Cocky had eventually got the case open, and our skipper was dressed less formally than at breakfast. We were in the airport hotel, so we walked to the terminal in search of dinner. Settling into our seats, in a large Italian pizza restaurant we studied the menu.

Cocky did it again. He stood up, waved at the waiter, and clicked his fingers. The waiter was at our table like a shot. Full of gallic fury, he spat out, 'You are a very rude person, I will not be serving you, or your friends, please leave, now.' Well done Cocky!! So, it was sandwiches, pepperoni, and chocolate milk from the petrol station for dinner.

It had been a long, uncomfortable, and quiet nights flying. The only conversation on the flight deck was reading check lists and making radio calls. Flying from Lyons to Brussels our unshakeable captain was clearly boiling over. 'Steve, you've got a PPL, haven't you? Swap seats with Cocky.' With me in the driving seat and Cocky in the flight engineers' seat, the inquisition started. Our captain grilled Cocky on the function and system associated with every switch and gauge on the flight deck. Cocky was struggling to find the answers.

It made a nice change for me not to be in the limelight. We started our descent into Brussels, I continued to fly the aeroplane. Turning onto final approach, I slowed us down and called for the flaps, Cocky looked at the skipper. 'What are you waiting for, he just asked for the flaps.' Cocky was gobsmacked, but he selected them. I called for the landing gear to be lowered and continued down to short finals. As we came over the threshold, I asked for a power reduction and started to flair. We touched down on the centre line, very gently, one wheel at a time, it was great.

As we slowed down and taxied towards our stand, the captain directed his look at Cocky. 'You must be feeling really embarrassed, the flight engineer just did a better job landing this plane than you have all week. You'd better pull your socks up.' It was worth getting chucked out of the restaurant, just to witness my boss's masterclass in tearing a strip off this recalcitrant first officer.

Whilst I was enjoying a little Schadenfreude, other Atlantique crews were having serious problems. G-LOFA and her crew were departing Berlin Schönefeld, en route to Cologne. In the climb, the ground engineer had reported some smoke or dust in the cargo compartment. Whilst this was being investigated, the situation became much more critical.

As the aircraft approached twelve thousand feet, it depressurised so violently that the flight deck door was ripped off its hinges. In isolation, this would be a scary thing to happen. It was made worse by thirty-five years' worth of dust and debris filling the air. The aircraft pitched down, rolled to the right and started shaking and buffeting. The crew realised that they only had limited control of the plane. Talking to the captain and flight engineer after the event, I got a detailed description of what had happened.

After the explosive decompression, the ground engineer had worked his way far enough down the freight bay, to see that the huge cargo door, which on this aircraft was at the rear of the fuselage, was either missing or open. In fact, it had blown open so violently that it was wrapped over the top of the fuselage.

The captain had to hold in a lot of aileron, rudder, and elevator on the control column just to maintain straight and level flight. Carefully manoeuvring the aircraft back to Schönefeld in this condition was a major achievement. This was a situation that could easily have ended very badly, had it not been for the professionalism and cool headedness of everybody on board.

The subsequent enquiry by the Air Accidents Investigation Branch concluded that the aircraft door indication wiring was at fault. As a result of several modifications over time, the indicator lights did not reflect the state of the door under all circumstances. This resulted in the aircraft getting airborne, with the door only partially locked. G-LOFA spent a long time in the hangar being repaired and modified before it could be allowed to fly again.

Steve Woodhouse

Base Training probably could have gone better.

Fatigue crack finally gave in. Flaw traced to manufacture in the 1960's

Chapter 22

Mile High Club.

As you may think, flying around in a large freight or passenger airliner is a tightly regulated thing to do. You are under constant scrutiny. Air Traffic Control watch your every move, they also check on your compliance with every instruction. Every word you say on the flight deck is recorded.

In recent years this has become even more controlled, with the introduction of Flight Data Monitoring (FDM). This system, built into all modern airliners, records every output on every instrument, the position of every switch, every control input. Make a mistake and the aeroplanes on board computer automatically reports it straight to your company's flight safety department. Immediately after that, your whole world will find out what you did. I can't think of another industry that works in such a closely scrutinised environment.

If you know the parameters these systems work to, it is possible to stretch the envelope to its limits. Sometimes in the name of efficiency, sometimes just for fun. Occasionally we got to fly our Electra's around empty, this was always a bit of a treat and taken advantage of. Oscillating the plane vertically by plus or minus two hundred feet, was enough to give a zero-gravity effect at the back of the freight deck, we occasionally tried this out. Any more than two hundred feet from your assigned altitude, triggered the warning lights on the ATC radar screen and got you a call from the controller. This day our ground engineer had brought his girlfriend along for a flight.

After a bit of whispering and giggling, the pair of them disappeared off the flight deck. Nothing was said, but we knew exactly where they were going, so we gave them a couple of minutes to 'warm up'. Then began pushing and pulling on the control column. Pull, plus two hundred feet, push, minus two hundred feet. We were in fits of laughter when they finally returned. Our engineer was grinning like a Cheshire cat, his girlfriend was nursing a huge bruise on her backside. Even in negative 'G', what goes up, eventually comes down, apparently with quite a thump.

Pulling onto the apron at Nantes, we could never have guessed how much attention we were soon going to attract. All went smoothly with the turn-round and we were loaded, ready to depart for Bordeaux. Our problems began when we tried to start the first engine, it was having none of it. We traced the fault down to the fuel ignition unit. A relay box about the size of a cigarette packet, it signals the fuel control valve and ignitor initiators. The good thing was, that although we needed this component to start the engine, it wasn't needed once the engine was running. What's more, we had four of them.

The solution was obvious, remove the defective unit, borrow a working one from a good engine, slave it in. Then, refit it to the original engine once it had done its job. No problem. I went onto the tarmac with the ground engineer. We had all the tools we needed, and a ladder. The cowlings on two of the engines were opened, and the defective bit removed. We then 'borrowed' the good fuel ignition unit from the adjacent engine and fitted it. I waved up to the captain to start the engine. Beautiful, it fired up perfectly. With the engine running next to us, me and the engineer took the fuel ignition unit off, secured the cables, closed the cowlings, and moved ourselves and our ladders to the next engine.

The ground crew were at the front of the aircraft, watching our progress in some disbelief. They had clearly told their mates that something unusual was going on. The ground crew of three blokes started to grow. Four, five, six, we were acquiring an audience. We refitted the part in its original place and closed the cowlings on the second engine. Climbing back aboard the plane we started the rest of the engines and left for Bordeaux. This had the signs of becoming a pain in the neck. The problem was simple, we had a broken aeroplane. However, with some extra effort, not to mention increased risk, by me and our engineer, it could be made to work. Most importantly in the company's decision-making process, this was at no extra cost. In all probability, the company would now do nothing to fix the fault.

As predicted, Op's had been in touch, if we could just 'nurse' the plane around the route, they promised a replacement part would be waiting for us when we arrived back at Brussels. We repeated the process the next evening in Bordeaux, to the amusement of the ground crew there. They knew we had a problem before we arrived at the aeroplane. The guys in Nantes had passed on the news. We also had to let the loaders and ground crew know, that we would need ten minutes longer than normal to get the engines started. During the engine starting, doors open, doors closed routine, the fuel ignition unit from the working engine came to grief, it fell off the ladder and landed on the tarmac. Fortunately, it bounced away from the spinning propeller, it was still a heart stopping moment. Watching it drop six feet to the ground, we had no idea which way it would jump, or where it would fly, if it were to hit the propeller.

Our problem was now compounded, we only had two remaining serviceable ignition units. Our start routine now had to incorporate a third engine; it was getting trickier by the hour. By the time we arrived back in Nantes, our welcoming committee had grown even more. The ground crew were joined by at least a dozen spectators, some in overalls, some in suits. They had arrived on bikes, in cars, on tractors, from every corner of the airport. As the loading progressed, the crowd grew. By the time we were ready to start the engines and leave, the small, remote apron was virtually surrounded with onlookers. They had even been joined by a fire engine and an ambulance. All waiting, hoping to see a crazy Englishman get chopped up by his own aeroplane.

Treating our newly acquired fans to a regal wave, we taxied out to take off. We arrived in Brussels to be met by a triumphant engineer brandishing a new, shiny fuel ignition unit. His face went very crinkly when we told him that he needed two.

We had done our bit, all we had to do now was drink coffee and wait a couple of hours for our jump seat home. Ending a stressful week was always a good feeling, the pressure was off. This was one of the rare times we were passengers in one of our Electra's and going directly to Coventry. That was a bonus, it would save an hour or two crammed in a taxi.

The wall adjacent to the runway, of hangar seven, was covered by a 1950's style prefab lean-to row of offices. One of these offices was used as an honesty bar, furnished with a threadbare, rank sofa and a worn-out pool table, it worked amazingly well. The fridge was filled with beer. When you finished work, if you fancied a drink, you just helped yourself to a can and dropped some change in the cash jar. The jar always contained money and the fridge always contained beer. Unlikely as it sounds, nobody would dream of abusing this facility and it worked well for years.

Taxiing to our parking spot on the apron outside the bar, we could see a reception committee. The Electra's taxi light swept along the wall as we turned to park. Greeting us in the very bright spotlight was a row of five or six bare arses. Another couple of crews had arranged a welcome home parade for us. All lined up facing the wall with their trousers around their ankles, very cheeky. That had to be worth a round of drinks.

Nuremberg was always a favourite place to visit, it's a typically traditional Bavarian city, in its architecture and customs. Inside the city walls, it is beautifully gothic, outside the city walls, it is a very modern industrial, educational, and financial development. Any city in which historically, the law required its citizens to brew huge volumes of beer gets my vote. We would typically arrive at the hotel here early in the morning, often before breakfast was served.

My way of passing an hour before breakfast, was usually to go out for a run, a lap of the city walls was about twenty-five minutes, so normally, two laps was perfect to work up an appetite. On this morning though, things were made very uncomfortable for me. I had completed one lap and was passing a wide, grassed area, with a few footpaths and some seating. I had spotted the group of people standing about drinking tins of beer, so I gave them a wide berth.

A large dog trotted out of the group towards the path in front of me, it was a big rottweiler. Showing no signs of aggression, this animal stood on the path I was running down, blocking my way, and facing me. I stopped running but continued to walk towards it. It responded by walking up to me, standing upright and putting its front paws on my shoulders. Having an uncontrolled, strange dog behaving this way in a public place is disconcerting to say the least.

Its dark brown eyes looked straight into mine, they showed nothing, no anger, no friendship, nothing. Its head was huge, twice as wide as mine. I could feel its weight pressing down on my shoulders. It's warm, foul breath in my face. I really didn't know what to do at this point. Any move by me was likely to end badly, so I just stood there for what felt like an age. I suppose the dog got bored, because it dropped down onto its four paws and trotted back to the group of vagrants. I walked on down the path until I'd passed the group and their dog, then continued with my run.

Whilst I was mulling over the dog event, I ran my second lap of the wall. Intimidating, it had been, but other than being shaken up a little, no harm was done, what's more there was nobody about who really gave a toss. That was the end of it. As I rounded the last corner, I headed at a trot over the pedestrian crossing towards the hotel. There was a snarling and strangled barking, rushing in my direction. A very distressed woman, with her dog's lead wrapped around her wrist, was being dragged into the road towards me.

The Alsatian on the other end of the lead was foaming at the mouth, clearly intent on getting its teeth into me. This time I didn't break my stride, I side stepped the vicious animal, avoiding its snapping jaws and continued jogging towards the hotel. Leaving the distraught woman to deal with her own horrible dog, it wasn't going to become my problem.

Anybody who goes running regularly, will have had similar encounters, but in Germany, where rules are generally followed to the letter, and twice in one short run! What was this place coming to? By the time I sat down for breakfast I was starving.

Early in the evening we were travelling back to the airport, I was in the front of the Mercedes taxi, with the captain and first officer in the back seat. It was proving to be a cringeworthy journey, our captain, Dick was in full flow. Dick had served in the Air Force as a pilot, and as a young officer he had flown with some of the old boys who had seen action in the second world war. This formed the basis of the story he was telling; It lasted all the way to the airport. His chum, Ginger, had apparently flown Lancaster bombers during the war. One dark night he had set off on a bombing raid to Cologne. Because of the atrocious weather over his original target, he had to go to his secondary target which was Nurnberg.

The church in the Nurnberg market square, still displays photographs of the area after the bombing raids it suffered. The whole city was entirely obliterated. Dick emphasised the salient points of his story, going into particularly minute detail about the navigational skill of his mate Ginger. I was sat next to the taxi driver, a native of Nurnberg. He would more than likely have lost relatives and property in these raids. Me and the first officer did our best to change the subject, but Dick was having none of that. He ploughed on with his story, 'He only dropped his bombs here because of the bad weather in Cologne.' He repeated for the fourth time, as if he was speaking to deaf imbeciles.

The taxi driver, who spoke good English, was clearly fuming. I was honestly amazed he kept his temper contained long enough to drop us at the airport. It was with a great sense of relief I got out of his cab. I'm sure he was just as happy to see the back of us, especially Dick.

Arriving on the Electra flight, deck we were met by Dave, our engineer. He had spent the afternoon doing maintenance work on the plane. He didn't look at all well. 'Are you ok Dave.' We asked. He clearly wasn't, he turned around and lifted the back of his t-shirt. 'Holey shit,' his back was red raw, covered with deep welts. 'What the fuck have you been doing', we spluttered. The previous evening after his dinner, Dave had wandered into the city. He'd had a drink or two and strolled around the inside of the city walls.

Not having any destination in mind, he found himself in the red-light area. The pretty girls were inviting him into their rooms, with a range of enticing promises. One of the girls was exceptionally attractive, and our engineer was hooked. Although Dave had not paid any particular attention to her speciality service, he thought, why not? He signalled his interest and she let him into the building and up to her room.

She was wearing very little, black panties, stockings, and high heels as he entered her boudoir. She wasted no time getting him undressed and Dave was being as helpful as he could. Sitting him facing the back of a kitchen chair she fastened his wrists and ankles to the chair legs and back of the seat with silky ropes.

Dave thought, 'This is going to be good.' Fraulein Whiplash then set about him with a riding crop. She certainly knew how to make it sting. Dave squealed in shock and pain, she took this as encouragement and carried on thrashing away even more enthusiastically. Dave begged her to stop, she didn't. Something had got lost in the translation. Eventually his time was up, this lesson in German etiquette cost him a hundred Deutschmarks. One for each scar.

Chapter 23

The End is Nigh.

Pulling onto stand in Hamburg was becoming a bit of a ritual. Once the chocks were in place, and the engines shut down, the airport fire service would produce four large drip trays and position them under our engines. Not satisfied with that, they would then appear on the flight deck with an invoice pad and issue a fine for spilling oil and fuel on their pristine bit of tarmac. I'm certain profiteering from environmentalism started in Germany.

As we checked into the hotel, we were told that breakfast would be an hour before it was ready. Not really a surprise, it was five o'clock in the morning. Off came the gold braid, company ties and anything else that could identify us. Then we adjourned across the road to a little bar that was still open. Standing around a high table with a cold beer, we were happily putting the world to rights. Our first officer was starting to flag. By now the table was covered in glasses. Neil then actually fell asleep, standing up, he just folded in half at the waist. Had he not been stopped by the empty beer glasses; he would have broken his nose on the table.

He had been threatening to do this for several minutes, shutting his eyes and then twitching back into consciousness between sips of beer. We were nudging each other and smirking at our narcoleptic friend. When he finally succumbed, the result was spectacular. His head crashed through the glasses on the table, smashing a couple, and scattering broken glass over the table and onto the floor, we all took a step back. He immediately bounced back to a bolt upright stance, with a startled, far away expression on his face. He had a big smiley shaped cut in the middle of his forehead, that was dribbling blood down between his eyes and dripping from his nose. The barman declared 'Ziss is ze funniest sing I haff seen all night,' then he produced another round of beers, on the house.

My night was rounded off nicely, when after breakfast, I was in the lift going up to my room. At first, I didn't pay too much attention to the lift music, then my ears pricked up. Yes, they were playing the theme tune to 'Dads Army' in a German hotel lift. I walked down the corridor to my room whistling, 'Who do you think you are kidding Mr Hitler.'

Neil wasn't the only first officer to provide us with entertainment in Hamburg. Jimmy managed it too. Jimmy was young, always on the hunt for a bit of skirt, and not short of chat. He thought his birthday and Christmas had come together when he started a very noisy, physical 'friendship' with one of the hotel waitresses. The gloss was taken off this liaison, when he learned that her husband was a jealous, East German merchant navy sailor. He had apparently knocked lumps off the little trollops' previous casual dalliances. What's more he was due back in port any day.

Jimmy was wishing he hadn't been so easily led astray by the contents of his shorts. He even resorted to pleading with crewing, to take him off the Hamburg route forever. As we don't generally get to choose where we go, or who we work with, this was a non-starter. Over dinner, us, his crewmates, weren't helping at all. Comments like, 'don't worry Jimmy, we'll ship your mangled remains home, for free, once he's done battering you.' This did nothing to boost our Casanovas confidence. Our ribbing was taking place as we sat in a Greek taverna, and to say the place was a bit strange would be an understatement.

Walking through a quiet part of town, we had selected this restaurant at random. It looked OK from the outside. The three of us walked in and were directed to a table by the barman. He then disappeared into the kitchen, there was a loud female shriek, followed by shouted Greek expletives. I don't speak any Greek, but I generally recognise swearing and abuse when I hear it. There was a crash of crockery, as a pile of plates hit the floor, followed by more female screamed abuse and the slamming of a door. The barman's head appeared around the kitchen door, he gave us a grin and a thumbs up. 'OK.' Was all he could say. Apparently, the only things available from the extensive menu, was pork chops and coca cola. So, we had those, it was pretty good, considering.

Ad-hoc work was still a big part of the company's business, and this continued to bring some random jobs our way. As we arrived in Cork the ATC man gave us the weather report. 'At the moment it's a little soft (wet). It's forecast for a stiff breeze later though.' Smart aleck controllers always ready with a joke. We were coming into Cork to collect the first consignment of Viagra to be imported into Britain. Ten tonnes of little blue pills, will that make the plane hard to steer, will you be able to get it up off the ground, I hope the weathers OK in East Midlands or you guys will be up all night.

The innuendos went on and on, everybody with a radio had a quip. By the time we left we had heard just about every imaginable Viagra joke. Even the bowser driver got in on the act, 'This fuel's a bit expensive, but it shouldn't leave you too hard up.' 'If you guys were to steal this cargo, would that make you hardened criminals.' I think that Pfizer are missing a trick. They could include jokes in their packaging, promoting their product, just like fortune cookies, but more accurate.

Things were changing at Air Atlantique, the company was being broken up by means of a management 'Buy-In'. Essentially the managers of each division within the company, were given the opportunity to buy their part of the business and operate it as a stand-alone company. The Electra Division was bought by two of the companies' senior business managers. The Electra's were by far the most profitable part of the company and under our new bosses were about to become even more so.

Working conditions for the Flight Crew were about to change, and pretty quickly. The first cash saving to be made by our new management, was at the detriment of our beloved expenses system. Under the system we all enjoyed, the captain paid all our down route expenses, meals, drinks, taxis, using his company credit card. We added up what we thought was our portion of the bill. Individual crew members then wrote the company a cheque each month for this estimated amount.

Our new Managing Director had enjoyed the benefits of this expenses scheme as much as anybody, he knew exactly how it could be abused. It was the first thing our 'poacher, turned gamekeeper' changed. He understood the value of cash though, so he introduced a new bonus scheme to keep the troops sweet.

The large parcel carriers we worked for, depend very heavily on things happening on time. These mammoth logistical systems mostly run like clockwork. If a consignment is delivered late, or ends up in the wrong place, it causes them a lot of extra work, and expense.

Atlantic Airlines, as we now were, had a plan to encourage its crews to be as efficient as possible, in order to ingratiate ourselves with the logistics companies we contracted to. They introduced an 'On-time departure bonus' of £10 a sector. Our on-time departure record was already astonishingly good, even flying old and sometimes unreliable aircraft. Our M.D. decided that this record must be maintained, or perhaps even improved upon.

The kicker was, this bonus was only paid to the captains. Apparently, the flight engineer, first officer and ground engineers played no tangible part in the departure process. Clearly nonsense. In the M.D.'s mind we were simply assets to be managed by our company/cash minded skippers. The captains obviously did all the hard work.

This didn't sit at all well with the two thirds of the flight crew who were disadvantaged. Only one captain stepped forward to argue the case for the whole crew to benefit. To emphasise his point, he was proud to put himself at the bottom of every 'On Time' league table the M.D. instigated. His objection to the scheme was simple; He already did the job as well as he could, this incentive just pressurised our skippers into rushing the procedures and cutting corners. He was soon to be proven absolutely right.

Because all the departure and flight records were handwritten, by the crew and the handling agent, it wasn't difficult to fudge the figures. A nod, 'Are you happy to call that on time?' to the ground crew supervisor, ensured that all sets of the documented figures agreed, and small delays could simply be lost. Major delays had to be admitted to, but they were rare. Our on-time departure record reached improbable heights, but at a cost.

Early one morning on Apron 57, (or as we knew it, coffin corner), a remote and desolate stand at Brussels airport, G-LOFC was being loaded. It was looking unlikely that it would leave on time. The captain had his head down and was cutting every possible corner to collect his tenner. With the freight doors closed and the paperwork handed to the groundcrew, he instructed the first officer to request taxi.

As the taxi clearance was being received and written down on the flight log, the captain released the parking brake, and the aircraft started moving forwards. There was chaos on the ground, people ran in all directions, some waved and screamed at the captain to stop, but it was too late. The right-hand inboard propeller hit the ground power unit parked to the right of the aircrafts nose.

A GPU weighs in at a couple of tonnes, about the size of a small van. It contains a big diesel engine and an equally big 115 volt, three phase generator, putting out about 90kva (260amps) of electrical power. A very solid lump of a thing, it could provide enough electricity to run a row of houses. This unit was connected to a tug, in which the driver was sitting. The damage to the GPU and the aircraft was substantial. The trauma experienced by the groundcrew, particularly the tug driver must have been immense.

The procedures for taxiing an airliner away from its stand once the engines are running are cast in stone. Disconnect the air start. Disconnect the GPU. Call ATC for taxi clearance; read back taxi clearance to ATC; confirm taxi clearance is as briefed and makes sense. Signal the groundcrew to remove the chocks from under the wheels. Signal the marshaller that you are ready to release the wheel brakes. The ground crew then check the area around the aircraft is clear of equipment and personnel. The flight crew check their respective sides of the aircraft for the same. Only when the captain is instructed to by the marshaller, does he release the aircraft wheel brakes, and follow the marshallers directions. There may be slight variations on this procedure from company to company, but it's generally accepted as universal.

Our captain skipped all these safety procedures and saved around ninety seconds. As the first officer wrote down the taxi clearance, he released the brakes and started rolling forwards. The plane stopped after a few feet, when the inboard propeller struck the ground power unit parked in front of it.

This resulted in a damaged airframe, a destroyed propeller, a damaged gearbox, the aircraft generator ripped off its' mountings by inertia and landing on the concrete apron, a damaged engine, a damaged GPU. The most important consequence was, it resulted in a furious tug driver and a team of groundcrew who would have happily killed our captain, if they hadn't been restrained by their workmates. After the inquisition, the 'On-Time Departure Bonus 'was scrapped.

By now, I was getting more experienced as a private pilot, and more confident in my role as the flight engineer. Watching my colleagues, I felt that being a commercial pilot wasn't beyond my capabilities. How hard could it be. If these guys can do it, so can I.

Mark, the flight engineer on the DC6, had already begun the groundwork towards his Commercial Pilots Licence. There was no reason why I shouldn't do the same. I started to use all my spare time studying for the CAA, ATPL navigation group exams. I also spoke to my work colleagues, letting it be known this was the way I was trying to go. They were all immensely supportive. Lending me study material and training notes. I had a chat with my boss, asking him if the company would be prepared to help me out.

Air Atlantique had the absolute best cadet pilot training scheme in the country for many years. It is one aspect of the company that stands head and shoulders above everybody else in the industry. Other Airlines are run by managers and accountants, even our national flag carrier scrapped its cadet pilot training when times got tough.

Atlantique didn't, our scheme was the only fully funded training program in the country. Add to that, the training was all carried out within the company, in our own flight school. We simply had access to the best of everything. Over the years I've sat next to a lot of pilots and I can say without any doubt that Atlantique trained cadet pilots stand head and shoulders above the crowd.

The Icarus Game

This may sound very biased and it probably is. In contrast, I've also sat next to some really crap pilots, and some that are just plain incompetent.

Atlantic Airlines were to continue this program for many years, producing pilots for our airline and other carriers around the world. Unfortunately, these days it's down to a partially funded scheme, the accountants are relentlessly taking over.

Arriving in Op's, for an ad-hoc charter to Rabat in northern Morocco, I met up with my crew. The freight was unusual, it was a huge, gilded concrete fountain, weighing several tonnes. It had been bought as a gift for the King of Morocco. It took a lot of straining and pushing to carefully position it in the freight bay without chipping the gold plating. The flight over to Africa had been very jovial, spending the whole trip joking and taking the mickey. We had been on the approach to the runway for the last thirty miles. Rabat has a very long runway and as we got closer, we were surprised just how green and lush the countryside was, for northern Africa.

As we crossed the threshold, we got the shock of our lives. The green pasture and marshland on either side of the runway, seemed to lift into the air. Huge flocks of very large birds took off either side of us. The 'go around' call was interspersed with expletives, as we watched thousands of flamingos, pelicans, and goosy sized birds flash by the side windows. We didn't want to hit one of those. We eventually landed and began to offload our cargo. When we told the loaders the gilt fountain was for King Hassan II, they were clearly very proud, and saw helping in the delivery of such an important gift as an honour.

This is not a reaction I saw anywhere else. Unfortunately, within a couple of weeks of his new fountain arriving, the old king died. Whether he ever saw it I don't know.

Chapter 24

The End is Here.

As well as studying for my ATPL navigation group exams, I also needed to fly regularly, to gain experience and hours in my logbook. To this end, I bought a half share in a light aeroplane. The other half was owed by one of our first officers. To qualify to sit the commercial pilot exams, I needed to double my existing flight hours, my co-owner needed to increase his hours, to speed up the conversion of his CPL to an ATPL. With only two shareholders the aeroplane was available whenever we wanted it. It was also the lightest, smallest, cheapest aeroplane we could find, and cost virtually nothing to run. Literally a few kilograms above the lower weight limit for an aircraft requiring a PPL, it was powered by a tiny two stroke motor.

We both racked up hundreds of hours flight time in this little fabric fun machine. Being small and light, made it a real handful to fly. We bought it at a good price, because the previous owner had crashed it into a hillside after an engine failure. He was now scared stiff of the thing. That didn't put us off at all.

We handed over our cash, put the 'Green Meanie' on a trailer, and drove it to Coventry. Atlantique starred again, they allowed us to park our little plane in the corner of one of their hangars. She was very happy in her new home; we folded her wings back and tucked her away in the corner of the hangar surrounded by other aeroplanes.

Steve Woodhouse

Being the owner-operator of a small plane is a double-edged sword. On one hand, it's brilliant, being able to push your plane out of the hangar whenever you want, flying anywhere that takes your fancy. On the other hand, you must maintain it in an airworthy condition, and that takes quite a bit of work. There is also the temptation to push your luck. On a couple of occasions, I got airborne in murky conditions that turned worse. Hedge hopping your way around the countryside, to stay out of the clouds, is best avoided.

They say that there are two types of pilot's flying tailwheel aircraft, those who have ground looped, and those who will. I plead guilty to being in the former group. I was returning to Coventry from a Sunday afternoon fly-in, shortly after I'd bought the aeroplane. I knew it could be a tricky thing to land at the best of times, but the wind speed had increased during the afternoon. Now it was blowing straight across the runway. Anywhere else this would not be too much of a problem, I'd just land across the runway into wind. Coventry didn't like that idea, insisting I land on the approved bit of tarmac, in the approved direction. I crossed the threshold with full left aileron and a big boot full of rudder in.

All went well, the left mainwheel and the tailwheel touched down together, and I was tracking nicely down the centreline. My problem happened very quickly, as soon as the right mainwheel touched the ground and the wings levelled, the wind got under the left wing and picked it up sharply. At the speeds the Kitfox flew, I was virtually down to taxi speed at this point. I kicked hard left on the rudder, spinning the nose ninety degrees left into wind, grinding away a bit of the right wingtip in the process. I stopped on all three wheels, on the runway and pointing into wind.

The Icarus Game

Taxiing in this breeze proved impossible, after I had apologised to ATC for scratching their runway, I had to shut down the engine, get out of the aeroplane, pick up the tail and walk it back to the hangar. How embarrassing. Far from being an issue for me, this crash course in cross wind landings was never forgotten, and over the years I regularly had to deal with much more severe conditions. No matter what size or type of aeroplane you fly, the same aerodynamic rules apply.

Meanwhile in Nurnberg we had found another game to keep us entertained, rollerblading. Abusing the continental 'free' tram system, we went south of the city to Zeppelin Feld, part of a large public park and lake complex. We soon got the hang of our hired rollerblades, searching out somewhere suitable to use them. Nearby was the Kongresshalle, a huge horseshoe shaped building, constructed for Hitler during the second world war. Around the outside of this mausoleum was a wide concourse laid in polished granite, bordered by arches and pillars. For an unused building this place was spectacular, and a perfect racetrack. The four of us lined up, we took off at a sprint, three flight crew and an engineer, there was a lot of pride at stake.

Mungo, the engineer was the first to come to grief, he had overcooked it on a corner, hurtled between the arches and down a side ramp. He was trying to run, wearing roller blades down a gravelly slope. As he reached the bottom of the ramp, he very nearly ran under the wheels of a passing transit van. By now I was in the lead, beating my forty a day captain and Cocky the F.O. He still had something to prove. We reached the end of the concourse and faced with a solid granite wall; we were still going as fast as we could. I tried to stop by turning my rollerblades sideways, ice skate style. It made no difference at all, I hit the wall at about twenty miles an hour and crumpled in a heap on the ground.

My colleagues arrived shortly afterwards. Cocky pointed and laughed, Jake lit a fag, and with great wisdom said. 'They don't work like ice skates do they. Can you breathe yet?'

We found Mungo at the bottom of the ramp, suffering from an acute dose of gravel rash. We weren't done yet, skating back to the skate hire stall in Zeppelin Feld we passed a skateboard half pipe with a couple of kids playing on it. It was made from wood with a rusty steel sheet as the skating surface. Cocky decided these youngsters needed a lesson in advanced half piping skills. They stepped aside to let the maestro work. Cocky set about it with a gusto, within two minutes he'd removed the skin from his knees, hips, hands, and shoulder blades. The kids were well impressed.

We had spent the week moving Euro bank notes around for the Federal bank, it was just before their introduction, and as you can imagine security was particularly tight. I have no idea what ten tonnes of five hundred Euro, inter-bank notes stacked on pallets is worth, but I know what it looks like.

At the end of the week, we arrived back at East Midlands. It was a quirk of the roster that really irritated a few of us. It was Friday night; we were rostered to finish work at ten in the evening. Arriving in East Midlands at nine forty-five, with fifteen minutes of post flight work to do, the company maintained we had finished by ten. We still had to get back to Coventry though.

The three of us were grumbling and scheming between ourselves. 'If we get back to Op's one second after midnight, I'm claiming a day off payment, that'll show the twats.' This was the gist of our moaning, whilst we sat in the crew room at East Midlands waiting for our ride home.

One of the cadet pilots arrived in a flustered state at a quarter past eleven. 'Sorry I'm late, I've been running errands for Op's. If we get a move on, I can get you back before midnight.' We'd already decided that wasn't going to happen, the day off payment was ours. 'Don't rush, get yourself a coffee.' Our Fugly was getting anxious, 'But, operations said you had to be back before midnight.' We stretched our coffee's out for a while, then left for Coventry. All the way home, the three of us badgered our browbeaten Fug into sticking to the speed limit. We strolled into Op's and promptly filed our day off payment claims.

Fugly's, is the nickname given to Atlantiques cadet pilots, they were under paid and worked like slaves, getting them ready for what lay in store. The name reputedly came about when the Managing Director of Air Atlantique saw the first group of cadets and said 'Humph, is that the best we can find, they're fucking ugly.' Fugly, stuck. Despite his gruff exterior, he was a stalwart supporter of the cadet scheme.

Our day off payment claims got the three of us summoned for a meeting with the M.D., he was not impressed. Jake turned up with several years' worth of backdated claims, where he'd been worked into a day off, and not been paid. Cocky brought a Dictaphone and threatened to go public with this kangaroo court. I turned up ready for a scrap.

The meeting turned out to be a damp squib. The M.D. accepted liberties were being taken by rostering, promising to investigate our grievance. Our claims would not be paid, but we'd made our point. Me and Jake shrugged it off, Cocky was not going to settle for less than his pound of flesh. He demanded his right to payment in full and a proper disciplinary. We left him to it.

The news none of us flight engineers wanted to hear came like a bolt from the blue. We were all going to be made redundant. By now there was five of us. The company had identified a saving to be made at our expense. By re-writing the flight procedures, and moving a couple of circuit breakers, they could dispense with the flight engineer completely. Reducing the crew requirement to a captain and first officer. It had taken forty years of operating Electra's for somebody to work this out. I was furious, even a carpark attendant gets replaced by a computer, I had been made jobless by a fucking circuit breaker. How pointless was I.

It was going to take six months to make this transition to two crew operations. Revised procedures had to be worked out, written up and approved by the CAA. The aircraft had to be modified and the crews trained. We would have jobs for a while but that was it. Some of the flight engineers started to work to rule in protest, others just found other jobs and left.

I'd had a job offer from British Caledonian, so I was totally unphased by the prospect of redundancy. I decided to simply continue enjoying my last few months with Atlantic. Unfortunately, by the time the chop came, British Caledonian had disappeared, that was a spanner in my works.

Things at work were going through a rough patch, this was also being reflected in my home life. After a couple of years living from a suitcase, my marriage which was already becoming stale and passionless was grinding into failure. I would come home at the end of the week to a frosty reception. Beyond paying for the roof over our heads, I seemed to have no function. This sterile environment turned even more sour when the prospect of redundancy was thrown into the mix.

Tracy started spending a lot of time at her mothers, at her sisters, virtually anywhere but at home. These excursions seemed to fit in with my roster nicely, when I was at work, she was at home. When I was at home, she was away 'visiting family'.

The crunch came when I received a phone call from mum. 'Do you have any idea what your wife is up to?' I did, but I'd been studying for my latest set of exams, I didn't have the capacity to deal with both issues. If my marriage was at an end, I wasn't going to waste any more time or energy on it. It was already on its second chance. Anyway, I took the view, that if anybody else was prepared to have an affair with her, they were welcome to pay for the privilege, permanently.

The decision was obvious, I was going to continue concentrating on work and getting my Commercial Pilots Licence, even though this now looked like a very speculative thing to do. When I eventually got Tracy on the end of the phone, she was clear in her intentions, 'You're a bastard and I'm leaving you. Don't try to get me to come home.'

Fair enough, I wouldn't dream of it. 'I'll be visiting Scarborough next weekend, where shall I drop off your belongings.'

The next conversation was going to be more problematic. My daughter was now a teenager and I had to tell her; her mum had cleared off. As far as I was concerned, she could live with me or live with her mum, it was entirely her choice. After a lot of tears and soul searching, she chose to stay with me. Her school, her friends and her life were in Rugby, so that seemed to be the obvious decision. Tracy was very shocked by this outcome, but it was Vicky's choice and I would stand by her.

I was now, a soon to be unemployed, single parent. Not an enviable position to be thrust into. I started trying to resolve the mess I was in. A phone call to the DSS highlighted the problems I was to face. 'My wife has left me and I'm now looking after my teenage daughter on my own, can you pay her child allowance to me please?' 'No, we always pay it to the mother.' 'But she's spending it taking her new boyfriend on holiday.' 'That's her business.' 'Can you pay it into a trust fund for my daughter?' 'No, we always pay it to the mother.' Trying to use logic on government departmental robots was clearly a waste of effort. This was just one example of a system that simply doesn't recognise single fathers. I was in for an immensely frustrating couple of years.

My job as a flight engineer had come to an end, I was going into Atlantic for the last time to collect my final pay cheque and P45. When I got there, I was met by the M.D. and Flight Op's Director. 'Why the long face Steve.' 'I'm here to say goodbye to everybody and collect my P45.' Then came a beautiful lifeline. 'You've done a good job over the years; how do you fancy training as a pilot.' I couldn't believe my ears, one minute my future looked miserable and precarious, then within a couple of seconds it looked full of possibilities and excitement.

Sitting down with them, we discussed my situation. I was now a single parent with a teenage child to support. I had a divorce to organise. They were amazingly pragmatic. Ground school and flight training would be at Coventry. I could get home every night for the next year, after that I'd need to make other arrangements. We sorted out the contractual details, who would pay for what, and over what time frame, it was all eminently possible.

'Take yourself over to Flight Training and they'll sort you out.' I was now the companies oldest ever Fugly. I charged around the company like a teenager on speed, telling everybody my great news. Most were pleased for me; some had no idea who I was.

This change of circumstances had an unforeseen bonus, when I gave my divorce lawyer all my financial details, my financial liabilities were now huge, my income was pitiful, my outgoings were still outrageous. There was no equity in the house, and no savings or investments. If you ever get divorced this is the best situation you can possibly be in. On paper I was worth less than nothing, this divorce was getting less financially stressful by the week. At last life was looking up.

Chapter 25

Flight Training.

Obtaining my private pilot's licence had been a fun project for a summer. Drifting around the sky in my Kitfox had reinforced the lessons I had learnt; it gave me a new-found sense of freedom. A freedom that was further enhanced by my newly acquired status as a born-again single man, albeit with a teenage monster living with me. It didn't take long to discover the joys of being a trainee pilot with his own house, own car, own aeroplane. Really! It was an effort to keep myself in check and concentrate on the job in hand.

Not being prone to getting bogged down by other people's actions is a real benefit, I'm the only person I know who barely noticed his own divorce. It was just a very minor distraction in an incredibly busy time. Now it was time to work, the first thing on the agenda was ground school.

Having already tried one self-studied attempt at the CAA ATPL Navigation Group Exams, I knew I had work to do. I did ok. I failed every paper. On the face of it this sounds bad, the pass mark on each paper is 75%, I had scored over 70% on every paper, I failed each one by the skin of my teeth. I only needed to improve my score by one or two points on each exam. This was still going to take a lot of work, but my confidence was high.

I was enrolled in Ground School at Coventry Airport. As I sat through the various lessons for each subject, the penny dropped.

Navigation Theory lost its mystery and made perfect sense. Meteorology and Climatology, started to become obvious, with the knowledge of a few basic facts about our physical world. Flight Planning was suddenly just an exercise in using a calculator as fast as your fingers would move. Air Law was a read and remember exercise, Human Factors, was explained in words of one syllable. As an Atlantique cadet the rules are simple. Pass everything first time or you're chopped, this focusses the mind.

The knowledge of this group of ground school instructors was striking, they were all ex-RAF navigators. Anybody who can make these subjects comprehendible and sound simple, has a deep understanding of their subject, and the knack of explaining the detail to the likes of me. Even Performance exams became understandable.

Sat at my desk, with Sandy sitting opposite me. He would run his pencil along the lines of a multi axis graph. Explaining the relationship between temperature, altitude, and engine efficiency. His detailed lessons describing the braking distance required to stop, from any speed, at any given point on the runway was impressive. I even understood what I was being taught. Doing this from his inverted viewpoint, whilst writing notes upside down and back to front so that I could read them was astonishing.

In a very formal setting at Gatwick, I spent three solid days sitting exams. Two hours exam, fifteen-minute break, next paper. I didn't speak to any of the other candidates while I was there, and I ignored all the post exam autopsies taking place at the coffee machine. Sit the paper, then start focussing on the next one. There's nothing you can do about the one you just sat; your answers are already cast in biro. It worked for me; my pass marks were all over 90%. Box ticked.

Now was the fun bit, flying training. This starts gently with a few navigation exercises and then ramps up in complexity. Commercial flying is very different to flying for fun. You are there to make money for your employer. Essentially this means you will fly the aeroplane, unless there is a very good reason not to. To this end my instructors would expect me to fly in all conditions, gone were the days when I could look out of the window and go to the pub instead of flying. It was the instructor's prerogative to cancel a training flight, until that happened it would go ahead.

The first part of the course is done in light, single engine aeroplanes, I was with my instructor taxiing out in the Maule MX7, the same one I had dismantled in Opa Locka. It was howling a gale and I was having to work very hard on the controls just to keep us on the taxiway. We sat at the holding point and Andy turned to me. 'Are you happy to take off in this.' 'I'm very apprehensive.' I replied. 'So am I, let's go back in, we'll plan for the same exercise again and take off at lunch time.' That was the only time I had a lesson cancelled because of the weather during the whole course.

The only real scare I got during the course, was practicing an unusual attitude recovery lesson in a Piper Warrior. These are usually very placid, benign aeroplanes to fly. On this day, I think we over cooked it a little. The exercise goes something like this. The instructor takes control of the plane, the student looks down at his own lap. The instructor throws the plane about a bit to disorientate the student, and then puts it into an unusual and inappropriate attitude, with the controls in all the wrong places.

He then calls, 'Recover.' The student has to work out which way up he is, weather he's pointing up or down, and what the engine is doing. Sort out the power, get the wings level, put the nose on the horizon, simple.

On this go, Andy had rolled us inverted, pulled back on the controls, until we were pointing at the ground, and opened the throttle. 'Recover.' I looked up at the rapidly approaching ground. Shut the throttle and pull back on the controls. This should have completed the 'reverse Immelmann' that Andy had started. Instead, we continued, vertically down, the airspeed increasing rapidly.

Pulling as hard as I could on the control column, I was getting nervous. I asked Andy to pull on his controls as well. Both of us had our control columns pulled back onto their hard stops but the aeroplane continued its accelerating, vertical dive. After what seemed like an eternity, the elevator started to bite, and the nose came up onto the horizon. We had lost over two thousand feet in a few seconds, and the airspeed indicator had gone off the clock. That made my heart pound. We returned to Coventry for a brew and a debrief.

We were spending more and more time with black out screens up around the windows, flying on instruments. At first this is disconcerting, but I soon became accustomed to the routine. Take off, screens up, do the planned lesson's exercises, return to Coventry, screens down, there's the runway, land. This was basic radio navigation, tracking NDB's And VOR's, learning how to correct for the wind and errors. This phase of my training culminated in a Basic Commercial Licence, General Flight Test.

The day of the test arrived and surprise, surprise, it was howling a gale. I'd been out in the Cessna 152 just before the examiner arrived and spent an hour hovering and flying backwards over various landmarks in Warwickshire. This flight test was going to need careful planning. Sixty knots of airspeed into a sixty-knot headwind gives you a groundspeed of zero knots. Sixty knots of airspeed with a sixty-knot tailwind gives you a groundspeed of one hundred and twenty knots. Simply put, if you fly too far downwind, you may not have enough fuel to get home.

The first leg of the test was a visual navigation exercise, that went fine, then up went the screens and we headed west for Ledbury. We arrived over the beacon and down came the screens, the examiner shut off the throttle for a practice forced landing. I went through the checks and drills, looked around me for a suitable landing place, there it was, a grass airstrip right below us.

Could I actually land off this PFL? I checked the wind, and flew a circuit pattern around the airstrip, it was spot on. I was a few hundred feet above the threshold, on finals, and perfectly set to land when the unbelievable happened. An aeroplane taxied out from behind the hangar on the field, trundled onto the runway and started to taxi towards us.

The dopey pilot clearly had no idea we were there. I looked at the examiner and shrugged my shoulders. Picking the biggest potato field I could see, I set up to land in that. It was going to be bumpy, but we would walk away from it. On the way back to Coventry we did a bit of general handling and that was it. The examiner commented on the exciting PFL, and the fact that the flight test was conducted in tough, windy conditions. I had my BCPL.

All work and no play isn't a healthy way to live. I was playing quite a lot. My flight training had settled into a steady routine, for the first time in a long while I was working nine to five. Vicky was settled too. She had found herself a job in the local pub. My social life was getting busier by the week and was starting to get worrying. I was meeting ladies of a certain age, mostly in their mid-thirties. They seemed to be either divorcees with children or professional single ladies. Either way their hormonal clocks were clanging ominously.

Contraception was becoming a real issue for me. There is no means for a man to prevent an unwanted pregnancy, without his partner being aware of it. If the girl claimed to be on the pill or using some other discreet means of birth control, as the bloke I was supposed to accept her word for it. It seemed to me that girls had a monopoly on controlling procreation.

I'm not that trusting, the last thing I needed was to be presented with another child. The answer for me was simple, get the snip. If it was an issue for future girlfriends as and when they found out, they were not the right partner for me.

The waiting list for a vasectomy on the NHS was eighteen months. Christ I could father dozens of kids in that time, the alimony bill would become astronomical. I was put in touch with BPAS (British Pregnancy Advisory Service) by my GP. A counselling session was booked. The councillor seemed surprised at my black and white view on the prospect of future kids. No, absolutely not, I can't think of anything less desirable. I was booked in for the procedure the following week.

Arriving at the private hospital I was shown to a cubical and changed out of my jeans into a gown. Almost straight away I was called into the operating room. The previous patient was leaving, and we passed in the doorway. Neither of us wanted to acknowledge the other, so we settled for a slight nod, 'aw'right.' The Nigerian surgeon didn't speak, the nurse did. She was really friendly and before I knew it, I was on the bed, with a sheet covering everything. Except for a hole framing the part that was being worked on. I was feeling very vulnerable and self-conscious. My pride and joy, displayed to the whole room by a hole in a green hospital sheet.

The nurse asked what I did for a living. I told her and that was it, she was off, 'Terrible about Concorde crashing, wasn't it?' I winced as the local anaesthetic went in, that stung a bit. 'That's the worst over.' said chatty nurse. There was a bit of tugging at the tubing in my wedding vegetables, these tubes felt as though they were connected to my tonsils and big toes. Click, snip, tug tie. That was it, the only visible evidence was a couple of stitches under my ball sack. From walking into the room, to passing the next guy coming in the doorway, 'aw'right,' had taken about six minutes. During this time chatty nurse had a good look at my privates and got my life story, speed dating could learn a few lessons from this girl.

This whole procedure had been no worse than going to the dentist for a filling. Co-codamol kept the pain at bay for the next few days and I spent the following weeks purging and draining the system. Doctors' orders. When I finally had two consecutive blank sperm counts, I received a certificate, I keep it with my cycling proficiency test. I no longer had to ask; 'Are you on the pill?' I really had no reason to care.

Now came the expensive part of the flying course, the multi engine rating, and IR (Instrument Rating). Progressing from a small single engine plane to a twin-engine plane is a big jump, they are bigger, heavier, more powerful and a lot faster. The first time out at the controls is great fun, the Cessna 310 that I was to learn in is a proper pocket rocket. It carries loads of fuel, has great engines, and goes where you point it.

The fun is short lived though, this training is for a purpose, and you're not allowed to forget that. Very soon, every take off was immediately followed by a simulated engine failure. The rest of the lesson would be flown on the remaining engine. To me, this seemed a bit of a swizz, you're paying for multi engine time and flying around on one engine.

Everything is just a bit more complicated, variable pitch propellers, fuel balancing, more instruments to monitor, all added to the workload. The exercises were familiar by this time, resolving the problems though was much more complex, everything happens at higher speeds. Soon I was certificated to fly multi engines and ready to start the Instrument Rating (IR).

A multi engine rating and IR, is the key qualification requirement for all commercial flying. This is a real test for anybody, the preparation is exhaustive, everything must be done precisely as the examiner will expect to see it. The initial IR flight test is the only test still carried out by the CAA's own permanent team of examiners.

Except for taking-off and the last phases of the landing, the whole flight, including dealing with abnormal situations and emergencies must be done with no visual reference to the outside world. Pretty much the whole time you are flying from now on, would be done behind screens covering all the aircraft's windows.

This is mentally exhausting, the screens go up during the taxi out, leaving a letter box sized hole to look through, as soon as the wheels leave the ground, this tiny window on the world is closed. Engine failure, continue for the next hour or two with the lesson. Fly the approach on instruments, if the instructor opens the letterbox window and you can see a runway, land on it. If he doesn't open the window, go around, and try again.

On the morning of the test, myself, and Chris the other cadet pilot who was going to be examined at the same time, were flown to Leeds by one of the other cadets. On the day of the IR test, the only flight the company allowed candidates to conduct was the test itself. They felt that your nerves were too shredded to be expected to do anything else. Besides, if you passed you were going to get absolutely rat arsed, if you failed you were going to be fired. Either way, they didn't want you at the controls.

As a passenger, I sat in the back of the 310 for the first test, Chris was examined from Leeds to Carlisle via Blackpool. We stopped for a brief lunch then I took over flying. My test was from Carlisle to Leeds via a whiz around Teesside's beacon. Everybody remembers that flight with the 'Exam' callsign, it's up there with your first solo. After we landed, as we walked back towards the terminal, our examiner, Henry, turned to us and said, 'Well done guys, you've both passed.' I could have kissed him. We then had to sit through an hour of detailed debriefing, finally we had our pass certificates in our sticky paws. We went and found our cadet, 'FUG, FLY US TO THE NEAREST PUB.' I was no longer a cadet, but I'll always be a Fugly.

Chapter 26

Recon'.

I now had the rather dubious distinction of holding one of the last BCPL's to be issued by the CAA under BCAR's. The UK was changing over to the European JAR licencing system. The biggest difference was, under the new rules once you passed your IR you were issued a CPL. I had to amass seven hundred hours flying to convert my BCPL to a CPL. This flying had to be in the 'aerial work' category. That is all kinds of flying that doesn't involve passengers or freight. The next course of Fugly's behind me were the first of the new JAR system. With their licences they could go straight onto flying 'public transport', passenger or freight aircraft.

The Atlantic Group had several options for aerial work flying. Either, instructing at one of the flying schools, in Inverness or Caernarfon. Or Atlantic Reconnaissance (Recon') at Inverness or at Coventry. I was offered the Recon' job at Coventry, and it suited me perfectly. There were several contracts at Atlantic Recon', the first one that I was involved with, was doing topographical surveys of the country using a LIDAR laser scanner. This produced a three-dimensional computer model of the landscape I flew over. These models had a lot of uses, from planning roads, railways and construction works, to planning flood defences.

Training for this job was thorough, but fun. I would go out on surveys and patrols with experienced pilots and learn from them. One morning I was called in for a patrol flight in the Cessna 404, I had already done a few of these, but I still had to wait for my captain/mentor. I'd filed the flight plan and was sat in the aeroplane when Jon fell out of the taxi, clattered up the steps, and crawled along the floor of the aeroplane. He only made it halfway to his seat before he passed out. It was four o'clock on a frosty Sunday morning, and he was still enjoying a Saturday night out when he was called into work. I radioed ATC for engine start and taxied out. We were going around the north side of the Isle of Man before he came to. He looked like shit, so I threw him the flask of hot water and a tube of MaxPax coffees.

Although I was based in Coventry these surveys could be anywhere, mostly they were around the UK, but not exclusively. The transit flights to and from survey sights could be long, it wasn't uncommon to be airborne for ten or twelve hours. The actual surveys involved flying up and down a grid of lines over the site. Using a tablet screen, displaying a map with a grid pattern overlaid on it on your lap, this was linked to a GPS system. The flying had to be incredibly accurate, tracking, speed and height control had to be spot on. It was tricky to get the hang of, but after a few hours I had it sorted.

Aerial work has some downsides, unlike public transport which is regulated, the crew has no limits on their flying or duty time. After a few months, this was starting to show. I was on permanent standby, twenty-four, seven. I'd get in from a survey, fall asleep on the sofa and a few hours later the phone would ring, then I'd be off again. Whizzing around the country in a twin-engine Cessna for a living was great, but I needed a break. I broached the subject with my manager, He was unhappy that I'd distracted him from counting his paperclips. 'Nobody else is available, you'll just have to keep going.'

Sod this. I put my tent and fishing rod in the car and turned off my phone. After a couple of days fishing in the West Country, I felt rejuvenated. When I came back, my bosses went mental over my unauthorised absence, but no matter. I was refreshed and ready to argue my corner. They had a genuine problem, the next group of cadets to qualify did so with JAR CPL's. This meant they could go straight onto public transport work, carrying freight or passengers, which was much more beneficial for the company. For now, I was stuck on Recon' with no signs of progression in the immediate future. Eventually another pilot was found, and I got a change of scenery.

The pollution patrol job was very different, it was still with Recon' but doing maritime patrols, looking for oil spillages around the coast. This could be because of accidents or deliberate acts of pollution by ships operators, like cleaning out tankers holds at sea. Cleaning out ships oil storage holds is massively expensive, and a specialist job done in ports, if the operators could get away with doing it at sea, they could save hundreds of thousands of pounds. If we caught them, it cost them a lot more.

Any incidents we found were videoed, photographed and all conversations with the ship's crew were recorded. This material was then passed to the coastguard and other maritime agencies for prosecution. Although this job still involved long hours airborne, it was generally better organised. There was the occasional callout, but these were not nearly as frequent.

As well as doing patrols, I was one of the company air taxi drivers, I was preparing to fly down to Southampton to pick up another crew. They had parked the Cessna Citation jet there after a charter and were coming home to Coventry. I was using the Piper Arrow PA28R, this was like the Warrior I had trained in, but had a variable pitch prop and a retractable undercarriage. After a quick familiarisation with the new controls, I was on my way.

Finding the crew in the VIP lounge, working their way through the remains of the Citations mini bar, I dragged them out to the plane. Trying my best to be serious and professional, I talked to the ATC officer during our departure. Half way through my radio call there was an almighty commotion behind me. My colleagues had shaken up a couple of cans of Budweiser and fired one into each of my ears, at the same time shouting 'wwwwaaaaazzzzuuuuupppp' at the top of their voices. I was dripping the whole way home. The aeroplane smelled great for weeks though.

It was Friday night in my local, I was having a pint or two with friends and putting the world to rights. The conversation had swung between motorbikes, politics, Big Brother, religion, heavy duty electrical power generation, and aeroplanes. Last orders had been called and we were all tucking into the final pint of the night. Then my phone rang, it was op's. My friends listened with incredulity to the conversation that followed.

Steve Woodhouse

'Steve, the DC6 is stuck in Bordeaux with a blown cylinder. Get into work now, you're taking the engineers and their kit down there.' 'Sorry I can't, I'm in the pub. I've had too much beer to drive.' 'That's OK we'll send a taxi.' That caused quite a bit of spluttering at the bar of the pub. 'You're not really going to fly, now, are you?' 'It looks that way, see you guy's next Friday.' I walked home and made myself an egg and bacon sandwich with a large coffee. Whilst I waited for the taxi, I walked around the garden to dispel the bulk of the booze.

An hour after the phone call I was stood at the op's counter, with the flight plan to Bordeaux on my clip board. The engineers walked in, took one look at their dishevelled pilot, and groaned. The flight down was going to take about three hours in the Cessna 310. By one thirty in the morning, we were loaded up and taxiing out. The engineers took it in turns to watch me like hawks. Every time I looked down at my clip board, I was poked in the shoulder from the back-seat occupants. Normally engineers can sleep anywhere, not tonight. By the time I got into bed at the hotel I was dead on my feet.

My old diesel Citroen was overdue a service, so I decided one Saturday morning to do it. It hadn't been done for a while; I would do a thorough job. On the road outside my house, I drove the front wheels onto a pair of ramps and got started, draining the oil. It had been such a long time since I'd last looked at the car, I decided to flush the engine thoroughly before filling it with fresh oil. I mixed some cheap oil with kerosene, then poured it into the oil filler to clean out all the engine's little tubes.

When I started the engine, I got an almighty shock. At first it ticked over normally, then without warning, it started screaming, the rev counter went straight off the clock. I leant through the drivers' window and turned off the key, it kept screaming. Leaping into the drivers' seat, I stood on the clutch, rammed the car into reverse gear, dropped the clutch and stamped as hard as I could on the brake pedal. The ramps shot out from under the front wheels and cartwheeled down the road.

The front of the car dropped to the ground, and the engine stalled, I was awake now. I climbed out of the car, looked up and down the quiet cul-de-sac. I wondered if anybody had noticed. The street was filled with thick smoke, the noise from the engine had been ear-splitting. The curtains were twitching. With a cup of tea in my hand I phoned a local diesel fitter to find out how seriously I'd cocked up. It took him a full minute to stop laughing.

He explained that the engine wasn't running on the fuel in the tank, but rather it was sucking the oil and kerosene mix from the sump past the piston rings. This totally bypassed the fuel injection system and rev limiter. I was lucky it hadn't exploded. 'Check the cylinder block and crankcase haven't separated,' was his last nugget of wisdom. It took most of the day to get the car running normally again. My trusty Citroen was old and worn out, so I started saving for a new car.

'Are you happy to be illuminated.' Was a phrase that was new to me, it turned out to be a great distraction from the day-to-day patrol work. The first time it happened, I was transiting RAF Lakenheath's military zone, under the control of the base ATC officer. I was three thousand feet above Suffolk, and about a hundred feet above a solid, level covering of cloud. It was early in the morning and I was enjoying the clear blue skies that stretched from horizon to horizon.

The American voice of the controller came over the radio. 'If you're happy to be illuminated, I've got a couple of guys to get airborne, is that OK with you.' I had no idea what to expect, but what the heck. 'Yup, that'll be fine.' 'Maintain your height, course, and speed. Don't worry, my guys know exactly where you are.'

Suddenly, my Cessna 404 was feeling very flimsy. A few seconds after the radio conversation, two McDonnell Douglas F-15's burst into the clear sky from the clouds beneath me, passing vertically in front of me, at most a couple of hundred yards away, one either side of my track. I got a clear view of the top of the pilot's bone dome helmets and watched as they rocketed straight up, with their afterburners blazing. They were out of my view as quickly as they had appeared. It was a singularly impressive sight from where I was sat. I was certainly happy they didn't consider me to be any kind of a threat.

The maritime job also involved monitoring known shipwreck sites for any sign of oil leakage. At one time I had two such sites to monitor. The first was the 'Logic Nene' which had come to grief in the River Nene at Sutton Bridge in Norfolk. During a manoeuvre to turn the boat around in the narrow river channel, the bow and stern had become wedged on opposite banks of the river. The tide went out and without the support of the water the ship broke in half.

This damage resulted in the fuel oil on board being dumped into the river. Because the river was tidal and discharged into a nature reserve in the Wash, there was clearly going to be a lot of concern about this situation. I made daily surveys of the river, using radar, video, and photographs to measure the thickness of the oil on the water's surface.

This involved flying up and down the river at low level, much to the delight of the news cameramen, who were parked up and down the banks of the Nene. On one flight, I passed behind the then secretary of state for transport, as he was describing to the assembled TV crews the action his department was taking to resolve the spillage, perfect timing.

Around the same time, I was doing regular trips to a site off the Northwest coast of Alderney. This was to monitor the leakage of chemicals from the 'Levoli Sun,' an Italian chemical tanker which had set sail from Southampton. The vessel was swamped in heavy seas and taken under tow by the French navy. Heading towards Normandy, the ship sank near the Casquet Ditch. The cargo was 6000 tonnes of styrene, and other volatile chemicals used in the manufacture of plastics.

An Italian ship sinking in British waters, under tow by the French, this got the various government ministries hot under the collar. I spent a few weeks flying our Secretary of State back and forth to meetings in Cherbourg. One such flight was memorable because as we crossed the Channel, we spotted a fishing boat emptying waste oil over the side. Dropping down to sea level our VIP passenger got the boats name and port of registration off the back of the offending vessel. 'Eureka.' It's not many people who get caught in the act of polluting our waters by the Secretary of State for Transport himself.

Chapter 27

Around the Coast.

Flying over the Dover Straights, in the Cessna 404 with my radar operator in the back of the plane. We were on a regular patrol when a call came through from the coastguard. They had an unidentified ship in the Channel that they wanted details on. The weather was too bad to launch the Coastguard aircraft based in Kent, but we were already airborne. Could we 'take a look?' We would certainly try. Flying over the coordinates we were given; I soon identified the vessel in question. We could see from the bow wave of the contact on the downward looking radar the direction the boat was sailing. We needed to get as close as we could to the stern of the ship so that we could read the name and port of registration painted across it.

The first part of this job was to ensure that we had a clear run towards the stern of the ship. To confirm this, I flew overhead the boat at fifteen hundred feet, marking her location on the sat nav, then continued flying in the opposite direction to which she was traveling. Checking the water behind the vessel was clear. I had to be certain, that there were no obstructions on our intended course inbound to the target. Just over four miles would ensure I didn't collide with anything floating about on the water below me.

Once I was happy the area was unobstructed, I started my descent through the dense layer of cloud. The altimeter wound down and I was making constant cross references to the radalt (radar altimeter). We could get very low using this technique. As we dropped below one hundred feet above the water surface, I could just about make out the waves below me, it was still very murky. We were flying at about a hundred and thirty knots, fifty feet above the water and fifty feet below the cloud base, towards the stern of an enormous container ship.

As I approached the ship, I could just about distinguish the paintwork of the hull at the stern. The superstructure disappeared above me into the clouds. It was colossal, and I was closing on it rapidly. Once I had the name of the St Petersburg registered behemoth, I banked hard right and started to climb away. Being in such close proximity to several thousands of tonnes of solid steel, whilst travelling at well over a hundred miles an hour, in poor visibility was something I only ever tried that one time. Future shipping identification requests were thought about carefully before I dived into the murk.

Occasionally I had to stand-in at Inverness for short times, to cover when their regular pilots were unavailable. This was always a pleasant distraction. Flying patrols around the Shetland Basin and other oil fields. It always amazed me just how busy this part of the North Sea was. Some rigs even have their own air traffic control zones to deal with the mass of helicopter flights, taking workers to and from the rigs. Enjoying the stunning scenery of the Highlands coast is a real treat, an opportunity I always took when it was offered.

Arthur was a lovely old boy who worked around the offices of Highland Airways as an odd-job-man, making himself a little beer money. But more importantly for him, as he was aircraft nuts, he was paid in flying hours in the schools Cessna 152.

He loved nothing more than to fly it himself, not allowing his lack of a licence, dodgy eyesight, or lack of auditory perception to hinder his passion. His method was simple. He'd find a company pilot at a loose end, make him a cup of tea, then ask the unwary airman to 'accompany' him on a flight.

I was warned, but hey, what's the worst that can happen. We met by the aeroplane that afternoon. Did I mind if he flew us around his favourite sights of Inverness? Of course not. 'Fill your boots, Arthur.' 'You'd better do the radio Steve, I'm a wee bit hard of hearing.' We started by flying up and down The River Ness, it was lovely. Then we ventured north across the Cromarty Firth, heading towards the Dornoch Firth. There were a couple of Air Force Tornados heading north off my right shoulder, that set the alarm bells ringing. Arthur continued his commentary as he flew. I had a quick look at the chart and saw with some consternation that Arthurs magical mystery tour was taking us directly towards the RAF Tain, bombing range.

'Arthur, I'm running a bit short on time. Can you take us back towards Inverness now, please?' 'Oh yes, of course. Are you enjoying your flight?' Leaving the Air Force behind us to make their craters, we drifted back towards the airport. I could see an impending issue, the windshield of our little aeroplane looked as though it had been scrubbed with a scouring pad. To line up on finals we were about to turn into the sun. I dialled up the ILS (instrument landing system) and waited for the inevitable.

'Oh, I cannae see a bloody thing.' Stammered Arthur as he turned us onto finals, the suns glare blanking out the windscreen. 'No bother Arthur, I have control.' I followed the ILS down, 'Can you see the runway yet Arthur?' 'Ah cannae see a bloody thing.' At six feet above the runway centreline, I asked again. Again, I got the same response. As I turned off the runway out of the sun, Arthur was delighted to be able to see the taxiway. He taxied us back to the flying school and beamed with delight as he described his latest flight to everybody.

Poor weather was very rarely a factor when it came to departing Coventry for a patrol. It could become an issue when it came to land though. On occasion I would have to drop into another airfield, then wait for the weather at home to improve before returning. I generally flew the same aeroplane for maritime patrols, so I was very familiar with its capabilities. On one memorable patrol though I was using the aircraft usually based in Inverness. Although it was the same Cessna 404 model, it had at least one significant difference that I was to discover later in the day.

Patrolling southbound, about twenty miles off the East Anglian coast, I flew into a huge snowstorm. I knew it was there from the weather reports I'd read prior to the flight. A frontal weather system was moving northwards through the southeast of the country. Kent and Essex were at a virtual standstill. As I entered the snow, I switched on all the aircrafts anti-icing systems.

These generally include such luxuries as, heated windshields, heated pitot probes, heated propellers, wing and tail plane inflatable boots or leading-edge heaters. I sat back confident that I'd taken all the necessary steps to keep myself safely airborne. This warm, fluffy feeling soon evaporated. A few minutes into the blizzard, the snow was building up on the windscreen and was soon a couple of inches thick. Any amount of ice and snow accumulating on an aircraft, can very quickly affect its ability to fly. The aerodynamics are made less effective and the extra weight can be huge. Less lift, more drag, more weight is never in the pilot's favour.

Going down is not really a good option in any circumstances, it's hitting the ground that's the painful bit of crashing. I tried to start a climb, increasing the power, and pitching the nose up, nothing happened. The altitude didn't change, the speed didn't change, the engines just got noisier.

The planes lack of control in pitch was the first noticeable change, it was getting very sensitive. Climbing to a higher altitude wasn't working, so I settled on maintaining the status quo. I was now about ten minutes into the snowstorm, at a hundred and forty knots, that's around fourteen miles every six minutes, a check on the weather chart showed the front to be about thirty miles wide. Was the half I'd flown through the worst of it? Or was the next half going to be more severe. Toss a coin.

The snow was building up all over the aeroplane, crucially on the tail surfaces. Controlling the flight path was becoming increasingly difficult. The control surfaces became covered in more and more ice and snow. Although the build-up was relatively slow, it was relentless. The airspeed started to reduce, so I added more and more power. Inevitably, the air speed indicator sank back towards the aircrafts critical flying speed.

Feeling my control of the plane was getting marginal, I was concentrating hard. With the amount of snow covering the airframe, the published minimum control speed and stalling speeds (V_{mca}, V_s) for the aeroplane were unlikely to work, the stalling speed was going to be a lot higher than normal. The stalling characteristics in an ice and snow-covered aeroplane are very different to a clean one. Fly any slower and I was in serious danger of dropping the aircraft out of the sky, losing all control. In training you stall by decreasing your airspeed, and recover the aircraft by increasing its airspeed, it's all very controllable. In this situation, covered in snow and ice, there would be no chance of recovering from a stall.

The only option left to me was to maintain my airspeed, I settled on a hundred and five knots. By now the power levers were fully forward, the airspeed was still creeping back, so I started a slow rate of descent. I just hoped that we would emerge from the snow before we ran out of sky and hit the water. A controlled, or at least semi-controlled ditching on the sea, was for me, preferable to an uncontrolled crash into it.

Watching the altimeter tick down, I was sweating. It was like watching the hands of a clock whilst waiting for a filling at the dentist. You know what's coming, and it's not going to be nice. You can't slow the clock down or make it stop, you just watch it and hope. I was working very hard, anxious to eke out every meter of forward travel I could from every foot of altitude I was losing.

As the altimeter passed through one thousand feet and still descending, I was composing the mayday call in my head. I knew my exact position, I had also estimated where I would hit the water. Five hundred feet above the waves was where I decided I'd transmit it. As I passed six hundred feet we popped out of the snow and into heavy rain. It was magical, the snow was washed off the airframe almost instantly. I had full control of the plane again. I eased back on the controls and held the speed steady, we started to climb. The mayday call could wait for another day.

The Icarus Game

When I parked the plane up at Coventry, I climbed out and looked more closely at the wing and tail plane de-icing. There was none! Where there should have been heater mats or inflatable boots there was a thick coat of matt black paint. No warning placard in the cockpit, no warning in the tech log, no anti-icing. Fucking Hell.

The Recon' job was working well for me and Vicky, I was getting home most days, she still had her weekend job in the local pub. I was chatting with my neighbours on Sunday morning and was surprised to learn there had been a commotion on my front garden the night before. I had been working all day, then was comatose all night. I woke Vicky up to find out what had happened.

Apparently, she had finished work and rather than let her walk home alone, a dozen or so concerned drinkers in the pub decided to escort her to her door. After all, there are some strange people on the streets late on a Saturday night. An argument from earlier in the evening re-ignited and turned into a full-scale brawl, complete with swinging handbags, all on my front garden. I'd slept through the whole thing.

Our Cessna had just been returned to us with a new shiny paint job, red and white with 'Coastguard' emblazoned down the side. It looked very smart and exceedingly official. We were trying it out, off the coast of Portsmouth when we spotted a warship. On closer inspection we could see she was a German Navy

Frigate/Destroyer. My radar operator contacted the ship on the radio, offering our services if they wanted to 'illuminate' us.

'That would be most useful' said the radio operator. We were asked to fly as low and as fast as we could, about five hundred meters away from the boat, up the starboard side, around the bow, then back down the port side. 'Ok, let us know when you are ready.' 'We are always ready.' Came the reply.

We descended level with the hull of the frigate, about fifty feet above the water and flew straight and level from stern to bow. I glanced across at the Destroyer, every piece of weaponry was pointing at us, tracking our speed and altitude exactly. It was very disconcerting looking down the barrels of huge naval anti-aircraft guns, and banks of surface to air missiles, they were all electronically locked onto our every move. There was no sneaking past this radar guided battery of munitions.

After this excitement we had one more small job to do, the coastguards office on the cliff top at Dover had requested a fly-by, so they could admire our new paint job. We spoke to this office a lot on the radio, but they rarely got to see us. We made sure they got a good clear close-up, of our shiny paintwork on our way past their lookout window on Dover's clifftops. I think they were suitably impressed.

After nearly twelve months flying for Recon', I'd amassed nine hundred hours airborne. Returning to Coventry from a patrol, I was called into Doug's office, he was the Flight Op's Director. 'I know you've done a lot more Recon' flying than normal, I hope you've enjoyed it. We've found a replacement for you, you're going on the next Electra course, back to Seattle.' I was delighted. It had taken over two years, but at last, I had come full circle, back onto the Electra as a first officer.

This time I wouldn't have to do the ground school, I'd already done that as a flight engineer. To comply with the current training requirements though I would have to sit the course final exams again. I was called into work and presented with a pile of exam papers to complete. I worked through them steadily; I hadn't been near an Electra for two years. Dredging through my memory, the technical details of the aeroplane gradually came back to the fore, finding the right answers stirred up the grey matter a little. I handed the completed papers to the head of ground training. After a brief chat about the one question I got wrong, on propellers, I was ready to head back to Seattle, for another session in the simulator.

Chapter 28

Electra Training.

Nothing had changed in Seattle since my first visit. We used the same hotel, the sim was exactly as I'd left it, some six years earlier. The coffee was just as good, I was happy. Our instructor for the next two weeks was Doug, Atlantic Airlines, Flight Op's Director. The course consisted of a mixture of freshly qualified cadets, me, and a couple of captain upgrades. I was by far the oldest candidate; I was also one of the most experienced in the engineering aspects of flying the aeroplane. As a flight engineer, I had flown with the trainee captains when they were first officers and knew the cadets from long car journeys to and from airports.

The course itself was not particularly memorable, we went through all the same scenarios, practiced the check lists that were required. The big difference came during the weekend break halfway through the course. Doug was a big fan of skiing and all things Canadian. He had arranged a team building weekend in Whistler.

Whistler is like Disneyland, with mountains and snow. A purpose-built ski resort in 'Beautiful British Columbia'. After a long drive we had a great time there, the snow was perfect, the weather and backdrop were stunning. There are bars, cafes, and restaurants to suit every taste. Doug had prepared an itinerary for us, which included all his favourite ski runs, bars and eateries. The one thing he neglected to consider was, it was Mountain Pride week.

The place was buzzing. There was an absolute profusion of loud effeminate conversations and some outrageous costumes. Imagine Village People on speed at Notting Hill, with snow. Everybody was having a great time, so we threw ourselves enthusiastically into the mix. The following morning, I was sat in the bar complex at the top of Whistler Mountain. Nursing a pounding skull with my stomach-turning summersaults. My cure of choice, was mountain air, accompanied by the biggest hot chocolate with whipped cream and marsh mallows on the menu.

There was a group of guys chatting at the next table. Enjoying the outdoor balcony, overlooking the glories of the Canadian Rockies. My attention was distracted from my hangover and cocoa, when I looked up at a giant of a man. For a moment, I thought Arnold Swartzaneger was stood in front of me. He had just appeared at the top of the steps, and in his bright pink, spandex ski suit, gold tiara and pink glittery ski boots he was hard to miss. 'Hello girls, the queen of Whistler is here, let's get this party started' he shouted in the campest way possible. I think I may have stared, just a bit.

We returned to Coventry for the next part of my training, 'Base Training', this was to be done on the aeroplane. On modern types of aircraft, this phase of training is done in all singing all dancing flight simulators. Our 'space-race' relic in Seattle was not fit for this. It was a fixed platform, with no graphics, so we had to do it on the plane. Flying training is the same no matter what the size of the aircraft.

It involves dealing with a list of mandatory manoeuvres and failures, most of which you hope will never actually happen in real life. As one of our TRI/TRE's (Type rated instructor/examiner) Doug was doing my flight training off the Scottish west coast, just south of Glasgow. It started relatively comfortably with some general handling, getting a feel for the controls, climbing, descending and regular turns. Progressing onto steep turns, stall recovery and asymmetric flight (failing engines). After a couple of hours throwing the machine around it was back to Belfast for tea and medals.

Although it's great fun, this training is very intense and incredibly expensive, try hiring an airliner for a couple of hours. You can buy a decent car for the same amount. For this reason, candidates are selected on the basis that they get it right first time. Otherwise, the whole training package costs more than the airlines are prepared to spend.

The following morning, we started with a short transit flight from Belfast to Prestwick, then it was straight into the circuit. Visual circuits started with a regular take off and circuit to land. Then it got more interesting, take off, engine failure, take off, flap failure, take off, fire in the freight bay, take off, engine fire.

This went on for a couple of hours, then we had a brief stop for a sandwich. In the afternoon all the morning's exercises were repeated, but with the windscreen obscured by white Perspex covers. Everything was done on the instruments. This session was rounded off with a couple of abnormal landings, one with no flaps, one on three engines. Another short break and all that was left was some night circuits and I was done.

The weather had been typically Scottish all day, wet and windy, no real problem it just meant I had to work a little harder. The night circuits were going fine, but after six hours of continuous failures and check lists, I was getting tired. My concentration was slipping, and Doug was getting a bit tetchy. Instead of landing exactly on the runway centreline, I was allowing the plane to drift a little bit downwind. I was still trying as hard as I could, but my brain was about fried. It was the last landing of the day; I came over the threshold with the left mainwheel over the centreline one too many times. Doug finally snapped.

'I have control.' He wanted to make his point, he jinked left and put us directly over the centreline, 'There, that's the centreline,' he said sharply. The Electra flared, touching down gently on the threshold of runway one-three. I was a little disappointed that my last landing of the day had been taken off me, this self-indulgence didn't last long though. It was clear that all was not well, Doug was feeding in more and more right rudder to keep us on the centreline. I could see through the mounting level of concentration on his face he was working hard. The aircraft was leaning heavily to the left, and the artificial horizon showed the wings were far from level. Something was seriously wrong with our aeroplane. At this point we didn't know what.

The radio confirmed all was not as it should be. ATC asked, 'Atlantic 188 Tango, are you ok?' I had now assumed the duties of the non-handling pilot, and couldn't think of a sensible answer, 'I don't know, we haven't finished crashing yet!!' Was the best I could manage.

As the speed decreased Doug was struggling harder to maintain the aircraft on the centreline, and eventually he ran out of rudder authority. Even with full asymmetric reverse applied to the right-hand engines, we continued to drift left towards the edge of the runway, and I couldn't resist a little poke at my trainer. I pointed out to my right, 'Doug mate, the centreline's over there.' As far as crashing goes, we were doing ok. We left the tarmac of the runway, sliding to a stop on the concrete verge, bordering the asphalt.

Things then got very noisy, as we ground to a standstill, the remaining stub of the left-hand undercarriage broke through a steel grate, dropping into a drainage channel. Both left-hand propeller tips hit the concrete and showered us in a hail of gravel, rattling off the fuselage and windows. Doug looked stunned; he stared ahead in disbelief. I leant across the flight deck and pulled the 'E'-handles, one at a time in quick succession. These big red handles shut down the engines and isolate the services from them. It all went quiet. Doug turned to me and asked, 'Are you ok?' 'Yes, I'm fine, are you ok?' Doug pressed on the radio transmit button, 'Mayday. Mayday. Mayday.' The whole episode lasted less than sixty seconds from start to finish.

We had just crashed a classic, fifty tonne, four engined airliner at Prestwick Airport, and lived. For a second or two we just sat, and took stock. Doug reached up to the overhead panel and turned off the electrical switches. It went dark. We picked up our flight bags and walked to the door at the rear of the freight deck. Doug motored the door open, he then positioned the aluminium ladder and climbed down. It was comical, because normally the door is about ten feet above the ground, now it was just three or four feet up. A large proportion of the ladder was protruding into the aircraft.

Following Doug down onto the concrete, I got my first look at the carnage. The left-hand undercarriage leg had broken in half. Or to be more precise the shock absorber had snapped off, leaving the leg's aluminium casting sat on the concrete.

The bogey, that is the axle assembly with both mainwheels had gone, they broke off and flew through the trailing edge flaps, destroying them. Then, before bouncing across the airfield they had hit the tailplane. Looking forwards at the engines I could see that both left hand propellers had lost their spinners and had damaged blades. The impact with the concrete had left them bent and mangled. That was it though. Given what had happened, the damage was superficial. It was certainly repairable.

As I was examining the two inch deep, six-inch-wide gouge, that we'd carved into half the length of Prestwick's newly re-surfaced runway, the fire brigade arrived. They dashed around shouting a lot and trying to take control. There was really no need. A bloke in a white helmet approached us and announced that he was going to cover our plane in foam. What for? It's not on fire. After some discussion he settled for spraying some dry powder around, on the promise that we would allow him to go nuts with his foam machine, if the plane erupted into flames. That seemed to keep him happy.

We needed to get the recovery of the aeroplane underway before anybody else decided to do it for us. Doug got his phone out and called op's. 'What do you mean, can we fly it back to Belfast. No! I'm stood next to the smoking wreckage as we speak.' As he spoke the engineering director from 'Polar Air

Cargo' turned up to see if they could help. He soon understood our predicament, 'You need to jack this side up and sit the stub of the undercarriage on a trolley to tow it away. I've got some jacks; can you get the right type of jacking adaptors.' Doug was listening to our conversation as he spoke on the phone. 'Get the engineers up here with a set of jacking pads.' Was his last instruction to op's.

We left the firemen looking after the scene and climbed into the ATC Land Rover. The main runway at Prestwick was now closed, so we got to drive the full length of the groove we'd ploughed into it. It went from the midpoint of the runway to the touchdown markers. 'Do you want to see your wheels?' asked the cheerful airfield op's driver. They're over there by the warning light.' Once me and Doug had looked closely at the axle and wheel assembly laying in the long grass, we both heaved a sigh of relief. It had fatigued and cracked all the way around, finally snapping off. We knew immediately, we were not in any way at fault.

We got a lift to the ATC tower and sat with the controller, drinking coffee whilst we waited for the engineers to arrive from Coventry. 'It looked spectacular guys; you were belting down the runway with a huge rooster tail of sparks following you.' We'd certainly brightened up his shift.

An hour later, one of our light twins landed, carrying the engineers and a set of jacking pads. By the time we got back to the plane, a tipper truck full of tarmac and a small group of builders had just finished filling the groove in the runway. 'When you're all done here boys, can you do my driveway with what's left over?' The weather had got even more Scottish, the wind and rain had turned into wind and snow.

Me and Doug climbed into the Cessna 310 twin, and hitched a ride back to Coventry. Things hadn't worked out too badly considering. The runway at Prestwick was only closed for four or five hours. G-LOFD was towed away and would be repaired. We had survived an airliner crash, and most importantly, I had finished my base training.

A week later I jumped out of the minibus at Belfast with Paul, my TRE (Type Rated Examiner), and looked up at the Electra in front of me. I was here to do my LPC (Licence Proficiency Test). It's a very formal, standardised flight test. The format and accuracy requirements are set in the CAA's big book of rules.

Essentially all 'Public Transport' pilots do these tests every six months. The last flight I'd done in an Electra was at Prestwick, and that hadn't gone too well. I fuelled the aircraft while Paul did the walk around, then we climbed aboard.

Paul went through the test requirements and briefing, it's a set format and something he would have done hundreds of times before. He rounded it off with, 'To fail today, Steve, you're going to have to do very badly, just don't crash the fucking thing!' The rest of the test went by in a blur of activity. Take off, engine failure, three engine precision approach to a three engine go around, airways bit, non-precision approach to land. LPC passed. I just had to hang around in the bar for a few hours, then get a lift back to Coventry in our Electra.

That was my Electra type rating as a first officer finished. What an achievement, I could now call myself an Airline Pilot. The type rating would be applied to my licence. Most of my flying from now on would be on the Electra and I was on cloud nine.

The Prestwick incident was not yet resolved, I was sat in front of the investigating officer from the AAIB (Air Accidents Investigation Branch), giving my account of what had happened. They already had the results from the metallurgy tests, and knew why the undercarriage leg had broken. It was a fault in the manufacturing process, forty years earlier. They had listened to the cockpit voice recorder and that tallied with our statements.

They had witness statements from the ATC tower and airfield Op's vehicles. Apparently, all the fucks and bangs on the voice recording were the right way round. Bang-fuck, you hadn't seen it coming. Fuck-bang, you knew it was about to happen. The interview finished with some reassuring words from the investigator. 'Statistically, you will only be involved in one AAIB investigation in your lifetime, you've just had yours.'

For the official air accident report go to:

https://www.gov.uk/aaib-reports/lockheed-l188c-electra-g-lofd-21-march-2001-at-1948-hrs

Printed copy in annex 1.

Chapter 29

You Can Take the Kid Out of the Council Estate…

The first few weeks flying online were taken up with 'Line Training.' This involves flying alongside a training captain, doing the regular job. It's much more relaxed than simulator training, getting newly qualified pilots into the routine of flying a freighter. Once your trainer is happy that you are comfortable in the job, he'll 'sign you off', then your name goes onto the roster with the regular flight crew.

We had arrived in Edinburgh in the small hours of the morning, unloaded our cargo and gone to the hotel. I was knackered, so after arranging to meet my captain for breakfast I went to bed. Snoring like a rhino, I was sound asleep when there was a loud screeching noise in my room. I buried my head under the pillow and tried to ignore it. It kept screeching. I picked up the phone and called reception to complain about the racket, no answer. The screeching continued.

Oh, for fucks sake! I got out of bed, pulled on my trousers, walked across the room to the door, and poked my head into the corridor. Oh shit, the corridor was thick with acrid smoke, the bloody hotel was on fire. I grabbed a jumper and jacket, making my way down the stairs and out into the car park. By now there was a crowd of guests milling about in various states of night attire, clothes, and undress.

Happy I'd taken my jumper but cursing the schoolboy error of forgetting my shoes. It was four o'clock in the morning and freezing cold. The cooks had set fire to a deep fat fryer in the kitchen, filling the building with chip fat smoke. The big question on everybody's lips was, 'Breakfast will still be served, won't it?'

My twin engine rating and single crew I.R. were still current, so from time to time I was called off the Electra to do the occasional taxi job. I enjoyed these; it was now a bit of a novelty. After a few months though these ratings lapsed, and I was exclusively flying the Electra.

In the early hours of the morning my phone rang, it was Op's. 'Steve, we need you to take the 310 to Brussels with an engineer.' 'Sorry mate, I can't help you, all of my single crew ratings have lapsed.' I put the phone down. Two minutes later I was woken again by the phone ringing. 'Steve, I've spoken to the M.D. and he says you're the only one available and you've got to do it.' Grumbling to myself I dressed for work and drove into the airport.

Standing in front of the Op's officer, wearing my sternest scowl, I repeated my protestations. 'My twin rating and single crew I.R. have lapsed, I am not qualified to fly your Cessna 310, are you sure you still want me to do this?' 'Yes mate, the M.D. says you have to.' I picked up the flight plan and walked out to the aeroplane.

When I got there, it was parked in a huge puddle. I bent down and dipped my finger in the liquid, it was AVGAS, high octane aviation fuel. It was running from the wing tank down the undercarriage and onto the tarmac. I went back to Op's and told them what I'd found. We rounded up a couple of bodies to help me move the aeroplane and clean up the mess.

Sliding the paperwork and 'tech log' back across the counter. I asked, 'Have you got another aeroplane for me, this one's broke?' The Op's officer sent me to find the 'tech log' for the other 310. I rooted around the offices and after waking up the Flight Training manager with a phone call, I found the logbook in her filing cabinet.

I went and found the plane, fuelled it, loaded the engineer and all his kit onboard and finally set off for Brussels. We taxied onto the stand next to the unserviceable Electra, where the engineer unloaded his gear and started work. I didn't need to wait for him, so I was on the radio calling for start clearance to return to Coventry when my phone rang.

It was the CEO. That was highly unusual, I generally didn't get past daily pleasantries with our senior management. 'Hi Steve, have you got the 'tech log' for the 310?' 'Yes, it's on the seat next to me.' He enquired. 'Is the plane ok?' 'Yes, it's fine, I've just flown it from Coventry to Brussels.' 'Ok, safe flight, bye.' That was weird.

Flying the 310 west up the Thames Estuary on my way back to Coventry, I was enjoying the views, being on my own in an aeroplane was a rare treat. Cruising towards me a thousand feet above my altitude was a Boeing 747 coming out of Stanstead. I looked up as this monster blocked out the sky passing directly overhead my little aircraft.

After landing and completing the post flight routine, I walked back into Op's. Waiting on the other side of the counter was our CEO. In his hands was a tech log for the aeroplane I'd just flown.

'Snap! My tech log says that 310 is in pieces, what does yours say?' Asked the boss. 'Mine says it's fine and I didn't notice anything missing.' I passed the flight paperwork to the Op's officer and the duplicate tech log to the CEO. 'I'll let you sort these out.'

Having two 'Tech logs' for the same aircraft is an absolute no-no. I then waited for the shit to hit the fan. It reminded me of my military days, with the Regimental Sergeant Major poking the young Marine with his pace stick. 'There's a piece of shit on the end of my stick young man.' 'Yes sir, but it's not at my end.'

It took a couple of weeks to percolate back, I was summoned to a meeting with the companies 'Head of Training Standards'. She was a straight-talking lady, with a lot of flying and training experience. I wasn't in a position to bullshit her. 'No, of course, I wasn't going to refuse the MD's order to fly his aeroplane, I want to be here for a while yet.' 'Yes, I told him my ratings had lapsed.' 'Yes, I did check the tech log, in detail and do a thorough walk around the aircraft.' 'No, I wasn't aware that aircraft had two tech logs.'

She was fuming, mostly with the company for demanding the inexcusable, and failing to control its aircrafts' maintenance documents properly. The following day, I was back in the 310 with an examiner, revalidating my twin rating and single crew I.R. That was my last flight in a light twin.

In Nuremburg I was flying the Electra with Richie, he is a genuinely nice man, but he hadn't grown up on the same planet as the rest of us. He was athletic and had a strong resemblance to Hugh Grant. Richie wanted to visit a teacher friend of his that he had been at university with. She was about half an hour away on the train. Did I know how to get to Bayreuth? Of course I did, and the trains here are free.

We climbed aboard the carriage and set off, the ticket inspector arrived so we told him our destination and reluctantly bought a ticket off him. The inspector then explained that, although we were on the right train, we were at the wrong end of it. At the next stop, the front of the train was going to Bayreuth, but the rear carriages were going to be attached to another train going elsewhere. Crikey, that stretched my German a bit. At the stop, we leapt out of the rear carriage of the train, ran down the platform, and re-boarded at the front.

Arriving at the right place was a result in my book. We headed to a café to meet Richie's' friend. Richie was keen to impress her with his mastery of the German language. When the waitress came to our table, she asked what we would like. Richie ordered for us. 'Drei café bitte, und haben sie eine tochter.' The waitress looked patiently at Richie. 'That's three coffees and yes, I have, but she's far too young for you.' 'If you'd like cake, that's torte. Tochter is daughter.' We fell about giggling at Richie's faux pas, I was very impressed with the cool way the waitress dealt with it.

The following afternoon, towards the end of a week flying around Germany, and having had a good day's sleep, me and Richie found ourselves wandering around Nuremberg again. We had exhausted most of the regular entertainment. I fancied a coffee, so I suggested a visit to Bar 2000. Bar 2000 was a strip club in the town, I had been there several times before. During the day it was a pleasant distraction, and they sold decent coffee. The girls performed their acts on a rotating stage surrounded by clear Perspex screens. 'No way.' Said Richie, as forcefully as he could. 'Last time I went in there, one of the girls whipped her knickers off and she had a knob!' 'No! That's never happened to me. You must have just been unlucky.'

I dragged him through the turnstile into the club. We settled down at our table with a coffee, as the next girl appeared on the stage. Like all the working girls, she was tall slim and very attractive. She gyrated to the drum and bass that was her chosen soundtrack, I enjoyed my coffee as we watched. Her act was ok, but after you've seen a few, you become more critical of the performance and less distracted by the nudity. As her clothing was discarded, her figure was clearly something she was very proud of, and rightly so. Then came the finale, off came her skimpy, lacy knickers. Richie glared at me. 'You bastard Woodhouse!' How was I supposed to know that we'd be looking at her man parts at the end of her act?

For a while, we had been staying in the same hotel in Cologne whenever we passed through the city. I always carried a tea making kit in my suitcase. A travel kettle, cup, tea bags and milk. A lot of places we stayed at didn't provide these, and I was too tight to order drinks from room service. I had lost my kettle in the same hotel the week before, so I went to reception to enquire whether it was in their lost property box. The receptionist looked at me as if I was an Alien. 'You has left ein cow in your room??' 'What, no, I've lost my kettle.' 'Ya, ein cattle is ein cow, is it not.' 'Not cattle, kettle.' I did a drawing on the note pad to try to break the language deadlock. I showed her my little sketch. 'Ahh, it is ein tee Kessel, not ein cow, no I don't has vun of those.'

Hotels were a constant source of frustration and amusement over the years. Because we flew all night and slept all day, we were always trying to sleep in the wrong place at the wrong time. Being woken up by housekeeping, a few hours after my head hit the pillow was a common occurrence. At first, I'd open the door and explain that I was sleeping off a night shift. After lots of years, having the 'Do Not Disturb' sign ignored I didn't bother. I tried shouting, 'Go away, I'm sleeping'. That didn't seem to work very well, so it turned into, 'Fuck off!' shouted from my bed. That worked better, especially with cleaners that didn't speak English, but could understand Anglo Saxon. I consider myself to be reasonably tolerant, but over time things can just grind me down, then I revert to good old Anglo Saxon. There's still a council house kid under this exterior.

This approach was largely successful, but not in Lyon, France. I was curled up under my duvet with the 'Ne Pas Deranger' sign hanging on my doorknob. There was a loud persistent banging on my door, followed by a shout of 'Housekeeping.' 'Fuck off, S'il vous plait.' I yelled from within my fluffy cocoon. The lock rattled and the door opened, in marched a large black lady. She completely ignored me, I sat baffled in the bed, trying to maintain some dignity under my duvet. She plugged in the vacuum and promptly cleaned around me, then she went on to clean the bathroom. As she left, I managed a 'Merci.' She ignored that too.

We checked into a modern, smart hotel in Vienna, on the banks of the Danube. This was another regular layover; the reception staff are very friendly and professional. I took my key and headed for my allocated room. When I opened the door and walked in, I was faced with a mess that would have been more expected in my teenage daughter's rancid pit. At first, I thought the bed was unmade, then I noticed the mop of black hair on the pillow. I shut the door as quietly as I could and returned with my bags to reception. 'Excuse me, there is a Chinaman in my bed.' I said to the mortified receptionist, as I slid the room key back across the counter towards her.

Sitting on the end of my bed in a Toulouse hotel I was staring in disbelief at the TV. I'd just woken up and was catching up on world events with CNN. In front of me was an airliner crashing through one of the towers of the World Trade Centre. As I watched, the enormity of this act was immediately apparent. Then another plane crashed through the remaining tower. The attack was chilling in its simplicity, and terrifying in its effectiveness. That evening, I would be flying an airliner around Europe along with hundreds of other pilots. How was this going to change my world. My job was already heavily preoccupied with mitigating risk, that workload was certainly going to rise.

Chapter 30

Fishy Fingers.

We had landed in Stavanger, me and Neil were there to collect a drilling bit and take it to Aberdeen. How hard can that be? When the crate containing the bit arrived at the aeroplane, we soon realised. It was about a meter square, and twenty meters long, weighing in at a couple of tonnes. The Norwegian loaders had it sussed though. They turned up with a load truck, winches, and rollers. In about half an hour they had quietly and carefully inched this huge, awkward, heavy box into position on the freight deck. These guys clearly knew their job. The drilling bit was destined to end up on an oil drilling platform in the North Sea.

We strapped it down and set off across the North Sea towards Aberdeen. So far so good. At this point the Atlantic Airlines MD and our Op's department got in on the act. Aberdeen Airport was going to shut at ten, we would arrive just after that, so the company had arranged an extension. We would land and park up, the airport could then close. The drilling bit would be unloaded first thing in the morning. Everybody was happy. Well almost. Our illustrious MD thought that he would impress the customer with our efficiency, so he promised them the drilling bit as soon as we arrived at Aberdeen.

The welcoming committee was larger than normal. With an uncharacteristic urgency they charged on board our plane. The securing straps were off in a jiffy, there was lots of yelling and shouting in Scottish. We watched amazed as they tried to manhandle the freight off the plane, it wouldn't budge. 'See you, this fuckin' fucker weighs a fuckin' tonne, we need mare fuckin' cunts up here tae throw the fucker off.' That was the gist of it.

It still didn't move. Then they came up with a bright idea. They wrapped a couple of tie-down straps around the box and attached them to the aircraft tug. Holy shit, these shaved monkeys were going to wreck the plane. We yelled at them to stop. 'We're doing what your boss has asked fae.' Came the reply as the tug reversed away from the plane.

The noise of ripping aluminium preceded the snapping of the nylon tie down straps. These things have a breaking strain of about ten tonnes. The steel ratchet mechanisms from the straps were hurtling down the fuselage at an astounding velocity, and smashing into the nine-g bulkhead with the force of an artillery round, leaving deep dents and gouges in the thick aluminium panel. Time to exit the killing zone.

Me and Neil ran off the aeroplane and out of the firing line as quickly as we could. If these idiots want to kill themselves, that's fine, but I'm not staying anywhere close to them. We grabbed the load supervisor who by this time, had given up trying to talk sense to his out-of-control team of loaders. 'Your guys are doing a lot of damage up there.' 'Aye, I know, but they were promised a wad of cash to get you unloaded, what do you expect?' It all made sense now.

Our boss had struck a deal with the Aberdeen loaders; an envelope of cash would be with them if they unloaded the drilling bit straight away. The faster they unloaded it, the fatter the envelope would be. We knew nothing of this as we landed and taxied in.

Neil got on the phone to Op's, just as the drilling bit crashed out of the aeroplane onto the tarmac. 'What are you idiots down there playing at?' He described the carnage in detail. 'Book us a taxi and a hotel, then send an engineer to Aberdeen.' The aircraft's floor and freight door were badly damaged, there was no way we could fly out of here with the plane in this state.

Geneva is a beautiful city to fly into, from one end you approach the runway over the lake, from the other end you approach the airport by flying down an Alpine valley. In the sunshine this is a glorious way to arrive somewhere for breakfast. It's a different experience in thick fog and howling winds, you are acutely aware of the mass of granite that lurks in the fog, waiting to crush you if you stray off track. With the wind in the wrong direction the turbulence was sufficient to loosen your teeth. The Swiss air traffic controllers are by nature very precise people, so we had a little game we played with them. The airport opened at five o'clock in the morning, we were scheduled to land at five o'clock in the morning.

Using the clock on the GPS, which is correct to a couple of milli-seconds we would time our approach, adjusting our speed to reach our decision height 200ft above the runway threshold at exactly five o'clock. Arrive a few seconds late and the airport was already open, the controller would contact us and clear us to land. Arrive a second early and the radio remained silent, you were going around. Get it right and the radio call went; 'Geneva, this is Eurotrans XXX, short finals.' 'Eurotrans XXX, you are cleared to land.' The wheels then touched the tarmac. Sometimes, you'd need to hold the plane off the ground in the flair for a second or two, until the radio call was complete. You must keep the job interesting somehow.

Me and Rich had set ourselves a small challenge, we were going to survive the entire week down route eating nothing but kebabs. It was going well, but things were about to backfire. We were in the back of a Nurnberg taxi heading for the hotel.

It was early in the morning and Rich was turning a funny colour, sort of light, yellowy green, then he started to wretch. 'Bitte, halten der auto, miene collegue ist krank.' Not great German but the driver got the idea and pulled over. Rich clamped his hand over his mouth and struggled out of the cab. He staggered over the footpath onto a used car lot, where he threw up on the bonnet of a Mercedes. I think he felt better after that.

Waiting around was a regular part of the job, waiting for a taxi, waiting for a crew bus, waiting for freight to arrive, waiting for a load team, you name it, we waited for it. Since 9/11 we were no longer allowed to walk out to our aircraft, we had to be driven by the handling agent. This obviously meant more waiting. At Cardiff we were waiting, yet again for the crew bus by the doors of the departure gates. My captain, an inveterate joker called Murphs spotted a microphone on the desk at a nearby gate.

The boredom of hanging around was just too much for him, coupled with the temptation of causing a stir in the departure lounge, he couldn't contain himself. He nipped across to the desk, pressed the button on the mike stand and spoke. 'Would Mr Hunt please come to the information desk, that's Mr Isaac Hunt to the information desk.' His words echoed loud and clear throughout the airport. He returned to my side and stood there like butter wouldn't melt. We were on this route all week.

Every night he'd dream up another message to broadcast, his imagination knew no bounds. 'There's a taxi waiting on the rank for Mr Richard Head, that's a taxi outside for Dick Head.' 'There is a delay to flight ABC123, this delay is for operational reasons, your captain is stuck on the toilet with explosive diarrhoea.' On it went every night. By the following week the airport management had finally worked out where the mystery tannoy messages were coming from and complained to Atlantic. Murphs was summoned for a ritual thrashing in the Flight Op's Directors office. 'It serves them right for leaving us standing about,' was his defence, this logic seemed to be received with a certain amount of sympathy.

The freight had arrived at Coventry from Canada, we were to transfer it onto our Electra and take it to Zaragoza in Spain. I met up with my captain, James, in Op's. We got into the crew bus across the airfield and sorted out loading this sensitive cargo. It was ten tonnes of hake, I had no idea what hake looked like, I just knew it was a fish. This fish arrived in polystyrene boxes, packed in ice, loaded onto wooden pallets, and wrapped in plastic film. We had a forklift to lift the pallets onto the freight roller deck, then using a pallet truck, we man-handled them down the fuselage. This was going fine until we tried to strap it all down. It proved to be impossible, with the straps loose, the boxes moved about easily, with the straps tightened, the fragile polystyrene boxes were crushed. Trying to secure this load was futile, we just hoped there wasn't too much turbulence on our route.

Crossing the Pyrenees, we started our descent into Zaragoza, it was a bright, clear, summers day and we could see the airport from miles away. James flew the arrival route and we were cleared to land, all was happy in our little world. Then in a Captainly sort of way, James made a decision. 'I can save a few minutes by vacating the runway at the first exit.' He slammed the props into full reverse and started pumping the brakes. What a twat. There was a thud behind us on the freight deck as our insecure load, which had survived the flight, gave into the inertia of hard braking and gravity. I gave James my most patient look, he already knew he had cocked it up.

We pulled onto stand and shut down the engines. It was now time to survey the fishy slurry that was engulfing our plane. I got out of my seat, climbed out of the flight deck, onto what should have been a roller deck at the front of the fuselage. I was ankle deep in fish, water, ice, and fishy snot. It smelled a bit like the seaside, wet and salty, but a lot less pungent than you may think.

The first two or three pallets had fallen over, behind that there were some pallets leant over at quite a jaunty angle. I splashed through the pond of fishy goo to the door operating mechanism, to open the freight door. On the tarmac was a cheery Spanish handling agent. He stopped smiling when a waterfall of fish detritus poured off the aircraft and swamped his feet. I don't know what the Spanish is for, 'What the fuck?', but I'm pretty sure that's what he said. (I just looked it up, it's 'que carajo'.)

The Icarus Game

Shrugging my shoulders, I gestured towards the captain, who still hadn't left his seat, and in a show of crew solidarity, made the universal dickhead sign with my hand and forehead. After kicking some of the now empty polystyrene boxes down to the loaders, I began scraping the fish and snotty gloop back into the boxes on the freight deck. Starting the task of stacking them back on the pallet. James appeared in the doorway, took a deep breath, and joined the messy job of refilling boxes. I couldn't contain myself any longer, try as I might the stifled giggles had to come out. 'What a prize twat you are!' was all that would come out of my mouth. James couldn't really disagree.

After lots of scraping and shovelling in the Spanish afternoon sun, the fish were back in their boxes. Hake are ugly things from the deep, I hope they taste better than they look. After three or four hours of Spanish heat the fresh salty smell of the seaside had turned a bit stale. We stank of foetid decomposing aquatic phlegm, we were also covered in dried out, crusty fish snot and scales.

The handling agent took us to the hotel, because he said the local taxi drivers wouldn't allow us in their cabs, on account of us stinking. The hotel was really plush, marble floors and chandeliers. The smart receptionist in his tightly fitting, tailored uniform, stepped back as we approached his counter. He had difficulty understanding how this pair of smelly vagrants could possibly claim to have a reservation in his five-star palace.

I climbed into the shower fully dressed, including my weatherproof jacket, armed with all the soap products I could find in the room, and some that I'd nicked from the housekeeping trolley in the corridor. I covered everything in lather as I peeled off the layers. Gradually the slime and odour seeped down the plughole.

Smelling altogether fresher, we met up for dinner later that evening. James gave work a call to find out what we were doing next. They wanted to find us a 'back load', so for now we were to stay in the hotel. After two days of drinking coffee and watching the Spanish workmen dig a hole outside our rooms, we were getting bored. Finally, Op's gave up on their 'back load' idea and told us to bring the aeroplane back to Coventry.

On arrival at the plane, I climbed the ladder and opened the crew door at the tail end of the fuselage. Oh. My. God. The stench was stomach turning, and it got worse. A gentle hum turned into a loud hum and got steadily louder; I was then engulfed by a swarm of blue bottles. The air around me turned black with flies, millions of them, all trying to get out of the door that I was trying to get in. I choked on the flies that had got into my throat, as I retreated down the ladder and brushed myself off. 'I think we need to give this a couple of minutes.' I croaked as I spat out a few wayward blue bottles.

The liquified nastiness of two days ago, had now seeped into every nook and cranny of the plane. It had truly become part of the fabric of the structure, joining the hydraulic fluid that constantly dribbled along the underside of the Electra's belly. The heat of the daytime sun took the temperature inside our big tin tube way into the fifties, putrefying anything organic very efficiently. It was a living writhing cesspit of nastiness inside. I took a deep breath and went into the plane, crunching my way through the dark, to the front and opened the freight door.

Once the interior was bathed in bright sunlight, the magnitude of the mess became clear. The floor, walls and roof of the cabin was crawling with flies and maggots. The flight home was going to be a couple of hours, with all the doors and windows shut and airtight. This was going to be memorable. Surprisingly after a while you just blank out the stench, I guess that's how teenagers survive in their bedrooms.

Entertaining myself on the way home, I constructed an effigy of James out of dead flies on my kneeboard, poking it repeatedly. We pulled up on the apron at Coventry, gathered our kit together and left the plane. As we descended the ladder, we were met by our ramp guys, they were there to remove the flat floor and prepare the plane for that night. 'She's all yours, we smiled and walked away.' They got to the top of the ladder and stopped. 'Jesus Christ! We can't work in that!'

Chapter 31

Smart Quips and Cockups.

Four o'clock in the morning is around the time that you feel at your most tired. More often than not, it's halfway through the last sector of the night. All the hustle and bustle is over. Your mind is drifting towards breakfast and bed. The rhythmic vibration of the airframe and propeller drone in your warm flight deck, is enough to send any insomniac into the land of nod. Trying to stay alert at the end of a long night is an ongoing battle.

We were in just this position, on our way down to Toulouse, me and Nik were running out of idle chat to keep us awake. Then the radio brought me out of my soporific trance. 'Eurotrans, call Marseilles on 123.45.' Responding to the call, I dialled in the new frequency. Putting on my chirpiest radio voice. 'Marseilles, Allo, Allo, this is the Eurotrans XXX, flight level two one zero.' The answer was priceless, 'Eurotrans XXX, listen very carefully, I shall say this only once. You are cleared direct Netro.' The controller was certainly more awake than I was.

Everybody is fallible, you may not like to admit it, but they are. Your surgeon will make mistakes, so will your pilot, so will your stockbroker. Not too often, and not always with disastrous consequences, but they will make mistakes. If you can't live with that knowledge, stay wrapped up in your duvet. Murphy is out there and he's waiting for the unwary, the under prepared and the overconfident.

Sitting next to Dirk on the flight deck, it was a filthy night. Lashing rain and high winds, we were approaching our decision height. Two hundred feet above the runway threshold at Metz. I was flying and Dirk was monitoring the approach, implementing check list actions, making check calls, and dealing with the radio. The plane was bouncing around, but the needles were spot on, we were configured to land, all checks complete and on speed. All we needed was a runway.

'Deeee sisshhh uunn.' 'Lights ahead, landing.' I loosened my grip on the power levers as we came over the approach lights at a hundred feet. I was just about to start gently backing off the power when it went very dark. There was no runway. I shoved the power levers forward and pulled the nose up. 'Go-around, flaps seventy-eight, set power.' Dirk did as I'd ordered, then he got on the radio. 'Eurotrans XXX is going around, where are the runway lights?' The radio went quiet. 'We haven't turned them on. I'm sorry about that. There!' The runway lit up brightly as we climbed away. It turned out that Metz is an ATC training centre, and the trainee controller had missed turning on the runway lighting as we approached. C'est la vie, blame the apprentice.

It was just a short hop from Coventry to Dublin, we were maxed out with freight, so we could only carry minimum fuel. This is fine, but if things go wrong, it does cut down your options. It was howling a gale as we approached the airport. The wind was reported at between sixty and seventy miles an hour, with a little mental trigonometry we had decided runway 'one six' was our best option. The Electra had a crosswind limit of twenty-six knots, we knew it could deal with a lot more than that. The crosswind on the day, we reckoned was nearer fifty-five knots.

We rattled and buffeted down the approach, I was looking behind the captain's head and out of the side window to see the runway. 'Anytime you're unhappy Steve, just go around.' Crossing the threshold was going to be the moment of truth. We were over the centreline holding a heading forty degrees off track and into the wind, I started putting in the rudder and tipping the wings into what felt like a hurricane. Eventually the fuselage was pointing down the runway and we were steady over the centreline, I put the into wind wheel onto the tarmac. The other wheels followed, as soon as all three wheels were on the ground, I pushed the column fully forward and hard over into wind. Then the power was reduced, and we held the centreline as we slowed down.

As we taxied onto stand, we saw the emergency vehicles heading out behind us. The aircraft following us down the approach, had gone off the side of the runway and had come to rest on the grass. We spent a couple of hours offloading our cargo in the wind and taxied out. 'Which runway would you like?' Asked the Irish controller. 'We'll stick with one six please.' 'Aaahhh, dat'l be your lucky runway then.'

It was around this time that my divorce was settled, two years of arguing over money and property was finally over. My first date with Gay, the hot, redheaded divorcee from over the road went really well. It also doubled up as a celebration of receiving my decree absolute. We hit it off straight away, even when she saw my more mischievous side, she wasn't deterred.

We were watching TV in my living room, when the phone rang. I picked up the handset. 'Hello, is that the Admiral Nelson?' Came the whiney, nasally question on the other end of the line. 'No, you've got the wrong number.' I put the phone down and returned to the sofa. The phone rang again. 'Hello, is that the Admiral Nelson?' 'No, you've still got the wrong number.' I tried to return to the sofa. The phone rang yet again as soon as I sat down. 'Is that the Admiral Nelson?' 'No, you are calling the wrong number.' Prat. I went to sit down, and the phone rang for the fourth time, I looked at the call minder, it was the village idiot again. I answered, 'Hello, this is the Admiral Nelson.' 'Oh good, I'd like to book a table for Valentine's Day.' 'Certainly sir, how many for?' 'I have a party of six.' 'What time would you like the table for.' 'Half past seven.' 'That's a table for six people, at seven thirty on Valentine's night, we'll see you tomorrow then, good bye.' Gay was flabbergasted, 'You can't do that!'... 'I just did.'

During the evening of the fifteenth of February my phone rang, it was the landlord of the Admiral Nelson. I fell about laughing as he cursed me for sending the dozy old fool to his pub, on the busiest night of the year. I felt sorry for the pub landlord, but the dozy simpleton who couldn't dial a phone number, gave me something to laugh about for a long time.

The Electra was loaded and ready to depart from Bergamo, in Italys we pulled off stand and started the 'taxi checklist' we hit a problem. The flaps were selected to the take-off position, they had just started moving, when they jammed, and the flap asymmetry warning light came on. That's frustrating. We stopped, shut down the engines and explained the problem to the handling agent. We would need the ground power unit for a bit longer, we'd call him once we had a plan. The captain called Op's and explained what was happening, then he had a chat with the engineers at Coventry.

After I'd pulled the asymmetry detection cable out from being wrapped around the screwjack, we spent the next hour in the hydraulic bay winding the flaps back in by hand. We knew that we could land at Coventry with no flaps, we had done that a few times before. Nobody had tried taking off without them though. How hard could it be. We thought over the normal take off profile, V1, V2 minus 5kts rotate, positive rate, gear up, VF flaps up. VF was at V1 plus twenty knots. If we rotated at VF minus five knots we would be into the normal flapless speeds as we left the ground. What's the worst that can happen?

We decided to give it a go. It was faultless, V1, V2, VF minus 5, rotate, we climbed smoothly over the Alps and were heading for home. At Coventry we calculated the speeds for a flapless landing, and all was well in our world. The Electra fleet had grown to six aircraft with a proportional increase in the number of crews that flew them, the company was always on the lookout for short cuts, to get our aging planes out of a hole when they broke down. This technique albeit unapproved, had a future. You don't have to cheat very often to turn a modest profit into a very healthy one, and seriously improve the airline's reliability figures.

Things were moving on very nicely with the hot redhead over the road. We were planning our first holiday. A week somewhere exotic would highlight any differences to our outlook on life. So far there had been none. Shaking all the money we could from our collective piggy banks, a week in the Seychelles was booked. We spent the entire week laughing at each other. I couldn't resist taking the micky, when Gay tried to describe the coral-reef we were snorkelling over to me, through her snorkel. I had been particularly impressed, when she hadn't been put off snorkelling, even when the woman on the boat told us to keep a good lookout for the sharks. Gay couldn't resist ridiculing me when I fell out of a coconut tree, missing acres of soft white sand and landing on the only rock on the beach.

Returning home, we knew that we had a future together. We had been entertaining the nosey neighbours for months, running back and forth between our two houses. It was now time to move in together. I spent two or three months knocking my house about to create enough rooms for all the kids, decorating each one under the direction of the respective teenager that was going to occupy it. My family was about to expand, from me and Vicky, to five of us. Gay along with her teenage son and daughter were moving in.

I met up with the captain in Op's for a charter to Saarbruchen, we were to fly out empty and return with a load of car parts. Somebodies 'just in time' production line was running just a bit too late. We were met in Op's by a tall well-spoken gentleman. He was the CAA 'Flight Op's Inspector' doing an un-announced check on the company. He was going to ride along with us on this trip, checking everything that we did. He started by going through our flight crew licences and the aircraft paperwork. It looked like the makings of a long day. By the time we took off, things were a lot more relaxed.

By his choice of clothing, it was clear that our inspector was more used to flying on passenger 757's than rattly, oil-soaked freighters. When he realised there was no catering on board, he was clearly disappointed. On the approach into Saarbruchen, I was taking in the sights, flying in daylight was a rare treat for us. I had drifted below the glideslope enough to set off the GPWS (Ground Proximity Warning System), the computer-generated female voice nagged me back onto the glide slope. We pulled onto stand and the handling agent took away our pallets to load them.

As we waited for our freight, the three of us had a coffee and shared petrol station sandwiches over a chat. The inspector admitted to us that he had drawn the short straw with this flight. 'You guys have developed a reputation around the Authority for operating on the fringes of legality. I hope today is going to be above board.' 'Of course, we wouldn't dream……'

The loaded pallets of freight appeared alongside the plane. What a mess. Instead of evenly distributing the cargo, the handler had rammed as much as he could onto half the pallets and spread what little there was left among the rest. The captain went with the agent back to the freight shed to redistribute our load.

We all set about pushing the freight onto the plane, 'These pallets are bloody heavy.' Said our inspector as he put his shoulder to the load. He was right, they could weigh in excess of a tonne and a half. Once there was some weight at the back of the plane lowering the tail, the freight deck levelled out and it was ok, but the first pallet generally had to be shoved uphill. Add to that, the customer had sent a couple of tonnes more cargo than they had declared, it was going to be hard work.

We arrived at Coventry with a thump and taxied onto stand. A solid arrival wasn't too much of a surprise to me, after all, I'd prepared the load sheet. The inspector declared himself to be happy with what he'd seen, and after a handshake he headed for his car.

For the previous eighteen months I'd been back and forth to the doctors and hospital. For years my neck had been noisy, clicking and grinding. I first went to the GP's after noticing that part of my right triceps had disappeared. The last meeting with the consultant neurosurgeon had been frightening. Studying the MRI scan he announced. 'In thirty years, I've never seen anybody with a neck like yours who wasn't in a wheelchair.'

My cervical spine was in tatters, a fractured vertebra, three ruptured and prolapsed intervertebral discs, one of which was displaced and cutting through my spinal cord. It was all highly unstable; one more serious event and I could be paralysed from the neck down. Not what you want to hear from a neurosurgeon. I tried to recall all the times I'd fallen off things, crashed into things, been hit by things, there was lots. My injuries couldn't be put down to a single event.

The 'good news' was, he could fix it. Titanium brackets and bone grafts featured heavily in his explanation of the surgery I needed. Me and Gay had just returned from a skiing holiday when the phone call from the hospital came. They'd had a cancellation, if I got to the hospital straight away and occupied my bed, nobody else could use it. My operation would be first thing in the morning. Coming out of the anaesthetic, looking up at a nurse who was rubbing orange juice onto my dried lips with a cotton bud, I tried wiggling my fingers and toes. They all worked, happy days. After six weeks recovery time I was back to work.

We were patiently waiting for our descent into Cologne, it was looking very tight. My captain was from Eastern Germany, his English was better than mine, which is a bit embarrassing. I learned my hybridised, gutter Anglo Saxon as I grew up. He learned his English at college and by watching English speaking movies. We were still at twenty thousand feet with less than fifty track miles to touchdown, with a healthy tail wind, it was going to require a steep dive to make the glideslope from here.

At last, the clearance came, I shut off the power and sat with the airspeed at two hundred and fifty knots. As the altimeter quickly unwound, our calculations showed we were getting closer to making our required height to start the final approach, as we progressed things improved, so we continued.

'We are descending very fast, Steve. I think we will make the glideslope.' 'I know mate, it's looking ok, just as well I did my IR in a Stuka.' Sometimes I wish I could keep my gob shut.

He starred during the following approach into the same airport. As we were close to the threshold he announced. 'I shall now demonstrate a greaser.' A greaser is a landing that is so gentle, you do not feel the wheels touch the ground. A rare thing. To announce it in advance was very optimistic. As it turned out the landing was ok, but not as predicted, 'Ein greaser.'

The Icarus Game

As we slowed down on the runway to taxi speeds, the captain requested a one eighty and backtrack. I could see what was coming, on the taxiway to our right, heading towards the same parking area as us, was a Lufthansa 737. We span through one hundred and eighty degrees, paralleling the 737 as we backtracked the runway.

We were closing on the Lufthansa, my captain eased open the power levers. As we pulled alongside the Boeing, the other captain saw us, and opened his throttles. Neck and neck, we were heading for the parking apron, at fifty knots. ATC had other ideas, 'Lufthansa XXX and Eurotrans XXX, this is not a racetrack, slow down. Eurotrans XXX you are to give way to the Lufthansa. Bloody favouritism.

'Eurotrans XXX, you are cleared direct Erlangen.' My navigational instruments were already set up for the approach, so I entered the waypoint into the GPS on the pedestal. It was the most basic of units, very simple to use, no fancy touch screens on our flight deck. I altered our heading and carried on the conversation with my first officer. We were heading into Nurnberg and flying directly into the sun, working nights has allowed me to watch a lot of sun rises. A few minutes later the controller was back on the radio.

'Eurotrans XXX, where are you going?' 'Erlangen!' my F.O. replied confidently into the radio. 'Not in a million years.' Came the response from the Bavarian controller. I looked down at the sat nav, ERL the VOR we were heading for was three thousand miles away, somewhere in China. I toggled through the list of ERL's and found the one in Germany, ten degrees right of our heading and two thousand nine hundred and fifty miles closer.

Chapter 32

Benny The Ball*.

Having been tremendously fortunate as a first officer. I'd survived a couple of years cocking the job up, and not fallen foul of the management. More importantly though, I'd flown with some incredibly good pilots. On the flip side I'd also flown with some bad ones. I knew what attributes and failings made up these diametrically opposed groups. When Doug called me into his office, it was to tell me that my days as a first officer were now behind me. I was unbelievably proud of myself. I was going to be the captain of a fifty-tonne airliner.

It had taken me nine years to go from rookie flight engineer to captain. The hours of study and practice had been more fun than hard work. I had developed sufficient technical and management skills and felt ready to make the transition. I was going to continue developing this knowledge further in the future, but for now, I was chuffed.

Joining my colleagues, travelling to Seattle for another session in the simulator, was different this time. It held very few mysteries. The complexities of the aeroplane were something, which over the last nine years, had become second nature. I had seen most of the scenarios we were about to enact in the simulator, for real. Sitting at the pointy end of an aeroplane that is failing piece by piece, gives you an incredible sense of self-reliance. I can't think of too many other situations in life or work, where you are so isolated when things go wrong.

Instead of booking us into the usual concrete village, airport hotel, Doug had found a quirky bed and breakfast. The house was an old timber building dating back to the turn of the twentieth century, almost to the gold rush. The people who ran it were into west coast gastronomy and history. It made the visit just a little more memorable.

The guests were varied, the American woman in the room over the hall, was determined to let everybody in the building know she was getting a good seeing too. During her less than private lovemaking bouts she hollered and yelled throughout, climaxing with a loud, 'Oooooohhh Baarrry' at her moment of glory. This was just a minor distraction from my preparation for the next sim session. Trying to pick Barry and his partner out at breakfast brightened up the start of our day.

With the simulator finished, my training was going smoothly, much to everybody's relief, no more ploughing up runways, please. During captain's line training, the candidate occupies the captain's seat, and is responsible for all decision making. The trainer adopts the role of a competent, if unmotivated first officer. Me and my trainer Mike, were far from unmotivated on this morning.

Approaching Toulouse, we were both looking at numerous purple splodges on the weather radar. These represented big

The Icarus Game

nasty, noisy thunderstorms. One was sat on the inbound track to our runway, there was another patch of weather on the reciprocal end. What to do, we could hold, and wait for it to move. There was no prevailing wind to shift it, so that might take a while. We could divert, if we really had to. The freight was for Toulouse, our breakfast was in Toulouse.

Plan 'C' then, tighten our seat belt straps, and fly through it. Not an ideal option if you're carrying passengers, they whinge like crazy if you bounce them about. Freight doesn't care. We established inbound for the runway and watched the weather get closer. We hit it with a bang, the hailstones were the size of marbles, the noise was deafening. Our real concern though was the strength of the impending updraught. The vertical speed indicator (VSI) shot up, I shut the power off completely, pushed the nose down, holding us on the flap limiting speed of 190 Knts. We were still climbing at two thousand feet a minute, the glideslope disappeared below us at an amazing pace, we were in a fifty-tonne glider.

Looking across the flight deck at each other, we both shrugged our shoulders. We just had to wait for the downdraught we knew was coming. It soon arrived. I pulled the nose up and applied full power, we still sank rapidly, then we popped out of the shower into clear air. I reset the power to an approach setting, put the nose on the horizon and checking the instruments. We were back on the glide, a glance out of the window showed two red lights and two white lights on the PAPI's, result. We landed and headed for one of my favourite breakfasts.

Your first flight as the captain, is a nerve-wracking experience, you're trying to apply everything you've learned over the previous years, praying to your gods that you don't screw up. You're being particularly nice to your plane, stroking her and whispering sweet nothings. If she's in a bad mood, suffering a touch of the hormonal imbalance, you're in for a hard time. I was now the guy that everybody would be turning to for answers.

We had left Liege, inbound to East Midlands, it had all gone smoothly. On touch-down I heaved a sigh of relief. As I lifted the power levers into the ground range, it all went pear shaped. Bloody typical. The red lights behind the No 2 'E' Handle lit up and the fire bell rang out. I called to Sohan, the first officer, for the engine fire drill, 'Silence the bell, E handle No 2.' While the first officer dealt with pulling levers, I vacated the runway and sent out the Mayday.

ATC directed us to a nice wide area of tarmac, and we parked up. The airport fire service was there as the engines finished winding down. I'd got the freight door open and directed the firemen to the No 2 engine. They had the cowls off and were looking all around the engine bay. There was no sign of flames.

The clamp holding the jet pipe to the turbine section had broken, leaving the jet pipe hanging loose in the bay. The red-hot gasses from the turbine were blowing straight into the engine bay instead of being blown overboard behind the wing. This is what triggered the fire warning on the flight deck.

The fire section left, and our engineer fitted a new 'V' band clamp onto the jet pipe, we were good to go. Rotating off the runway at East Midlands, I was being extra nice to the Lecky Bird,

'Ok, you've had your fun for one day, please don't try to kill me again tonight.'

As captain you know the rules, ignorance of these rules is not a defence, it's just ignorance. I knew better, but I still did it. There was no fuelling policy at Atlantic, you uplifted what you needed. We were in Exeter to collect parcels going to East Midlands. I had collected the aircraft from Bournemouth, departing thinking I could fuel up in Exeter.

We pulled onto stand and called up a fuel truck, the bad news came over the radio. 'The fuel truck driver finishes work at ten o'clock. Do you want us to call him out? There will be an extra charge of one thousand pounds.' A grand to get a truck driver out of his bed, what are these profiteering idiots on. We checked the fuel on board using the dip sticks under the wings, very carefully. We checked the flight plan fuel calculations. We rechecked the weather, 'Tell the fueller to stay in bed, we've got what we need.'

As we approached East Midlands, the fuel gauges, which were virtually useless on the Electra, showed empty tanks all around. Our fuel calculations showed we had fuel, but it was getting tight. Aircraft fuel tanks are odd-shaped things, squeezed into all the voids they can fit in. There is always a small amount of unusable fuel onboard. As we descended on finals the fuel pump lights started to flicker on and off. This meant they were starting to cavitate. The weather was a bit murky, but we had the runway in sight, I opened all the fuel transfer valves. This allowed any engine to take fuel from any tank that still had fuel in it. As we landed and the nosewheel of the aircraft lowered, the fuel in the tanks shifted and the fuel pump lights went out. We taxied in and I was cursing myself for cutting it so fine, I wouldn't do that again just to save the company a few quid.

At Coventry, Atlantic had one piece of ground equipment that stood out from the crowd. The air starter. Most air starters consist of a big diesel engine driving an air compressor. This provides enough air flow and pressure to drive the aircraft starter motors. Atlantic's air start was a beast, it consisted of a gas turbine engine, we think it came out of an old helicopter and the pressurised air was drawn from the turbine's compressor. The whole thing was mounted in a tin box on a trolley. To use it, it was parked alongside the aircraft under the first officer's window. On a good day it roared ferociously and blasted a huge wall of blue flames past the first officer's right ear. On a bad day it coughed and banged, spewing flames in all directions.

The ground crew were rightly scared of this contraption, they would hit the start button and dive behind the tractor. Taking cover until the thing was running with a degree of stability. Watching new first officers who'd never had the jet-start experience trying to scramble out of their seats, in fear of their lives always gave me a good laugh. It's loads more dramatic than sending the apprentice to stores for a set of fallopian tubes.

'Touchdown zone, flooded. Midpoint, flooded. Stop end, flooded.' This was the runway weather report that greeted us at Liege, along with howling, gale force winds. I was happy the aircraft could cope with these atrocious conditions. It was extreme, but that's all part of the fun. We came down the approach with a torrent of water rushing up the windshield, the wipers were making no impression on it at all.

Touching down on the part of the airfield lake that looked most like a runway we started to slow down. As the airspeed decayed the aerodynamic control of the plane reduced. The wheels though had not yet touched the tarmac, we were aquaplaning. The nose wheel steering was having no effect and the gale force wind caught the tail of the aircraft, and at 100kts we weathercocked into wind.

We were about to be blown backwards off the side of the runway. I called 'Go around, flaps seventy-eight' and pushed the power levers hard forward. As the aircraft accelerated, we regained control and rotated back into the air. That was close, fortunately my first officer was experienced and reacted absolutely correctly. Any hesitation could have been embarrassing. I was saved from the ignominy of 'going farming'.

During the next foggy, windy night in Liege I was a little more wary. I was being followed down the approach by our Flight Op's Director, so I was keen not to cock it up. I'd flown down to minimums on the instruments, and we had only just seen the approach lighting. I knew I was a bit left of the centreline, so rather than risk a jink to the right at low altitude, I 'went around' for another go. I was sure I'd get stick in the crew room from the boss for not nailing the ILS, but that's life.

As we came out of the low cloud the second time, I was right over the centreline and landed. We were gently rolling down to taxi speed when I saw the other Electra on the taxiway coming towards us, backtracking from the other end of the runway. How had he ended up there? I couldn't resist asking. The first officer had done the same as me, come out of the cloud left of the centreline. He however, had elected to land, and after some weaving back overhead the runway, finally touched down halfway along it, rolling out at the far end. I'd had a let off, but it didn't stop me taking the piss royally.

We needed a holiday; I had been working away a lot. So, me and Gay took ourselves to the USA for a couple of weeks. No phone, no email, we hired a car and drove all around the North-eastern corner. New York, Boston, Niagara, Pittsburgh, Washington, it was a great road trip. We covered two and a half thousand miles, all without a sat nav or incident, spending our last night in Manhattan.

Our flight home was early in the morning, by five o'clock we were on the road and driving through the Queens Midtown Tunnel, under the East River towards JFK Airport. As we emerged from the tunnel, there was a vast expanse of tarmac and a row of toll booths. The direction signs for these booths are buried amongst a mass of Pepsi and Dr pepper adverts. I aimed for one in the middle, Gay had a handful of loose change for me to throw into the cash basket.

The booth I'd chosen, was one that only accepted the EZ Pass electronic payment, which we didn't have. At this time in the morning, we were the only car around, so I backed away and drove to the next booth that did accept cash.

Oh dear. I stopped at the red light and lowered my window, the light changed green and I was just about to drive forwards to the barrier when there was a voice in my left ear. 'Don't you be driving away from me, sir.' Came the distinctive Noo Yoiyk accent. I glanced over my left shoulder and was looking straight down the barrel of a large calibre handgun. Ooooh shit. 'Is this your ve-hic-le sir?' 'No officer, it's a rental.' 'Keep your hands on the wheel, sir.'

The NYPD over do the politeness thing. When you've got a gun stuck in somebodies' ear, there's really no need to call them sir. Fuck me, I thought, I'm about to get shot by Benny the Ball*. Gay wasn't helping, sat in the passenger seat trying to stifle a giggle.

The officer then very kindly reeled off my list of 'Violations'. 'You arrived at a toll booth without the means to pay, you reversed away from a toll booth, you crossed a solid white line.' He rattled off five or six misdemeanours, that I was clearly guilty of. 'How long are you staying in the United States for?' 'We're not officer, we're on our way to the airport now to get our flight home.' The officer settled for a brief lecture on the potential cost of my multiple violations, then put his gun away. As we drove away, Gay turned to me and said, 'He was just trying to intimidate you.' 'It bloody worked!'

*Benny the Ball- Fictional character out of the 1970's children's cartoon 'Top Cat'.

Chapter 33

Mr Woo.

My willingness to deviate from the company's standard flight profiles and procedures from time to time, had not gone unnoticed. If you want to learn how not to crash an aeroplane, occasionally you need to scare yourself by getting close to the edge of the performance envelope. In modern aircraft this is mostly done in the simulator, but we had to do our learning in the plane. Sit in the comfort zone, fat, dumb and happy and you may think you're doing ok, but in reality, you're learning nothing. Sooner or later, you'll find yourself in uncharted territory and if it's your first time out there, it's scary.

If my first officer wanted to try an approach onto a short, narrow runway when the weather was filthy, I would arrange the flying schedule for the day so they could. I knew my capabilities, where my lines in the sand were drawn. They were usually far enough beyond where my crewmate wanted to go, to give us a fighting chance of success. It wasn't long after my promotion to captain when I was asked to do the 'Line Training' job. This involved flying with first officers and captains immediately after they had completed their simulator and base training. Getting them through the first few hours in the aeroplane, on the job.

Flying out of desolate freight hubs has one distinct advantage, there's usually nobody watching. This gives opportunities for fun, without loads of phone calls to the company, from irate whingers who have never had a day's excitement in their lives.

Valladolid in northern Spain, is as desolate an airfield as you will find. The first time I landed there I thought it was an abandoned film set for western movies. There was not a living soul in sight. My first officer was a capable, experienced guy and when he asked if we could depart using the 'hooligan departure' profile, I had no problem with that.

The hooligan departure, was a home-grown profile that differed significantly from standard. The standard profile is all about noise abatement, fuel efficiency and obstacle clearance, the hooligan departure is all about having fun. I had him talk me through what he was going to do, I just needed to point out to him that it was forty degrees Celsius outside, so our performance would be a lot less sprightly than he might expect. I rounded off the briefing with, 'Any failures, we revert to the standard profile.' All was good and we taxied out.

V1, rotate. Lift the wheels off the ground, level out at fifty feet, gear up. Vf, flaps up. Start pushing forward on the control column, to counter the change in pitch while the flaps are travelling, maintain fifty feet above the ground. Accelerate to 250kts, pitch the nose up to thirty degrees. Hold this attitude until the speed decays to two hundred knots, then lower the nose and climb away at two hundred and ten knots, job done.

All would have been well apart from one unforeseen thing. Because of the high outside air temperature, the subsequent lack of performance meant we crossed the airfield boundary fence at fifty feet and flew out of sight of ATC, across the barren moonscape. The controller thought we had crashed, so he hit the 'big red emergency button.' Only to see us climb away a few seconds later. He had mobilised the airport fire section and woken up the Madrid fire department. When the inevitable snotagram arrived, I sent a suitably apologetic reply.

Flying over the Ionian Sea towards Crete can hardly be considered work, as we descended into Chania my workload went up marginally. The first officer announced, he would like to fly a visual approach, rather than follow the instrument procedure. It was a glorious day so why not? First officers flying visual approaches will get the captain into trouble, very quickly, if he's not ahead of the game. I set up my instruments for the instrument approach, 'just in case,' and followed our progress carefully on the charts.

'Tell them we're on finals.' Came the confident instruction from the first officer. 'Nope!' I replied. 'Why not? There's the runway.' He protested pointing at the strip of tarmac in front of us. 'Because that's not the runway, the runways over there.' I pointed to our left at a wider, pale concrete strip. 'You are trying to land on the taxiway.' 'Are you sure?' 'Yep, it's on my ILS.' We stepped across to our left, and I called the tower. 'Atlantic 188, two miles, finals.' 'Atlantic 188, you are cleared to land.' We taxied in and then the fun started.

The load was sensitive enough for our General Manager to accompany us, that was ok by me. He was good company and his credit card would get a spanking over dinner. We were carrying a consignment of anti-aircraft missiles for the Greek military, the missiles themselves are safe enough to transport, but the nose of each missile is packed with clever electronics which must be handled very gently. The detonators are also sensitive, packed in a separate small box. The missile boxes are covered with plastic stick-on tell-tale shock sensors, to highlight any rough treatment.

The detonators, we kept safe under our manager's seat. If there was a problem, he would be the first to know.

We were met on arrival by the handling agent, and a senior officer from the Greek navy. He was pleased to be receiving some new toys to play with. Until that was, an officer from the Greek army turned up, announcing that the missiles were in fact his toys. The two officers fought it out, while we jumped into a taxi and headed into town to find food and beer.

The following month I was flying another load of the same type of missiles into Ankara, Turkey. Arming both sides engaged in a long running state of tension wasn't going to register on my moral compass. As far as I was concerned these missiles could be fired at anybody. So long as it's not me, I don't have a problem. I was struggling to hear the controller as I flew down the approach, because the local Turkish taxi company seemed to be using the ATC radio frequency for their cabs.

Checking into the Ankara Hilton, I couldn't help but notice it was all brand new, the receptionist answered my unasked question, 'This part of the building has just been rebuilt, after Al-Kaieda bombed it.' It must be said, the rebuild is fabulous, the place is palatial.

Things at work outside of the flying were moving on at a pace, I was already well established in the 'Line Training' post, this was interesting in its own way. Flying with people who have a marginal grasp of their surroundings is always going to need a higher level of concentration.

Now, I was promoted again, to the Electra Fleet Captain. This added a new level of responsibility and complexity to my role. Updating technical manuals seemed to take up an inordinate amount of time. Comments from the Flight Op's Director like, whilst your sat at the computer Steve, can you just knock out a company newsletter didn't help either.

Having spent the week flying in the DHL network I was finishing in Brussels. I thought my work was done, when my phone rang, it was Op's, 'Steve can you fuel up the plane and bring it to Coventry, ASAP.' 'Ok, fax me the flight plan, how much fuel do I need?' 'Fill it up.' What? This was highly irregular. Filling the tanks would limit the freight load we could carry significantly. And leaving the DHL network with our tanks full of their fuel was very naughty. 'Are you sure? This is a strange way to operate.' 'It's what I've been told to ask you to do.' Even the bowser driver commented on how much fuel I uplifted. I dropped the aeroplane at Coventry and went home for the weekend.

On Monday evening I was back at work, picking up the same aeroplane, to take it back into the DHL network. Funny thing though, it had barely enough fuel in the tanks to get to Brussels. When I pulled onto stand, I called up a bowser, the DHL ramp manager on the radio sounded confused. 'But you took fuel on Friday.' 'Are you sure, I'm on the plane now and the tanks are empty.' He clearly had no clue the aircraft had left, and subsequently re-joined the DHL network.

The Icarus Game

Although I had a very good idea what Atlantic were doing, I saw it as being between our company and the companies that employed us. Not something I was going to shout about at the time. At the end of the day, the fuel wasn't mis-appropriated until our accounts people failed to pay for it.

We now had seven Aircraft on the fleet, so swapping them between networks to mask the fuelling irregularities was simple. Each time we did this little stunt, it netted about fifteen thousand litres of Avtur, around ten thousand pounds sterling at the time. After about six months the parcel companies had worked out that we weren't playing it straight. Whenever a fuel bowser turned up at our aircraft, a ramp manager would also be there, with his clip board. We were in the spotlight. Assuming we took an aircraft's worth of fuel each week for six months, well, you do the sums. It would all be additional profit on our own charters.

One of the most regular mechanical failures we had, was the starter motors. These tiny turbines are powered by compressed air, supplied from the ground air start machine, or cross bled air from our own engine turbines. Rather like air powered drills. For their size, these motors were immensely powerful, about the size of a beer glass they create over two hundred horsepower. This is used to spin up the engine and propeller, to its start-up speeds.

If the starter shaft sheared, which they did occasionally, you were stuck. We tried a lot of variations on windmill starting the engines with some success. The technique started with the three good engines running, accelerate down the runway, unfeather the failed engine's propeller and wait for it to start rotating and fire up. Not very scientific, but it usually worked and got you out of a hole.

Jumping out of the crew bus at Liverpool, I was met by the captain of a failed windmill start attempt. He was clearly shaken, and I wasn't surprised. We walked around his aeroplane; it was a mess. All four mainwheel brake units were burnt out, all four mainwheel tyres were destroyed, both nosewheel tyres were also trashed. He had spent too much time unfeathering the prop while he accelerated down the runway. The prop started turning very late in the process, the plane ended up going a lot faster than he had planned. Running out of tarmac very quickly.

He realised at the last minute that the engine wasn't going to start. Reversing on his symmetrical live engines and standing hard on the brakes, he slowed the plane down just enough to vacate the runway at the end. Instead of ending up in the Mersey, he screeched around the sharp ninety degree exit from the runway at breakneck speed. The hard breaking overheated and burned out the wheel brakes melting the tyres, the sharp turn off the runway overstressed and destroyed the nosewheel tyres.

After the engineers had fixed the starter, replaced the brake units and given me a new set of rubber, I was airborne and going to Liege for the week.

Liverpool was a regular stopover for us, the company had an apartment there, that we used in preference to a hotel. Since 9/11 getting in and out of airports had generally become a chore. Dealing with airport security is no fun, particularly when some security operatives see flight crew as a target to take out their own frustrations on. Dealing with their petty hassles every day soon gets tedious.

At Liverpool, freight crews were kept segregated from the passengers. We had to enter the apron via a remote security post. The security operatives there were as obnoxious as any, plus there was a lot of them. The security hut was just that, a porta cabin, equipped with all the usual walk-through arches and x-ray machines.

It also had a surplus of bolshie security bodies, who I'd already had disagreements with. Their pet hate is liquids, I like a coffee in the cruise. It doesn't seem much to ask for in my workplace. My flask of hot water was not going onto any plane if they got their way. I tried turning up with an empty flask, asking nicely, 'Can I use your kettle to fill up my flask please?' 'No, if I let you, everybody will want to use my kettle.' That got their kettle filled with washing up liquid as I passed it.

These petty annoyances were just part of the job, some people can rise above it, not me. We were going through the security hut one evening and there was a local football match on the television. There was even more fat, lazy security bodies in the hut than normal, crowding around the telly. We were waiting ages to get through. As we were the only ones there, it was irritating. One of the bodies who was looking at his phone piped up, 'Hey, who's 'Mr Woo?'' That was the Bluetooth I.D. on my phone. This was an opportunity for a wind up I couldn't resist.

The following night the security post was overstuffed with football watching security bodies again. This time, when we walked in there was pandemonium. The TV watching crowd started shouting and waving their arms in the air. It wasn't because Liverpool had scored this time though.

'Fookin' ell. Wah the fook.' It was fat boy with the phone. 'It fookin' sez 'ere. 'Lazy scouse twats!!'' I'd changed my Bluetooth I.D. Collecting my x-rayed bag I strolled out onto the apron, smiling.

The Icarus Game

L188 Electra flight simulator. Based in Seattle

Above: GLOFC fitted with spray booms.

Spray training in the Bristol Channel at 100ft

The Icarus Game

Above: East Midlands Fire Dept. deals with a fire warning on my first flight as a Captain.

Below: Brussels Fire Dept. keep a safe distance, while our engineer puts out the fire.

The drugs dog leaves, whilst the other Wroclaw immigration officers try to repack the load they had dismantled.

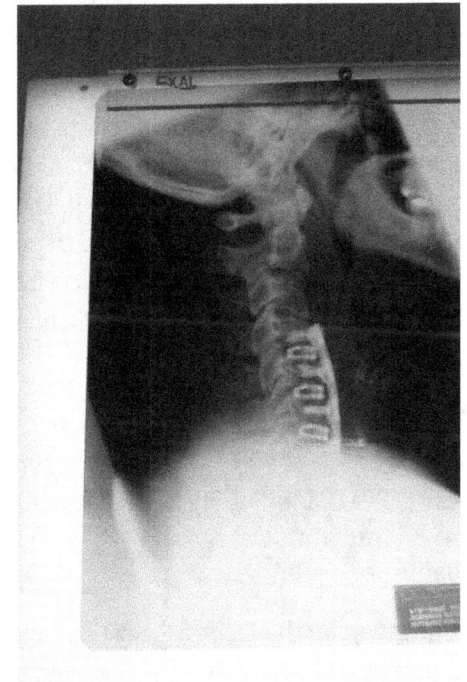

My neck, after the neurosurgeon had screwed it back together.

Chapter 34

Odd Jobs.

As the Fleet Captain, part of my work involved screening pilot job applications and CV's. As a public service notice, I can tell you what my waste bin liked best. Red, green, or purple ink, all got filed straight away under B1N. Italic or other hard to read fonts, B1N. Documents that take more than five minutes to read, B1N. Standard letters sent to, 'Dear Captain XXXX.' If you can't change XXXX to my name on your word processor, don't expect an answer.

One of our other management pilots had experienced our perennial problem with security at Edinburgh. They had confiscated his flask. He asked me if, as I was going to be there that day, could I recover it for him. Of course I could. I arrived at the airport and took a detour to security, requesting the return of my colleague's property. It was handed to me by a particularly surly individual in uniform.

He gave me a long-winded lecture on the dangers of drinks containers on aeroplanes, and the (non-existent) security regulations regarding carrying empty thermos flasks. This lecture was followed by, 'I've just passed my IR, who do I write to at Atlantic for a job.'

 'I'm Steve, I'm the Electra Fleet Captain, you can write to me.'
'I'll give you this now then.' He handed me his CV. I thanked him

for considering us as his potential future employer, walked around the corner and dropped his CV in the first bin I passed.

Conducting pilot job interviews was an eye opener, if you want a job as flight crew, at least try to act the part. One of our stipulations at the time was, that candidates should live within an hour or so of Coventry airport. The guy sat across the desk from me lived eighty miles away. 'If you get this job, will you consider relocating closer to work?' 'No, I can drive here in less than an hour, easily.' Time, distance, speed calculations are pilots' stock in trade sums. This innumerate street racer clearly hadn't worked that out. 'Thank you for your time, goodbye.'

Generally, I liked to start interviews with an easy, ice breaker. 'Can you tell me what you've been doing over the last year?' I would expect a response that was vaguely flying related. I've been towing gliders, instructing, collecting supermarket trolleys to fund my hours building, would all be good answers. One candidate obviously misunderstood the question. 'I've had a terrible year, both my parents died, and I've been dealing with the probate. I didn't actually have a breakdown, but my GP put me on tranquilisers just in case. 'Did I want to fly alongside this suicidal, manic depressive, no thanks.

I knew I was in for a long painful night before I left Op's. The job was to fly to Belfast, Aldergrove. Collect a consignment of munitions, take them to Teesside, then load them onto another aeroplane. We were going to park our plane up and fly the freshly loaded one to Prestwick. Another crew would collect it from there and fly it across the Atlantic, to the USA. There were two problems that we as a company thought we had dealt with.

The first was at Aldergrove. We were to be loaded on the military site. The taxiways on the military side of the airfield were narrow, there was also a four-foot-high wooden post on the side of the taxiway exiting the runway. This was part of the RVR (runway visual range) measuring system. The second issue was that Teesside Airport would be closed when we arrived there.

We wrote to Belfast ATC, notifying them that we needed a particular routing onto the military site, to avoid the RVR post. We also wrote to and spoke with the Senior ATC officer at Teesside.

Taking off from Coventry I had this plan firmly in my head. As soon as we landed at Aldergrove I was on the radio. 'Atlantic 188, request exit the runway via the crosswind runway, to enter the military site at the southern end.' 'Negative.' Came the reply from the controller, 'I need you to enter via the northern entrance.'

He clearly hadn't read the memo. After querying the instruction and being told to get on with it because there was a 737 following me down the approach. I rolled out down the runway and turned left onto the narrow, obstructed taxiway, then stopped. I shut down the engine that was going to hit the marker post and called ATC for a marshaller.

The 737 trying to land behind us had to go around, my tail was overhanging the runway, the ATC officer was in a state of speechlessness. The best he could manage was, 'I'm reporting you to the CAA.' That was a letter I'd like to see; he'd cocked up royally. As he was intent on reporting the incident, I also had to file a report with my version of events, that would be entertaining.

The reporting system used by the CAA is known as an MOR, Mandatory Occurrence Report. These reports cover all safety and security issues, including near misses, crashes, serious accidents and fatalities. After carefully manoeuvring my now static propeller around the wooden post and taxiing onto the apron, we were loaded up.

Calling Atlantic Op's, I let them know we were ready to depart. 'You'll have normal ATC coverage until you reach Teesside, there will be an approach controller but nobody in the tower. You should see a vehicle doing a runway inspection as you come down the approach. Once he's off the runway you can land at your own discretion. Then follow the truck to your parking.' The flight went without a hitch, the arrival into Teesside was just as I'd discussed with our Op's officer.

We loaded the freight onto the other Electra, ready for its trans-Atlantic crossing, then we secured our inbound aircraft for somebody else to collect later that day. It all worked very well as far as I was concerned. As we landed at Prestwick, I had to point out the long black scar on the runway to my first officer. 'See that, I did that!'

As soon as I'd parked up and turned my phone on, it started to ring, 'Steve, somebody's reported you for landing an airliner at Teesside when the airport was closed.' 'Have they, you're saying it like it's my problem, you lot had better get your story straight,

The Icarus Game

I'll file a report.' One night's flying and two MOR's, I think that's probably a record.

The flight from Brussels to Marseilles should have been a routine trip. Had it not been for the plane catching fire, again. This time it was memorable, more for the comedy value than it being a serious incident. We had our taxi clearance and were making our way across Brussels airport. This can be quite a long taxi sometimes.

As we taxied out, the first officer was running the check lists as normal. He started coughing and spluttering as he was reading. Looking up at the air conditioning vent I could see mist coming into the cockpit. He insisted it was smoke, I insisted it was just condensation. As the condensation got thicker, I had to concede that he may be right.

I had the FO put out a Mayday call to ATC. They instructed us to park on a large area of empty tarmac, at the side of the taxiway. The memory items on the checklist for smoke in the cockpit are very simple, 'Don facemask, oxygen 100%, turn off recirculation fan, close flight deck door vent.' I was in the process of doing these as I steered the aircraft off the taxiway. My FO had other ideas, he opened his sliding side window, stood on his seat, stuck his head and torso out of the window, and started screaming blue murder that he was going to die.

His action had an unexpected benefit for me. Even on the ground the engine driven compressors (EDC's) were pumping air into the fuselage. Most of this was vented overboard until we got airborne, but a residual amount would slightly pressurise the plane on the ground. By opening his side window, the FO had provided a route for this air to escape, taking the smoke with it. Air and smoke poured around the FO's waist and out of his window, leaving my side of the cockpit smoke free.

The fire section arrived on the scene and surrounded us with fire engines, about a hundred meters away from the aircraft. I opened the freight door and smoke poured like a waterfall from the freight deck that I was stood on, down onto the tarmac. I beckoned the fireman over, they wouldn't move. Eventually our engineer, Gandalf, appeared with the fire extinguisher from his van in his hand. I shouted a description of what had happened to him, he then disappeared under the plane, into the electrical bay. He reappeared a few seconds later with a discharged fire extinguisher, shouting to me that the recirculation fan had been on fire, but it was out now. He was going to look in the spares pack and try to find another one.

During this whole episode, the airport firemen never left their fire engines. Nor did they attempt to help us or extinguish the fire. Add to that, my first officer never even managed to get off his seat, waste of space doesn't even start to describe this guy. After a couple of hours, Gandalf had a new recirculation fan fitted and working. Had it not been for our engineers' efforts, the plane could easily have burnt to the ground.

My first officer was by now behaving like a sulky, stroppy teenager. I dragged him away from his laptop, out of the crew room and back to the aeroplane. He was hard work to get flying at the best of times, but when things were going wrong, he was a real harbinger of doom.

As we arrived at the aircraft, I was challenged by a man introducing himself as the Airport Director. He wore a suit and clearly knew little about operating aeroplanes. 'I can't allow you to start your engines, until you guarantee me your aeroplane won't catch fire again.' There was no way I could promise that, as soon as you put fuel and sparks together, something will happen. Most of the time it's what you expect, sometimes not. 'Can you make the same guarantee for that aeroplane?' I asked pointing at a Brussels Airlines Airbus. 'No, of course I can't.' 'We'll just have to hope it doesn't then.' He got back into his car, muttering to himself. It was a long night, my FO refused to acknowledge my existence during the next few sectors. That's just the way it goes sometimes.

Brussels Airport had problems of its own, for months there had been regular protests outside the freight area. The locals were objecting to the noise of aircraft taking off at night. We would watch them marching up and down with their placards chanting and shouting. 'Stop flying at night.'

To be honest they got no sympathy from us, if you don't like aeroplanes, don't live near an airport. These protests carried on for months. Then it all changed, the protesters had got their wish. DHL announced that they were closing their hub at Brussels, moving the whole operation to Leipzig in Eastern Germany. The entire staff would have to relocate, or find new jobs. The protests continued, only the placards and chants changed. 'Save our jobs.'

Spray training was always something to relish, it was a chance to fly in a very different style to normal. Atlantic had a contract, which was linked to the pollution patrols I had flown in the

Cessna 404. The contract was to spray dispersant chemicals onto oil spillages at sea. Previously this job had been done by the DC3's. Now we had a specially modified Electra for the task. The aircraft was equipped with spray booms at the rear. The cargo compartment was filled with around ten thousand litres of dispersant in tanks, and a huge pump. This aircraft and its crew were on constant standby, we always had to have a trained crew available.

Training was usually done during the Christmas lull and was great fun. We would fill the dispersant tanks with water and take the aircraft to a quiet, deserted piece of coast. There we could practice the flight profiles we would use when flying at low level over an oil spill. To be effective we had to be at one hundred feet and one hundred and fifty knots, this gave the dispersal pattern the oil clean up agencies wanted. The spray operation was controlled by the incident manager, in a light twin engined aircraft sat high above us. He would guide us onto the area of the oil slick that needed the most dispersant.

At first flying with your propellers just above the surface of the water is disconcerting. After a while you become accustomed to it and relax a little. It's vital that our pilots were comfortable with the sensations of being so close to the water. We also practiced exactly what we would do if anything went wrong. The Electra is a very stable platform and ideal for this kind of work. The spray pump was voice operated, 'pump on…now.' This got the engineer in the jump seat to press the green button. We had no shortage of volunteer engineers for this job.

The Icarus Game

The company's willingness to take on unusual jobs, was the single best thing about working at Atlantic. It appealed to my need to have a fresh challenge now and again. I couldn't imagine doing the same thing year on year. One unusual challenge took me north, to within 250 miles of the Arctic Circle in January. We were flying between Umea in northern Sweden and Stockholm for the Swedish Post Office. The temperature never rose above minus fifteen all the time we were there, it did get a lot colder though.

Normally snow is cleared off the runway before you can take off, here they simply pack the snow down flat and take off from it. This was the first time I had landed or taken off from a snow-covered runway. The hardest part is height and depth perception, everything is flat and white. Landing fifty tonnes of aeroplane on snow and not even scuffing the surface, is a strange concept to get your head around. Surprisingly, taxiing on compacted snow is not that different to tarmac.

Plugging the hire car engine heaters into a power socket, every time you stopped, to prevent it freezing solid, was an indication of the severity of the cold. A short drive to the coast was another clue as to just how cold it was, this is the only time I've stood on solid, frozen sea water.

It was Julian's sector to fly us back north, the weather was atrocious. It was blowing a blizzard, straight across our packed snow runway. The airport sprayed lines on the snow in purple dye to help us orientate ourselves. Without this help a difficult job would be impossible. The blizzard was driven by winds that were on our limits to land on tarmac, we were landing on ice and snow. Julian did a lovely job bringing us down the ILS and put us on the snow as gently as you can imagine. We taxied to the freight shed. Before we were allowed to open the doors to unload, the aircraft had the be encased in a huge canvass awning. That's wild.

Chapter 35

Hassi Messaoud.

The taxi driver couldn't believe his ears when I gave him the address of the hotel. It was six in the morning and we'd just finished a night shift ending in Malmo. 'Are you sure? That's not a hotel I normally take passengers to.' 'Yeh, it's where the company has booked us into.' We climbed out of the cab and collected our bags from the boot. The hotel looked like a typical back street residence, with a sign over the door, 'Hotel Europa'. We walked in and joined the queue. Looking bizarrely out of place in our blazers and gold braid.

The brown vinyl floor, led to a green, chipped faux marble, laminated chipboard reception desk. The other guests in front of us were carrying their lives in plastic shopping bags, paying for their accommodation using DSS vouchers. None of us felt like making a fuss, we were all dog tired. We checked in, collected some cheese and crackers from the vending machines and went to our rooms. These were in a similar style to the reception. This was definitely not the standard of hotel that was in my terms of employment.

After a day's sleep, we went in search of dinner, I needed to make a phone call to Op's. 'What the fuck were you thinking when you booked that hotel? Can you please find somewhere else for us by tomorrow morning?' I gave the Op's officer a detailed description of the hotel's shortcomings as I saw them.

Steve Woodhouse

The following morning as we left the aeroplane, I called Op's, 'Which hotel are we in today?' 'Sorry mate, it's the same one as yesterday, I didn't have time to change it.'

Climbing into the cab with my colleagues I turned to the driver, 'Take us to the most expensive hotel in Malmo please.'

We pulled up outside the Scandic Koenig, the driver had been right, this was smart. A vast reception, marble floors, chandeliers, immaculately dressed reception staff. I handed my company credit card over and asked if they had four rooms. 'Do you have a reservation, sir.' 'No, I'm afraid not, we're here at short notice.' 'No problem, sir.' After a good breakfast I went to my room. Spending the next hour swimming up and down my Olympic sized sunken bath, it was ace. When we checked out the following evening I thought, this is going to sting, I was right.

The company never said a word, but they never booked me into another scruffy hostel either.

'Hassi Messaoud? Where's that?' We had been chartered to take a huge oil pipeline shut off valve to a BP terminal in Algeria. As I collected our paperwork, I signed for, and stuffed a wad of five thousand US dollars into my pocket. This was to pay the airways and handling bills on arrival. It was early one Sunday morning. I'd never been to Algeria before, so I was looking forward to adding it to my list of places visited. There was a degree of urgency to this charter, because the inoperative shut off valve in the African desert, controlled the flow of oil being exported from the country. While the existing valve was broken, no oil was flowing from the region.

The Icarus Game

The flight down was great. Taking off from Coventry, flying south, across the Channel, right down Europe, and across the Mediterranean. We crossed the North African coast and flew deep into the Sahara Desert. Leaving the cool, damp, green of England and flying a vintage airliner over the different landscapes of central and southern Europe, over the bright blue Mediterranean Sea, and into the desert scape of north Africa is as good as flying gets.

We were greeted on the ground by the enthusiastic Algerian handling agent, everybody was pleased to see the valve we were carrying. It was quickly unloaded and sent to the BP compound. I was taken by the agent to the ATC building to settle the landing fees. My wad of dollars started to deplete. After being presented with an assortment of charges and paying them, I found myself in the handling agent's office, looking at his bill.

Ahh, this was about to get awkward. I was holding the agents bill for $2500. I had left Coventry with twice that amount in my pocket, I was now down to fifteen hundred. I asked if he could explain why his bill was so high, he detailed every item on it. Then announced that this bill did not include his personal commission. That was generous of him. I took out my wallet and slid the company AmEx card across the desk towards him. 'What's this? I need cash, US dollars.' 'I only have $1500 in cash.' At this point our fledging friendship took a dive.

'This is very bad; you can go to jail for not paying my bill.' The prospect of spending any time at all in an Algerian jail did not appeal. I had vivid flashbacks to watching the movie, 'Midnight Express'. 'I can arrange for Atlantic to transfer the money to you, that's not a problem.' 'No, I need cash. You are not leaving here until I am paid.' 'That might take a while, can you book me and my crew into a hotel?' 'No, you are not leaving this office until I am paid.' I looked around the office, no windows, grey painted brickwork, concrete floor, grey steel and Formica utility furniture. No air conditioning, over forty degrees centigrade, and a cast iron radiator, he must be kidding. Apparently, he wasn't.

He got up and left the room. The door was blocked by a paramilitary in a beret and blue grey fatigues carrying a machine gun. His overalls were faded, and his gun looked old and in poor condition, no doubt it worked just fine. I looked at the company's mobile phone on the desk in front of me, the battery was only half charged. I called Op's and got Barney, the American Op's officer. 'Barney, hi, it's Steve, I've got a problem.' I went on to explain my predicament, adding that my first officer and Gandalf the engineer were still outside on the aeroplane. Barney was his usual laid-back self, 'Gee, that's a problem, leave it with me.'

Why the agent thought I needed an armed jailer I don't know, I couldn't go anywhere even if I wanted to. The aircraft couldn't leave without ATC clearance, or a groundcrew with an air start machine. I certainly had no plans to walk across hundreds of miles of desert dressed as a pilot.

As I saw it, until the cash arrived, I was screwed, I was also hot, sweaty, hungry, and thirsty. My phone rang. 'Hi Steve, it's Barney, I'm trying to sort out a plan to get you guys out of there, but there's nobody else in the office on a Sunday.' Cheers Barney, I didn't feel any better. I had flown back into the stone age and was being held hostage. All over a measly thousand bucks. Fuck, I'd stuffed more than that into lap dancers' garters over the last few years.

The Icarus Game

As the afternoon drifted into evening, I became more and more familiar with my hot, airless cell. These were not good hosts, not so much as a glass of water, a cup of tea was well beyond them. I had been incarcerated for hours, was this just the start of a long, long wait for release. My mind was drifting to the stories of Gary Waite or John Peters and John Nichol, I clearly remembered the images on the TV of these bruised, maltreated guys and I thought how much worse my situation could become. I was cursing the presence of the radiator, why would anybody want one of those in the middle of the bloody Sahara Desert.

My phone rang again, jolting me from my stupor. 'Hi Steve, it's Barney, I've tried to speak to the British Consulate in Algeria, but there's nobody working on a Sunday.' Cheers Barney, my phone battery is running down, please only call me if you have good news.'

As far as I could work out, the Algerians now had their pipeline valve, they had no further use for me, my crew, or my aeroplane. They would happily leave us to rot. My armed guard was by now looking a lot less alert, he had stepped back from the doorway and was leant against the far wall of the corridor. I wandered to the door and tried to strike up a conversation with him. 'Hi, I'm Steve, what's your name?' He looked startled. I figured a jittery bloke with a machine gun was probably not what I wanted outside my makeshift prison, I went back to my seat and sat quietly.

I couldn't see how this situation was going to be resolved. It was certainly out of my hands. Time was passing very slowly. High on my priority list was getting a drink, I'd been sweating it out in this dank oven for hours. Separated from my crew, I had no idea how they were being treated.

My phone rang again, 'Hi Steve, it's Barney, I've spoken to the duty manager at the BP compound in Hassi Messaoud, he's on your case.' He was apparently going to have a whip round at the oil terminal and try to come up with some dollars. I doubted he would be successful. I should have had more faith. A couple of hours passed, and a group of people appeared in my gaol. At the front of the crowd was an Australian or perhaps New Zealander, he introduced himself as the BP depot, duty manager. I missed his name, I think it was John, whatever his name, he was a star. The Algerian agent was at the back of the crowd looking very sheepish.

John explained to me quietly that, 'All these people understand is force of numbers.' Hence the crowd. He had rounded up as many people as he could at short notice, marched into the airport with his posse and demanded to see me. This guy had a serious set of balls. He turned to the agent. 'I don't have your money; I can get it by Wednesday. If these guys don't leave right now, you'll never get it. Ok.' After a bit of discussion, John produced a promissory letter and made a show of having everybody in the room sign it.

At last, I was finally free to leave, after ten hours solitary confinement, in a sweat box, with nothing to eat or drink, under armed guard. The relief was colossal. As we all walked out of the terminal building towards the aeroplane, John turned to me and said, 'Whatever happens, don't still be in Algeria after midnight, they will throw you in jail and it'll take years to get you out.' I took him at his word and shook his hand, thanking the rest of his contingent. I made a point of ignoring the agent.

As I approached the aeroplane I was met by Gandalf. He led me to the bottom of the ladder, where another paramilitary stood with his gun. Gandalf introduced him, 'This is Abdul, I've been teaching him English.' 'That's great mate.' I turned to Abdul.' 'What English have you learnt?' The guard straightened up and enunciated, 'Wanker. Motherfucker.' Clear as you like, Gandalf was a good teacher.

Walking onto the flight deck, I climbed into my seat, and asked the first officer to call for start clearance. He enquired, 'Have you checked the fuel and done the walk around?' 'Nope, we're just getting out of this fucking shithole.' As we flew north, I checked the fuel and routing. We had enough fuel for the five-hour trip home, but we would be well out of duty. I asked the other guys, 'Would you like to divert somewhere for a night stop, or shall we go straight home?' I didn't care which option they chose, as soon as we landed, I was having a cold beer either way.

I was pleased to get home to Gay, she was already in bed by the time I got in. 'How was your day darling?' I told her all about it, she was getting used to my crazy, random work experiences. Even so, this one was definitely more radical than normal. I asked her, 'How was your day?' 'Quiet.' 'That's good, night night.'

Being struck by lightning is something that happens to aeroplanes now and again. I've had it happen regularly, once, or twice a year. Usually it's predictable, the weather radar shows up weather cells very clearly. Tonight, I was with a new first officer, Hugh from Dublin. He was cheerful company and full of blarney. We were descending into Liege through a stormy summer night, we'd turned on all the anti-icing systems and were trying our best to avoid the worst of the weather.

It was proving difficult, there was a line of thunderstorms across our path. I picked the biggest gap in the purple splodges on the radar screen and set a course for it. As we approached the squall line, the static around the aircraft increased. On the Electra, St Elmo's fire was a common phenomenon, it took the form of a sharp crack, like a gun shot and a blue flash starting from the wiper blade and tracking diagonally up the windscreen, through the heating element. This was often just a warning that worse was to come.

Hugh hadn't seen this before, he jumped out of his skin as the static build up discharged right in front of his eyes. 'Oh, Holy Jesus!' Was all he could say. We were in dense cloud and I was watching the radar screen, staying as far from the storm cells as I could. The clouds lit up around us every few seconds as the storm raged through the sky. Hugh's faith in the Good Lord was commendable, but we were not on his 'nice list' tonight.

I could see the faint blue glow forming on the top of the nose cone in front of me. I was halfway through telling Hugh to shut his eyes and look inside the flight deck, when there was a deafening crack and the brightest blue flash that engulfed the front of the plane.

Despite Hugh's supplications to the Almighty, we had been smitten by a bolt from the heavens. Hugh looked towards me, his pupils were still fully dilated from becoming accustomed to the dark flight deck, but his retinas were overwhelmed by the intensely bright flash, he was clearly shaken by the experience. 'Don't worry Hugh, you'll be able to see again just fine, in a minute or two.' We were met on the stand by the engineer. 'How is she?' It always made me smile how the engineers never asked after my health, just the wellbeing of the aircraft. 'Can you take a good look at the weather radar, please?' 'Of course, what's wrong with it?' 'It just got struck by lightning!'

The lightning strike had burnt several small holes through the glass fibre radome, put a hole through the radar scanner and damaged the wiring inside. It also temporarily melted Hugh's retinas. The storm was headed for the UK. So, we would be going through it again on the way home.

Chapter 36

Second Time Around.

By now, me and Gay had been together for quite a few years. Our three kids had grown up and drifted away, doing their own things. We now had the time to think about ourselves. Marriage was something we had discussed, deferring it until our other commitments had been dealt with. Now was our time. Neither of us wanted a big wedding, but we both wanted something to cement our dissipating family together. We decided a family holiday, with our wedding in the middle was the answer. We looked at the brochures and decided on Tobago, the capital of Tobago is Scarborough, perfect. My home from home in the Caribbean.

Arriving in the sun was a treat for all five of us, jumping into a couple of old, open topped Cadillac's, for the journey from the airport to the all-inclusive resort, started things off in fine style. Whilst the rest of the family were entertained on the beach or in the health spa, my treat of choice was scuba diving, in the crystal-clear water on the reefs around the island. The day before the wedding, which was to take place on the beach, I went on another diving trip.

The dive boat was anchored just off the beach, in chest deep water. I was with the other members of the dive, carrying the equipment through the water on our shoulders, out to the boat. There was a bit of a swell, and I was passing air tanks up to the divemaster on the boat. I miss timed my throw. As I threw the metal air tank up to the crewman, a wave lifted the boat, the tank bounced off the gunwale and dropped onto my face. Ow, that stung, it hit me square on the bridge of my nose, unzipping the skin instantly. Oh dear, I was in serious trouble now. I would be appearing in my wedding photos with two black eyes and a split open nose, looking like one of Mike Tyson's opponents.

For the rest of the dive, I was nicknamed shark bait. My face mask was filled with blood and water for most of the time. I couldn't even empty it out, for fear of attracting too much attention from the local predators. When I returned to our room Gay was seriously unimpressed. This was right up there with the other stupid things I'd done. The wedding photographer had his work cut out, photoshopping my self-inflicted facial deformities.

The Electra attracted quite a bit of attention as we landed at Wroclaw, in Poland. We were there to collect a load of cow hides, that were to be used to upholster cars. Atlantic had been chartered to fly them across Europe to Valencia. We went through the usual routines; I went with the agent and paid the landing fees, while George my first officer refuelled the plane. Then we waited for the freight to arrive. Then we waited some more. We got a message from Op's, half the freight was here, but it was being held up at the customs shed. This was going to take a while. As we waited the sun came up and it was a lovely day. Not so much for our plane though, it was old and leaky at the best of times. Fill her with fuel, sit her in the sun and she leaked worse than a government press office.

Steve Woodhouse

We went around the plane putting drip trays and buckets under the trickles of fuel. Our engineer, who was a contractor, had little experience with old aeroplanes and was getting very anxious. 'It shouldn't be leaking like this.' I tried to calm him down. He diagnosed a cracked main spar. This shaved chimp was the worst kind of mechanical hypochondriac. I went onto the flight deck and hid the tech log, just in time as it happened. 'I'm going to have to tech this plane.' Announced our engineer. He was supposed to be there to help, he wasn't licenced, or type rated, he was a prize pain in the arse. I told him to go away and polish his spanners, or something along those lines. 'Tecking' the leaking, imaginary 'cracked main spar' was the last thing I needed. I knew the aeroplane was behaving exactly as I would expect.

The only thing tecking this aeroplane would achieve is a mass of paperwork, an assortment of deferrals and exemptions to allow me to fly it. Either way I would still be at the controls, just carrying a few ounces more paper. I have been here plenty of times before. Get back to base and the company would then dig out a random set of x-rays, put the appropriate registration on it and declare the plane fit for service.

I phoned our engineering director and asked him why he'd employed this prick. 'He was the only applicant.' Was his honest reply. At that moment Hypo-mech appeared on the flight deck. 'I'm not flying any further on this wreck, I'm out of here.' He picked up his kit, walked across to the terminal, booked himself onto a budget flight to East Midlands, and was gone. I was glad to see the back of him.

Sitting on the apron, leaking fuel for hours is a good way to attract attention. A van pulled up alongside the plane and a uniformed officer got out. 'I need to search your plane for drugs.' This was going to be interesting. I explained that he was welcome to, but wasting his time. The plane had spent years flying around South America, Bolivia, Columbia, before we had bought it in Miami. He let his spaniel loose on the freight deck and it went crackers. We watched as this little dog yapped and scampered around the cabin; it was literally climbing the walls.

Every joint in this aeroplane contained residual traces of cocaine, or whatever else they grow in South America. The drugs officer would never find an elusive package, there wasn't one, his dog couldn't point at a specific place to look, it was driving the poor creature nuts. In the end they had to leave before the dog died of hypertension.

The first half of our freight arrived, and we loaded it onboard. Then we carried on waiting. A golf buggy arrived with a couple of burly characters wearing army style combat clothing. They were immigration officers and they wanted to search our freight. It had to be unloaded so they could be thorough. This all stank, somebody hadn't had their back hander, and was now making a pain in the neck of themselves. I contacted the loaders and had the freight offloaded onto the tarmac. The immigration officers started to dismantle the entire load, the banding tapes were cut, and each hide was moved. I was running out of patience. Eventually the big, camouflaged official announced they were finished.

'No, you haven't.' I said as I stood in front of him, a little too close for his comfort. I then went on to explain to him that the freight was no longer fit for air transport, and what's more, HE was going to put it back together! I don't think he had been poked in the chest by a relatively small, but very arsey

Yorkshireman before. His gun wasn't going to help him here. He really didn't know what to make of me. It's surprising what you can get away with when you wear gold braid and put your mind to it. I watched for the next hour, as the two immigration imbeciles, tried to reassemble our load with a roll of sticky tape.

As the freight was going back onto the plane, a car pulled up with the customs shed manager in it. She looked to me, as though she had been an Eastern European shot putter in a previous life. 'There is a problem with the paperwork for your freight.' This was the third piece of harassment I'd had that day. I explained that the paperwork was her job not mine, and what's more if the freight didn't appear soon, it would be staying in Poland. We would simply leave, empty.

Atlantic starred at this point. We had been sat on the aircraft all day and were running out of duty. Op's idea was genius, if we say you were in a hotel all day, you can start a fresh duty period when the freight arrives. Brilliant, why didn't I think of that, maybe because I didn't fancy staying awake and working thirty-six hours straight, 'Not a chance!'

Atlantic had little choice, the customer was given their options. They decided to fly another crew out to replace us. The Polish officials that had tried to give us a hard time, looked on as the Lear jet containing a fresh crew taxied up alongside our Electra. We handed the aircraft and by now a full load of freight to our colleagues and climbed aboard our executive ride home.

It had taken me twenty minutes to reach the start line, by the time I got there the leading elite runners, and eventual winner Hendrik Ramaala were already half way around the course. I had been running since I was a kid, this was my first major event. I had no doubts I could finish the Great North Run, asking for sponsorship was obvious, I was going to do it anyway. Raising some money for a good cause in the process was a no brainer. I was amazed just how generous my friends were.

The build up to the event and the race itself was a weekend carnival. Newcastle puts on a fantastic show every time this event is staged. Running in a crowd of fifty thousand people, past bands playing and people cheering their support, is an experience everybody should try at least once. By the six mile point I was aching all over, as I passed a motorised wheelchair equipped with oxygen bottles, I looked across at the occupant, he was driving the thing with his chin. My only thought then was, get a grip Woodhouse, if this fella can make such a monumental effort, so can you. Two hours thirteen minutes and three seconds after the start I was done. I was knackered but felt a million dollars.

The Electra was a lovely aircraft to fly, and in its earlier incarnation as a passenger airliner it was state of the art. Lockheed did a beautiful job in creating a luxury aircraft for the sixties. Unfortunately, I missed her heyday, getting to fly her after the nice furnishings had been ripped out, and the aeroplane was converted into a freighter.

One of the biggest bones of contention about this conversion was the decision to remove the toilet. After all, night freight involved long hours in the flight deck and lots of coffee. The diuretic effects of this were obvious to everybody, except Atlantic's management. The answer was obvious and cheap, a bucket in the courier station would be perfectly adequate. Not the most aesthetic, but functional. This worked fine until the first encounter with a bit of turbulence. Then the flaw in the plan could be smelled by everybody.

This was upgraded by somebody who enjoyed camping, and decided the new solution was to use a porta potty. A stroke of genius that was to create one of the company legends. True or not, it was frequently told in the wee hours, miles above the earth. The porta potty is simply a toilet bowl above a storage canister all moulded in plastic. The two compartments being separated by a plastic flap. Once you'd used the toilet you pulled the handle on the front and the flap slid away, dropping the contents of the bowl into the storage container. The flap was then slid back into position ready for the next user.

One minor thing eluded the person with this brainwave. An aeroplane does not have the same characteristics as a caravan, it is pressurised. On the night in question, one of the founding directors of the company, decided that the time had come for him to christen the porta potty. It worked perfectly, the lid was raised, the pan was filled with recycled MaxPax coffee, and all was well. Our luckless boss pulled the flap to drop the bowl contents into the bowels of the bog.

At a couple of miles above the ground, the pressure difference between the storage canister and the aeroplane cabin was significant. The weeks old contents of the toilet were nicely pressurised. The explosive, effervescent shower of effluent that followed, covered not only the courier station, but also our managing director. Being an old farmer, he brushed himself down and his response was typically pragmatic. 'Huumph, that bog needs sorting out.' The solution, a small hole drilled in the flap to equalize the pressure. This arrangement lasted for years.

One rather more practical problem was never really sorted out though. Whose job it was, to empty the honey pot (toilet). Clearly filling it up, was mostly the responsibility of the flight crew. Trying to prise your average sky god out of their comfortable seat, to empty the bog, however, is an uphill struggle. Topping up and draining fluids on the aircraft is a servicing function, and servicing is carried out by the engineers. Therefore clearly, emptying the pisspot, was an engineer's job. You can imagine the response to this well constructed piece of logic. 'Empty your own pisspot.' Consequently, it rarely got done.

The week had been a breeze. Running around the DHL network to and from Brussels and Scandinavia. Towards the end of the week the toilet was starting to overflow. This is something that is hard to ignore, so I called up the handling agent in Brussels, requesting the honey wagon on arrival. We pulled onto stand on a remote apron known as coffin corner to the crews of the leaky, aging freighters that used it, and were met by the usual buzz of activity.

Loaders, fuel trucks, handling agents and the honey wagon. Once the aircraft was unloaded and the initial frenetic activity was over, I was faced with a bemusing sight. A figure jumped from the access ladder onto our loading deck. He was full of energy and without a doubt the happiest Belgian I had ever met. He was the airport toilet servicing truck operator. Clad from head to foot in rubber waterproof clothing and wearing Wellington boots, he looked like a man who had found his true vocation in life. His arrival was announced with a fanfare of explanation. 'I have come to service your toilet.' He thrust a rubber glove encased hand in my direction. My hands immediately retreated into the sleeves of my shirt.

The toilet service truck is a custom-built vehicle with a storage tank that can hold several thousand litres of waste. Coupled to an assortment of pumps, pipes, and valves, to extract the contents of a Jumbo Jets toilets very quickly. I directed my new best friend to the overflowing mess in the courier station. He grinned at me as he brushed past, clutching twenty-five litres of fermenting urine in his hands, and disappeared down the ladder.

He poured this into the waste tank on his truck. He then turned to me as he shouted, 'You want blue (disinfectant)?' Why not, in for a penny and all that. He positioned our toilet under a large pipe and opened a valve. The wrong valve apparently. Within a couple of seconds, the entire contents of the truck's storage tank was deposited on the ground, washing over the operator's welly clad feet. You wouldn't believe how far toilet waste spreads. The happy Belgian did the only sensible thing he could. He threw his hands in the air and danced around in the stinking slurry, whilst shouting expletives at his 'Stupid fucking truck'.

I started to gain a new found respect for airport ground staff after that chaos. Hard working people, doing a challenging job, often in horrible conditions. All with a healthy dose of humour.

Chapter 37

End of the Atlantic Line.

The job with Atlantic had been brilliant. Varied, exciting. Not to mention, slightly mental at times. Working around the edges of legality, had never bothered me. Most misdemeanours can be rectified with a little creative book keeping or turning a blind eye. Stretched duty periods, flying semi-serviceable aeroplanes, slight excesses in the freight carried. All these things can be lost in the mass of documentation. Even if you know where to look, you'd be hard pressed to find them.

For me, the end of the line came after a brief row with the General Manager. The aircraft was prepared for its nightly short flight to Belfast. When the freight arrived, the load team supervisor came to me and said, 'We've got a problem with this load, there's no security seals on the lorries container.' This meant that as far as me and the load supervisor were concerned, this cargo had not been security screened.

Even if it had, there was no safeguard to ensure that it hadn't been tampered with on its way to the airport. Imagine strolling onto a flight with whatever you want to carry in your baggage, and not having to go through any kind of security checks. This would be unthinkable, but it's what was about to happen with this load. As the captain of that flight, it was my responsibility to ensure all the safeguards guaranteeing a safe flight, and the wellbeing of everybody working around the aeroplane were upheld.

Calling Op's, I explained the situation. The customers depot that loaded the trailer had screening facilities, along with the correct approvals, but they had cocked up, badly. The Op's officer called the customer and then got back to me. 'The customer says that the freight has been screened, they just forgot to seal the trailer. You've got to take it as it is.'

'Not a fucking chance. You can return the load to the customer to re-screen it and seal it, or we can screen it here, at the airport.' This argument went on for ages. I wasn't taking this suspect freight anywhere.

After this protracted discussion with Op's, I asked the loaders to take the freight to their x-ray facility and screen it. The company could argue the toss in the morning. Finally, we got underway, albeit a couple of hours late. I was to leave the plane in Belfast and get a scheduled flight home later in the morning. By the time I walked back into Op's at Coventry I was knackered. The general manager was waiting for me, he was fuming. 'You don't decide what we carry on our aeroplanes.' He raged. 'You don't even need to know what the freight contains.' I guess the customer was trying to cover their mistake by shifting the blame onto me. I was having none of that. 'Whatever I carry, it must be security screened, that load wasn't.'

I went home re-living the events of that shift. The more I thought about it, the more aggrieved I felt. I wasn't going to be pressured into breaking the law so seriously by my employer, ever. The security screening of freight, passengers and baggage is covered by International anti-terrorism legislation. This is not a set of rules it's healthy to break. The more I thought about it, the angrier I got. I had a few hours' sleep and drove back into work. I wasn't going to remonstrate with the general manager again, that would be a waste of time. I went and sat down with the company's security manager.

The outcome of this long and detailed meeting was…… nothing. A bit of teeth sucking and shoulder shrugging. It may have just been a simple mistake. My action had prevented any breach of the law. I went home, got onto the internet, and filled out a few job applications with other companies. This was one liberty too many for me.

The following week I was back in Leipzig, passing the days as best I could with my first officer. Exploring the area we found ourselves in, was my favourite part of the job. To break the week up I'd hired a car. I grabbed my FO and headed across Eastern Germany. We were going to spend the afternoon in Colditz Castle. It was somewhere I was aware of from the TV series 'Colditz,' when I was a kid. Looking up from the coffee shop in the town square, you had to be impressed by this imposing building on top of the hill overlooking Colditz town. It's a very long way from Blighty.

We had booked ourselves onto a guided tour and were sat outside the solitary confinement cells, waiting for our guide. Part of the castle is now used as a hostel and offices. A 'management sort' in a suit and tie walked past us, he looked down on me and my FO like we were something he'd trod in. I couldn't resist it, as he marched away from us, I whistled the theme tune from 'The Great Escape.' I could see the veins on his neck pulsating as he opened his office door.

We spent the rest of that afternoon being shown around the castle by a very knowledgeable German lady. She showed us all the escape tunnels they knew about. They think there may still be one or two tunnels they haven't found yet. Apparently, they didn't find the radio set, that was hidden in an attic, until renovation work in 1985 uncovered it. The tunnels were not what I expected, they were incredibly ingenious. Some were even carved through the fabric of the castle, cutting through ancient oak beams and solid granite bedrock. All excavated with makeshift tools, in virtual silence. Some of the escape attempts were very well planned, others, spur of the moment ventures.

Standing in the cells that hadn't changed since my childhood wartime heroes had left them was humbling. POW's like, Douglas Bader, Airey Neave, David Stirling, and a host of others were held captive there. Looking at the pictures they had drawn on the walls during their incarceration, staring through their windows, their eyes, at the enemy surrounding them. Trying to imagine the feelings of desolation, defiance, and their determination to get back into the fight.

My job applications had born fruit. Within a few weeks I was sitting in a flight simulator at Farnborough. Being put through my paces by one of Flybe's examiners, the sim ride was straight forward. The next stage was a series of personality profile type tests, followed by an interview. This was conducted by a Flybe management pilot and the HR manager at Exeter.

It mainly consisted of technical and air law type questions. All the type of stuff I'd paid little attention to for years, by now it was second nature. Flybe were expanding rapidly and were short of pilots, at the end of the interview I was asked, 'Do you know if any of your colleagues would be interested in working here?' 'I doubt it, they all laughed at me when I said I was coming to you for an interview.' Probably not the best way to conclude the meeting, the interviewers smiled through gritted teeth.

Before the end of the week, I got the phone call offering me a job as a Dash 8 Q400 Captain. I didn't have to think too long before accepting it. Gone were the days of living out of a suitcase. Short haul flying involved getting home most nights. Ok salary. Beautiful.

If I thought flying brand new aeroplanes was going to be hassle free, I was in for a disappointment. The Bombardier Dash8 Q400 was beset with niggles. The whole thing was computerised, anything that was remotely out of tolerance set off a ding and a warning light. It could be frustrating, pulling circuit breakers or shutting everything down and starting again to get rid of nuisance warnings, with a cabin full of passengers. Everything had to be done by the book, gone were the days of common sense and discretion. Now the rules were all black and white and remarkably, they were applied.

This way of flying was going to take a bit of getting used to, so was the aeroplane. It flew ok, but it landed like a shopping trolley. After I'd completed my initial training, I was happy it wasn't anything I was doing. Experienced pilots were regularly clattering the thing onto the tarmac, with comments like, 'I spend more on chiropractors than I do on my ex-wife.'

Spending time on the M6 in a taxi was getting more regular, Flybe's pilot shortage meant a lot of travelling from base to base, standing in for non-existent colleagues. I was sat in the back of a nice Mercedes being driven to Manchester by a particularly annoying Indian. I knew he was Indian because England were playing India in a test match in Calcutta and doing lamentably. Two hours of being told how crap England were, and how great the masterful Indian side was, was starting to get on my tits. I wished that I knew enough about the game to argue with him, but I didn't.

My stint in Manchester was done for now, the suitcase I thought I'd got rid of was getting as much use as ever. As the lift reached the top floor of the multi-story carpark, I checked the hire car keys in my hand. The lift door tried to open, got half way and closed, then it opened half way and closed again. This had a certain comedy value, but I wanted to get home, I put my boot against one door, grabbed the other with both hands and forced them apart. A length of pressed steel dropped from above my head and clattered to the floor. I stepped over the debris on the ground, found my car and drove back to Birmingham.

As we took off from Birmingham, the EGPWS (Enhanced Ground Proximity Warning System) started shouting at me. 'Terrain. Terrain. Pull Up.' Of course, it could detect the ground, we had just taken off. It blasts out is warning over the loud speaker in the flight deck and through our headsets, there's no way to avoid it's nagging. We ignored it the best we could and continue our climb. After a couple of minutes disturbing the passengers in the front half of the plane, it finally shuts up. As we start our descent into Glasgow, the thing starts shouting again, it was like having a noisy retard on the bus, that everybody wishes would just sod off. We're still fifteen thousand feet above hitting the Scottish granite, and ignoring the warning some more.

The Icarus Game

On the ground, we test the system, and it works perfectly. This is going to be a long day. Going back to Birmingham the thing kicks off again. This time I get the engineers to check it out, it's fine. We set off for Dusseldorf and hope we've heard the last of the EGPWS nag. As we start our approach into Dusseldorf, the machine goes ding. The flap asymmetry light is on and the flaps have jammed, just as they had started extending. A flapless landing is no great hardship, but it does mean we have to go around. We need to make some changes to the landing speed settings and re-brief the approach.

After setting ourselves up, I apologise to the passengers, and start our second go at landing. As we settle into the descent, I can see the nose is very high, these aircraft are known to belt the tarmac tail first in the right circumstances (known as a tail strike, it happens when you have more than seven degrees nose up, at touchdown). I add five knots to our speed and the nose lowered slightly; I was happier now. We landed, taxied to our stand, and disembark the by now relieved passengers. This plane was being a pain, I was glad to hand it to the engineers and walk off it.

As we walked down the steps my phone rang, it was Flybe Op's. We want you and your crew to take the plane on the next stand and fly it to Birmingham. By now I was feeling jaded, we'd had three spurious EGPWS warnings and a flap asymmetry resulting in a nonstandard landing. This all adds to the tiredness and fatigue levels of the crew. I turned to Richie and asked how he felt, 'Knackered mate.' 'Me too.' Did we want to spend the night in Dusseldorf or fly one more sector back to Brum? Reluctantly we agreed to fly home.

We spent the flight trying to keep ourselves alert, mostly by talking nonsense, we were not at our best as we approached

Birmingham. Through the drowsy haze of our collective brains, we had not been concentrating nearly enough, and were rudely brought back to reality by the nagging EGPWS. 'Too Low, Flaps.' Hang on, this is a different plane. The ground was very close, the plane had flown down the ILS on autopilot. Oh shit, Flaps fifteen, Gear down, landing checks. We touched down as the last check on the landing check list was completed, four miles later than it should have been. As we taxied in, we knew we were in trouble, the FDM (Flight Data Monitoring) system would grass us up to the company. We filed our reports from the crew room and waited for the inevitable snotagram from Flight Safety.

We had the joy of a day trip to Exeter, to explain our shortcomings to the Flight Safety Manager. Watching the FDM animation of our flights, we got to re-live the flapless approach into Dusseldorf. For which I received a rollicking, for deviating from the published landing speeds. We then re-lived the sleepy approach into Birmingham, we both got a rollicking for that one. I got an extra dose for agreeing to the flight in the first place. Our punishment was to write an article for the company flight safety magazine.

As we left the office, we passed another crew in the corridor, 'Hi guy's, what have you done?' 'We had a tail strike at Gatwick.' They had flown the aeroplane we dumped in Dusseldorf, had another flap asymmetry, followed the published speeds and wacked the runway with the plane's tail on touchdown.

Chapter 38

I Love Passengers.

My SCCM (Senior Cabin Crew Member or No1) was a physically muscular, large, proud, gay man. He had worked as cabin crew for a lot of years and was very professional, he was also a lot of fun. My experience of cabin crew at this time, gay or otherwise was limited.

Pulling onto stand in Jersey at nine in the morning, we were met by the handling agent. He gave me the passenger numbers and load sheet, adding that one passenger had been offloaded for being drunk. The No1 heard this and praised the passenger's dedication to his hobby, 'Too drunk to fly, at nine in the morning, that's a good effort. Let me have a chat with him.' Lloyd left the plane and walked across to the departure lounge.

A few minutes later he emerged with his arm draped around the drunks' shoulder. He was whispering in his campest voice into the terrified looking passengers' ear. 'Now then darling, you're not going to give me any bother, are you?' The drunk was sat in the front seat opposite the SCCM for the flight back to Brum. He didn't take his petrified gaze off Lloyd. In fact, he barely blinked.

Having passengers arrested was one aspect of the job nobody had told me to expect. The first incident was trivial, an arsey passenger had got the hump, when he was told he had to pay for a bottle of water. He threw the bottle at the SCCM, yelling his annoyance at her. He was displeased. She told me the story, and the Airport Police boarded the plane, and arrested him for assault when we arrived on stand. He was lucky he only got arrested, some of the girls would have rammed the water bottle down his throat.

The next incident was altogether more suspicious. We were in the cruise going to Hanover, when the No1 called on the interphone. Two of the passengers were acting very suspiciously. I asked her to explain.

One had been in the toilet for the last twenty minutes, and wouldn't respond to repeated bangs on the door. The other was stood in front of the rear galley, preventing the No3 from leaving her seat. They were both travelling together and shared the same surnames. She described them as being physical, large men and said they were very intimidating.

Switching on the seatbelt sign, I made the usual PA. 'Ladies and gentlemen, this is the captain. We are expecting a little turbulence, so I have put the seat belt signs on, please return to your seats, and fasten your seat belts.' Everybody on the flight complied, except our two likely lads. By now the brother in the toilet had re-joined the main cabin, taking over the rear galley post, the other brother had moved to the front cabin crew station and was standing over the SCCM. They ignored all requests from the girls to retake their seats.

This behaviour was highly unusual, it was setting alarm bells ringing in my head, had they planted or retrieved something in the toilet. Were they intending to escalate their actions to violence. Were they providing a distraction for somebody else. Were they trying to work out how the cabin communication equipment worked? I had no idea, but there was no way they were going to intimidate my crew, and not get some hassle themselves. I arranged for the German Polizei to meet the aircraft on stand. As soon as the brakes went on and the engines wound down, I was out of my seat.

I told the No1 to stand behind me on the flight deck, I took her position in the exit. Thanking passengers as they left the plane and went down the steps. The Police were arranged in two rows, so the passengers had to file between them. As the two brothers passed me, I stopped the other passengers, stepped behind them and followed them down the steps, signalling to the Police that these were the two passengers I wanted questioned. They were arrested and taken away.

Then I had to explain my suspicions to a senior airport police officer, detailing the events during the flight. We carried out a search of the aeroplane, paying particular attention to the area's this pair had been. I set about the toilet cubicle with a screwdriver, removing all the trim panels. The police went through the plane with explosives and drugs, sniffer dogs. The whole process delayed us by two hours. It had created a lot of extra work for everybody, especially the cabin crew.

The following day I was on the same route, I was watching the passengers disembark at Birmingham, and there they were, walking away from the plane. Despite the events of the day before, and the mass of paperwork it created, Flybe didn't even have the good sense to revoke this pair of alpha male clowns' tickets.

Flybe started a new route into Waterford, I had to dig out a map to find it, it's in Ireland. During the pre-flight briefing me and my FO had a good look at the airport plan. It was our first time going there, I didn't want to discover anything unusual when it was too late. The first thing that struck me was the length and width of the runway. It's short and narrow, it's also downhill. We were heavy, with a full complement of passengers and luggage.

The weather when we arrived was filthy, gale force winds and horizontal monsoon rains. One thing I hadn't considered was the effect of the terrain around the airfield with the high winds. Turbulent doesn't really cover it. As we came down the approach my FO went quiet, which was unusual for her, I could see she was very nervous, so I gave her some checks to do to keep her busy. We banged and crashed all the way down the approach, keeping us on the centreline and going straight was requiring a lot of pedalling. We touched down and slowed to taxi speed, to the sound of loud applause from the passenger cabin. That was a first.

After a few weeks, somebody more observant than the rest of us, pointed out the Dash 8 needed a thirty-meter-wide runway, the width of the runway at Waterford was twenty-nine meters. The answer, send the maintenance man out with a van full of gravel and a shovel. Dig a half meter wide trench either side of the paved surface and fill it in with gravel. Apparently, that's cheaper than using tarmac.

We were sitting on stand, on the southeast apron at Edinburgh, looking at the door in the terminal building, waiting for our passengers to emerge from it. Everything was ready to go, ramp agents with yellow vests were stopping traffic to allow the passengers to cross the road, I was draining the last of my cuppa. The first of our passengers were being directed to their seats by the No1, we were even on time!

Holy shit, my FO and me both saw it together, a baggage cart had hurtled behind our ground power unit, travelling across the front of the aeroplane. Ploughing through the waiting queue of passengers, crashing to a stop against the steel railings.

Some of the passengers were thrown into the air as the truck mowed them down. It was carnage. I had my headset on in a second and was talking to ATC, 'We need, police, ambulances and fire trucks with lifting and cutting gear.' By the time I'd grabbed my yellow vest and got to the passengers on the ground, the handling agents and the first police unit were arriving. There was a lot of confusion, people hobbling about and dazed, one woman was on the ground and clearly needing help, she had taken the full force of the collision.

We took charge of the passengers that could get onto the plane, they were looked after by the cabin crew, those on the other side of the incident were taken back into the terminal and checked over by the ramp agents. This cleared the area for the ambulance crews and police to do their jobs. The truck driver was arrested and taken away. The accident was all over in a couple of seconds, one woman needed hospital care, everybody else was treated by the paramedics at the scene. Within an hour we had the passengers that still wanted to travel boarded and were on our way. Another day living the dream.

Steve Woodhouse

It was Christmas market season in Dusseldorf, we were taking a tram ride into the city centre to enjoy the festive spirit, hot chocolate, and cakes. I was sticking with the, all continental public transport is free line, but the girls insisted on buying tickets. I handed them a handful of loose change and they set about feeding it into the ticket machine on the tram. I saw the pack of transport inspectors get on the tram, and for the first time, totally ignored them. For once I had actually bought a ticket.

The inspectors came over to our group and we handed our tickets to them. 'These are short journey tickets, you have travelled too far on them, the fine is fifty euros, each.' Consternation swept through the girls, a fifty euro's fine, at Christmas, what about the kids presents. The inspectors were indifferent and insisted on payment. We don't have the money, we told them. At the next stop we were herded off the tram and marched across town to a cash point. This was a different sort of trip to the Christmas market.

We all grumbled as we handed over our cash, bloody jumped-up fascists, no heart, ruined the kids Christmas, mutter, mutter. We had all paid up, except Rhona, she clung tightly to her cash and flatly refused to hand it over. She apologised to the rest of us and then told the inspectors that she wasn't paying, so there. Unfazed the inspectors set us off on another forced march across town, this time to the nearest Polizei station. We waited while the inspector explained to the duty police officer, what a bunch of fare dodging crooks we were. Rhona was identified as the most hardened criminal amongst us for not wishing to pay the fine. The policeman explained in crystal clear English that she had two choices. Graciously pay the fine or spend the night in the cells, then explain herself to the magistrate in the morning.

The Icarus Game

This was getting better by the minute. Rhona finally capitulated, she handed over the crumpled notes, one at a time.

Another thirty minutes and our airport standby would be over. Endless, tedious hours sat around in the crew room waiting for the phone to ring was almost done. Then the phone rang, 'Don't you just hate it when that happens?' I said as the FO took the message from Op's. We were to fly an empty aeroplane to Southampton, drop it off and get a taxi back to Birmingham, that was going to take seven or eight hours.

Having printed off the paperwork we went out to the plane and tossed a coin to decide who would fly it. We rotated from the runway and selected the landing gear up, then our problems started. The three green undercarriage position lights (gear down and locked) turned red (gear travelling), the two main gear lights went out (gear up and locked), the nose leg however made loud banging noises, as it tried but failed to latch up. Pan, Pan, Pan. Out went the radio call to air traffic. We needed to fly around the airport for a while to sort ourselves out. We were sent out of the way of the other traffic, taking up a large holding pattern.

We had loads of fuel, giving us the luxury of time to work systematically through our situation. Talking over the problem between ourselves and reading the checklist, allowed us to come up with a plan. The main gear was working just fine, the nose gear was the problem, it was still hammering away in the wheel bay as we spoke. First, we had to try to lower the undercarriage, there is a set procedure for doing this in abnormal or emergency situations, so we followed it. It took an age for the undercarriage to drop under its own weight. We now had three wheels to land on, but no nose wheel steering. The cabin pressurization wasn't working either, but that wasn't a problem for us.

Landing as slowly as we could seemed like a sensible thing to do, so that would need full flaps, we were also going to stop on the runway. This meant we would need a tractor and towing arm to take us back to stand. We explained our plan to the controller, he told the ramp team and our engineers what we intended to do. It worked exactly as we hoped. After a gentle touchdown we stopped on the runway, shut down the engines and a tractor and towing arm came out to meet us. The engineer struggled for a few minutes to get the towing arm fitted. The nose gear, shock absorber had collapsed, leaving the front of the plane about six inches lower than normal.

Eventually we made it to the maintenance hangar. Our engineer crawled into the nosewheel bay, after a minute or two he re-appeared holding a big black Maglite. Whoever had worked in there last, had left it wedged on top of the undercarriage leg. That was an expensive oversight. On the Dash this would be out of sight during any normal inspection. As the nose leg was retracting under hydraulic pressure, the torch had sheared off the nitrogen charging valve, dumping the pressure from the shock absorber. It had then been rammed through the pressure bulkhead by the huge force of the travelling nose undercarriage leg. Remarkably when we tried it, the torch still worked, but the plane was knackered, for a while.

Flybe's Op's department had a lot in common with Atlantic, neither of them were shy at dragging flight crew out of bed to go to work. It didn't matter to them if you were on duty or not, they just needed a pilot. This was becoming a frequent occurrence and it was irritating. I resorted to turning my phone off on a night. They clearly weren't going to take the hint.

At three in the morning, I was woken from my deep sleep, on a day off, by the doorbell ringing. Who would ring my front door bell at this hour? I rummaged about and found some trousers, went downstairs, and opened the front door. There was a complete stranger stood on my doorstep. 'I'm here to collect you.' 'What !!!'

'I'm your taxi driver, Flybe have sent me to take you to Birmingham airport.' 'Wait in your car, keep the meter running, I'll be twenty minutes.' Unbelievable, even by Flybe's low standards.

Chapter 39

New Start.

Me and Gay had been living together for a couple of years, we both had homes which we had inherited from previous marriages. They were nice houses, but relics from our past lives. They were directly opposite each other in a quiet cul-de-sac. We alternated living between them to the bemusement of our curious neighbours.

Once the kids had moved out and were doing their own thing, we decided it was time to look for a home that we could make ours. We both wanted a project house and after a short search we found Rose Cottage. An idyllic Victorian cottage set in an acre of garden in need of a lot of TLC. It was a stone's throw from the Grand Union Canal and near a canal side pub, we thought it was perfect. We sold my house and moved into Gay's, using the proceeds from my sale as the deposit on our new home to be.

We started renovating the cottage, soon discovering the magnitude of the job we had taken on. The structural surveys highlighted a few faults, but once the old carpets and flooring were thrown out, and the floorboards lifted, it was obvious the place was about to collapse in on itself. The electrics were outdated and positively lethal, it was a small miracle the place hadn't burned down. The central heating was leaking and had been installed during the stone age. Worse than this though, large areas of the woodwork in the house was riddled with woodworm. Suddenly, we were faced with a property that needed gutting and rebuilding.

Undaunted, we started the renovation, by driving back and forth from Gay's house to Rose Cottage at every opportunity to work on it. Although it was only fifteen minutes' drive, the cumulative wasted time really dented our productivity, it was very tempting not to bother going at all for small jobs and progress was painfully slow. Clearly, we had to come up with a better plan.

There was an old static caravan in the garden, and the best of the outbuildings on the site was a large, prefabricated concrete garage. We made both structures watertight and started to move in, stacking all our possessions in the garage and living in the caravan. Within a few weeks we were living there full time, and Gay's house was on the market.

The work started in earnest and I was doing most of it myself to keep the costs down. The plumbing, heating and electrics were all ripped out. Then a start was made on the structure. The woodworm was treated, and the rotten timbers were replaced. All the time this work was going on there was a horrible stench in the house. Stale dog piss. We had noticed it when we first acquired the property, but couldn't work out where it was coming from. At first, we thought it was the carpets or curtains, they all went to the local tip, but the house still stank. After I discovered all the ceiling joists needed replacement, the source of the odour became apparent.

To replace the joists, I had to pull down all the old lath and plaster ceilings. It was a filthy job. Once the living room ceiling had gone to the dump the smell stopped. Above the living room was the master bedroom, and the previous owner kept a Doberman in the house. It had seemingly taken to using the bedroom as a toilet. The urine seeped through the floorboards and soaked into the living room ceiling. Disgusting. On the plus side the stink and general poor condition of the house, did help bring the price we paid for the property down significantly. There's always a silver lining.

Our timing couldn't have been worse, the summer was behind us and winter setting in. It was to be one of the coldest winters on record. The kitchen and bathroom were in the house, but we lived and slept in the caravan. We both continued to do fulltime jobs as well as the renovation.

When I was on early's, the fifty-yard dash from the caravan to the house for a shower was usually about three o'clock in the morning. Doing this in my dressing gown and flip flops was a rude way to wake up. As the coldest winter in years tightened its icy grip, the mercury dropped to minus fifteen, and this was augmented by several inches of snow. My daybreak sprint to the shower got quicker. Gay complained one morning that her nose had frozen to the duvet. I was stuck in a hotel in Belfast at the time, surrounded by four-star opulence and doing my best to be sympathetic. I'm not good at sympathy and have a habit of finding the most inappropriate things amusing.

Very soon after we moved in, we discovered that our next-door neighbours, the Boddington family, owned a border terrier called Meg. This dog was very noisy and evidently a very stressed little creature. It was routinely put out in their back garden in the morning and left there until late into the evening. They clearly didn't want the animal in the house with them, but had no

The Icarus Game

problem inflicting it on their neighbours. The dog on the other hand obviously needed a lot of attention that it wasn't receiving.

During the summer months it would be outside up to twelve hours a day. When outside it would run around the garden trying to yap itself inside out continuously. It appeared to have endless energy. The barking was very loud, high pitched and impossible to ignore. It was the other side of our paddock, seventy-five yards away and could still be heard clearly over the traffic noise on the nearby A5. When I was trying to work outside, I could only put up with it for a couple of hours, then I had to find something to do indoors.

After about twelve months, I had to do something about the dog's noise for my own sanity. I went next door and spoke to Alan, again, face to face in his office. I asked him as politely as I could to please quieten his dog down. He said he would try, but nothing changed. What kind of response did I expect from a used car dealer.

On the face of it, Alan was an amenable, sociable type of chap. In reality, he had a real chip on his shoulder. Although he'd built up a reasonably successful used car dealing business, he really resented anybody else that was trying to do well for themselves. One neighbour, a single woman with a severely disabled child, was the target of a lot of spite from Alan. He fancied himself as lord of the manor, and would readily bully anybody he disliked. Including apparently, single women with disabled children. One such attack backfired on him.

It was shortly after we moved in, and there was a group of neighbours on the Boddingtons driveway enjoying a barbeque. This was a neighbourhood event to celebrate the recent street naming, and was well attended. As the evening drew on Alan produced some fireworks, mostly large rockets. Initially these were fired straight up above the party. But soon the trajectory started to change, and the occasional rocket would be aimed, accidentally on purpose at the target of Alan's dislike, in this case the home of the single woman and disabled son down the road.

Aiming rockets on a flat course is not so simple, so he tried a few methods. One was to tuck the stick of the firework under the windscreen wiper blade of a 4X4 on his driveway, then lighting the touch paper. Perfect, he thought as the rocket shot just above the unfortunate woman's rooftop. He then cursed when he realised that the heat from the rocket had wrecked the paintwork and melted the windscreen on his own car. I smiled at this little act of karma.

This open act of aggression in front of his neighbours was clearly intended to send a message. Nobody at the event wanted to reprimand him, and potentially become a target themselves. Being new to the area I certainly didn't intend to rock the boat. Not yet anyway.

The yapping dog continued unchecked, so I got in touch with the local council's environmental department and was advised to keep a diary, and read the information on their web site. Dawn 'til dusk, seven days a week, didn't need writing down to remember. I think because we lived in an isolated spot, there weren't many other neighbours to complain to the council.

Obviously because not many people lived here, the environmental officers didn't respond constructively at all. You can only leave so many messages on answer phones before you work out it's a waste of time. This was infuriating. I spoke to

The Icarus Game

other neighbours and the consensus was the dog was a nuisance. Very much the fly in the ointment. Getting them to complain though was fruitless, nobody wanted to upset their selfish, narcissistic neighbours.

The renovation was progressing well, and eventually we had done enough to move into part of the house. We had heating and running water. Luxury. Overall, the building work took about two years, the result was just what we had imagined. We were delighted with our efforts.

The house had taken shape and now it was time to look outside. We had a three-quarter acre paddock, about a quarter of an acre of garden, and some tumble-down outbuildings to play with. This was new to us and we really didn't have a clue where to start. Even with a heavy-duty ride on mower, the grass in the paddock took four hours to cut, and if it was left more than a week or two it was an even harder job. There was also a couple of hundred meters of spiky hawthorn hedge to trim and some pretty big trees around the place. A lot of hours working outside. All with the constant soundtrack of yapping dog.

We thought a few sheep in the paddock would keep the grass trimmed and ease the workload a little. So as a trial I spoke to a local farmer and offered him some grazing for his sheep. He had a dozen rams that he wanted to keep separated from his ewes, so he brought them around. I had no idea that sheep could be this big and powerful. Although they were docile enough, if they decided to push past you, they were muscular enough to do it.

I had gone out for a ride on my motorbike with friends on this sunny Sunday afternoon. Gay was sitting in the living room watching television and doing some knitting. She was engrossed in her own little world, when she became aware that she was being watched. Glancing up from her knitting towards the patio doors, she needed a second or two to process what she was seeing; she nearly dropped a stitch. There were half a dozen large white woolly faces peering into the living room at her. I had left the gate between the garden and the paddock open and the rams had gone exploring. Gay had never been around livestock before, and was at a loss what to do. She decided to shoo them back into the paddock from her chair. That did nothing.

She had no choice but to put down her knitting and go outside to deal with them. Sheep generally don't like things that aren't sheep, and if they are approached will simply move away. This was exactly what they did when Gay came out of the back door. Before she knew it, she ended up with a small flock of rams at the bottom of the garden. Even further from the paddock gate than they had started. She then spent the rest of the afternoon herding them up and down the garden, until eventually they wandered back into the paddock. They seemed indifferent to their excursion; Gay was worn out.

Having animals around the place was great, but there was a problem. The sheep always congregated as far from the neighbour's boundary as they could, and stayed there. The yapping dog was a real threat as far as these animals were concerned, they stayed as far away from it as they could. I certainly sympathised with them. They were only grazing a small area of the paddock and soon the grass was so short, it was not giving them the nutrition they needed. I had to contact the farmer and ask him to take his rams back. He had some choice advise what to do with the Boddingtons and their pest of a dog.

The Icarus Game

Shortly after the sheep had gone, I was in the vegetable patch trying to keep the weeds at bay. After the usual couple of hours racket from next doors dog I decided not to give in to the neighbours, so I telephoned the house. George their son answered the phone, I asked for Alison. 'She can't hear the phone' he explained, because she was wearing her headphones. To block out the canine cacophony with loud music. When she eventually came to the phone, I asked if she could please take her dog in from the garden, and quieten it down. She clearly wasn't happy at anybody having the nerve to complain about her precious creature. The dog was taken in, but within twenty or thirty minutes it was back out, continuing to be a noisy nuisance.

The house was coming on nicely, so it made sense to start on the lifestyle aspects of our enterprise. We quite fancied some livestock and having no experience whatsoever we started with some chickens. I built a run for them out of timber and wire, making it as fox proof as I could. Inside the run was a small wooden henhouse. We got two chickens to start with and began learning how to keep them.

We were both quite taken with the personalities of the different birds, and referred to them as the two fat ladies, Clarissa, and Jennifer. They were kept in a free-range sort of way, having the run of the paddock and garden during the day. We put them in their house on a night, calling them in by rattling a tin of food. It always made us laugh watching them run towards us. Their legs and bodies were out of sync and totally out of proportion. When one eventually died, we replaced her with another two. Our little flock did very well, until one day I realised we had unwanted visitors in the chicken run.

Chapter 40

Heart Attack.

Rats are a feature of the canal; they live all along the bank. I'd caught a few around the small holding. Generally, if I saw one, I would just shoot it. These latest visitors were totally brazen though, they had dug a tunnel and built a nest right under the hen house. I wasn't putting up with that. My first line of attack was to go into the hen house, armed with a shovel and an air rifle. My plan was simple. Dig up the tunnels and nest. Anything that moved in striking distance got hit with the shovel. Anything that ran away got shot. It worked just fine. One rat lobotomised with my spade and one shot was a good hour's sport.

Thinking I'd seen the last of our rodent visitors, I was to be disappointed. Within a few weeks they were back. This infestation was going to need a bit more ingenuity to resolve. I hatched plan 'B'. A bit of explosive arson should do the trick. I got a large fizzy drinks bottle and cut the base off it. Attached a meter of hose to the spout and turned the whole thing upside down to make a sort of long funnel. I wrapped the hose in oil and petrol-soaked cloth to fashion a fuse.

The cloth wrapped hose was then pushed into the tunnel and on into the middle of the rat's nest. The entrance hole around the tube was sealed with a spade full of gravel to prevent escapees. A gallon of unleaded was then poured into the bottle and flowed through the hose into the heart of rat land. I put a match to the oily cloth and retreated.

Whoomph, it worked a treat. Bits of mud and flames shot from the various tunnels and the ground shook. It was like a mini version of the Somme. I looked around to see if the neighbours had noticed the earth moving. For some of them it would have been a first if they did. Happy with my efforts I retired for a brew.

That kept the long-tailed buggers at bay for a few months, but rats are persistent creatures and they returned. I tried traps with some success. I had already decided against poison because I only wanted the rat's dead, not any other indiscriminate wildlife. It was back to the spade and airgun plan. I went into the chicken run and started digging.

Almost immediately, Roland was out of his tunnel and running around the chicken run. The greedy little git had gorged itself on so much chicken food, it could no longer squeeze through the wire mesh walls. In my wellies and shorts I chased after the rat that was in full flight, bouncing off the chicken wire walls. I must have looked a proper sight. They are very quick and agile critters. It was like playing squash with a shovel as the racquet and a rat as the ball. After a long, tactical rally the flat blade of my favourite Spear and Jackson came down squarely on the rat with such force the wooden handle broke. That took the edge off my pyric victory.

After chasing around for quite a few minutes, I was breathing hard with the effort. I'd played a lot of sport over the years, and being out of breath from physical exertion was a familiar sensation. I dropped the rats spatchcocked body into the compost bin, and walked into the kitchen grumbling to myself over the misfortune of my broken spade. I was still finding it hard to catch my breath while I put the kettle on.

After ten minutes had passed, I was getting concerned. I would normally expect my breathing and heart rate to return to normal after a minute or two. My heart was racing, and my breathing was becoming shallower and more of an effort.

Slipping out of my wellies I went through to the living room. All I could manage was to lay on the sofa. My breathing was becoming shallower and an aching pain was developing in my chest and left triceps. I had done enough first aid briefings over the years to recognise the symptoms. There was no way I was turning up in casualty looking like a rural vagrant, so I wheezed my way upstairs and got into some decent clothes.

At this point any normal, sane person would have dialled 999 and sat back to wait for the ambulance. Mr 'I can take care of myself' had other ideas. I got into my car and drove to the local doctor's surgery. Sometimes me and a thinking straight don't go well together.

Walking into the waiting room, I said to the receptionist 'I needed to see a doctor.' She looked up from her computer monitor and said, 'the next bookable appointment is a week on Thursday at 11:00'. 'I don't want an appointment; I need to see a doctor now.' As I clearly couldn't breathe or stand up to well, she relented and called the nurse. The nurse led me into a treatment room and connected an ECG monitor. The doctor arrived with his stethoscope, had a quick listen to my chest and asked the nurse to call an ambulance. I was then given an aspirin and a puff on a GTN (glyceryl trinitrate) inhaler. Everything was done quietly and calmly. Apart from the pain, I felt relaxed about the situation.

Steve Woodhouse

The nurse asked if I'd like her to call my wife, to let her know what was going on while we waited for the ambulance.

Shuffling out to the ambulance with the help of a paramedic, I was settled down on the gurney. It was an all-female crew, driver, medic, and a trainee. The journey to Northampton General was a right giggle. Once the girls found out how I gave myself a coronary, things got a lot more jovial. The driver was getting stick from her crew for abiding with the speed limits even with the blue lights and sirens blazing away. She had just been nicked for speeding and was scared to collect any more points on her licence. She'd lose her job if she did.

When we arrived at casualty the farce continued. I was wheeled out of the ambulance on a trolley, then accompanied into casualty by the three paramedics. We were given a numbered ticket, and all of us had to wait for the triage nurse. So, for half an hour the ambulance and its crew were stuck at Northampton General casualty department, unavailable to respond to another call until I'd been accepted as a patient by the hospital. I was still in casualty when Gay arrived. She had rushed straight from work and was very worried about me. After she saw I was still breathing and checked I had clean pants and socks on, she calmed down a bit.

Several hours sitting in a corridor, was followed by more ECG's, more doctors with stethoscopes, I was finally seen by a cardiologist. He bet his wages that I had suffered no more than a bout of indigestion, he never did pay up. As a precaution I was sent to the cardiology ward for observation. The diagnosis for a heart attack is quite a prolonged business. Symptomatic diagnosis (can you tell me where it hurts) is unreliable so the clinicians rely on a blood test. They are looking for the presence of an enzyme called troponin. This is released by the heart into the bloodstream, and tested for about twelve hours after the heart has suffered a trauma.

The blood test result came back after around fifteen minutes, it was positive. The ward staff started with blood thinning injections of Clexane every ten or fifteen minutes, and I was booked in for an angiogram the next day. This ended up being cancelled because outpatients take priority over patients on the ward. The good cardiologists are incredibly busy. The useless ones are left downstairs to misdiagnose heart attacks.

I was wheeled into the treatment room a day later for my angiogram. The room was quite large, with a separate control room along one side behind a wall of glass. The main treatment room was dominated by an X-ray machine and a bank of TV monitors. I was being treated by a surgeon and couple of nurses. The consultant was in the control room and in contact with the main area via an intercom. During the usual pleasantries, 'this won't take long, you won't feel a thing', I was given a sedative and a local anaesthetic in my right wrist.

They certainly had this down to a fine art and were wasting no time. The surgeon set about my wrist with a scalpel and after some difficulty found my radial artery into which he inserted a wire. The wire is a fine capillary tube that is used to introduce contrast dye into the bloodstream. This makes your blood visible to X-rays. I was laid on my back watching the TV monitors, absolutely fascinated. It took the surgeon just a second or two to get the wire from my wrist, through my arteries past my collar bone and into my heart. I could see its rapid progress on the real time X-ray. This also showed my own heart beating on the TVs.

The consultant was giving directions to the surgeon via the intercom. 'Take a look in this artery". "I need a measurement from that artery'. Fairly quickly, they had a clear picture of what had happened. Over the years a layer of plaque had built up inside my coronary arteries, being deposited in increasing amounts on the inside of my arterial walls. At some point this plaque layer had cracked, my blood thought this crack was an injury. It then did what blood does and formed a clot over the cracked plaque. This clot blocked the artery (the LAD, left anterior descending) preventing blood from reaching a vital heart muscle. The muscle stopped contracting. My heart was no longer pumping blood around my body the way it should. I'd had a myocardial infarction or an M.I.

This, I felt was grossly unfair. I was only fifty years old; I didn't smoke at all. I'd never used recreational drugs; I didn't drink excessively. I had a healthy diet and had done plenty of exercise all my life. I may as well have enjoyed myself and not worried about the outcome. What a rip off my healthy lifestyle had been.

During the procedure, I was chatting with the medical team, when they found out about the whole rat saga the piss taking went to a whole new level. I was treated with a large dose of a blood thinning drug called ReoPro which is made from mouse antibodies. "Your heart attack was caused by a rat and we're going to mend you with a mouse. Ha Ha Ha. Medical humour is an acquired taste. Within a few hours I was known by the entire ward staff as the rat man in bed eight.

After staying on the cardiology ward for a few more days, I was scheduled for another angiogram, to see if the ReoPro had done its job. The pain had subsided, and my breathing was back to normal. I even managed to walk around a little on the ward.

Laid out on a hospital trolley wearing a regulation gown, I was wheeled into the same treatment room for the second angiogram. I was under the care of the same consultant as before, but the surgical team was different. Another sedative and local anaesthetic in my right wrist and the surgeon started digging in my arm with his scalpel. I explained that the last time the surgeon had found it tricky to locate my radial artery, so he decided to go in through my femoral artery. This runs up the inside of your leg in very close proximity to your delicate nether region.

He told the nurses to apply another local anaesthetic to the top of my leg. The nurses were both in their thirties, the one with the syringe in her hand was wearing glasses. I looked at them and grinned. In my best pilot's voice said, 'ladies if you're going to poke around down there, I'd better warn you, it's an impressive sight'. They looked at each other and giggled. Then the nurse armed with the syringe lifted my gown. Both nurses burst into hysterical laughter. There was really no need for that. Glasses nurse with the little prick in her hand was laughing so much, tears were rolling down her cheeks and smudging her lenses. As she was just about to stick her needle into my leg very close to my pride and joy, I was rethinking the wisdom of being a smart mouthed twat.

The wire was threaded in through my leg, and in no time was back in my heart. The examination showed the drugs had worked and the blood clot was dissipated. At the end of the procedure came the bit I hadn't expected. The surgeon took what looked like a plumber's mastic gun, and stuffed it into the hole in my leg. Some of these medical instruments are very familiar to me now. He then filled my femoral artery with a collagen plug to stop the bleeding. That made me squeal.

Everybody was laughing and wishing me well as I left the treatment room. I like to think I may have brightened their day up a little. I was wheeled back onto the ward and feeling no worse for the whole experience. I'd been back on the ward for about half an hour when I was aware of a wet sensation around the top of my legs. I lifted the blankets to look. I was just hoping that I hadn't wet myself. It took a few seconds to process what I saw. Fluid was oozing from the incision in my leg. It looked like very dilute blackcurrant juice. It was in fact my very diluted, watery blood and the wet patch on the sheet was growing at an alarming rate.

I pressed the call bell by my side and before I knew it three nurses were around my bed. One of the nurses put on some latex gloves and pressed the heal of her hand hard onto the leaking wound. They were discussing between themselves how long it would take for my highly volatile blood to clot, and stop running out of the artery. A long time was the joint consensus. This was my lucky day. Lots of nurses taking a close interest in the top of my leg. I always try to find a positive view were ever I find myself.

Chapter 41

Sick Leave.

When I called Flybe to let them know my situation, the level of optimism was quite amazing. "Ok I'm sure you'll be back to work in no time. Take care". It was like I'd called in sick with a cold. I knew my medical situation was serious, I'd been lucky to survive. Being relatively young and physically fit had apparently counted heavily in my favour. The next few months were going to be an uphill struggle to recovery. My future as a pilot was also in doubt. I knew the CAA would have a rigid set of rules to deal with my predicament. The most important thing for me to do before I left hospital, was to collect every piece of information I could lay my hands on. Details of my diagnosis and treatment had to be handed to the licence regulators on a plate, if I was to keep my career.

Explaining this to my consultant during one of his ward visits, he was more than happy to provide all the information I needed. When I was discharged though, the ward manager was a lot less forthcoming. He told me I would have to request the information from the hospital administrators. Despite my feeble condition I couldn't accept that, so I simply refused to get off my bed or leave the ward.

The ward staff were at a loss what to do. How would it look for them if they tried to move a sick bloke with a dicky ticker, and I had another cardiac in the process? Not good. After an hour or so, my sit in bore results. The consultant appeared at my bedside and I explained to him why I was still blocking his bed. 'Oh, that's your paperwork on the desk'. It had all been prepared, but the ward staff hadn't been told what to do with it. Paperwork and medication in hand, Gay helped me with the slow shuffle out of the cardiac ward and into the car.

After a couple of days at home I started to feel a little more confident in my abilities, so Gay and me talked about her going back to work. Following a phone call to the CAA I was told that my medical certificate was suspended, which wasn't a surprise. The next day a letter arrived telling me I was medically unfit to fly, and my license was suspended for the next six months. That was the earliest time they would even discuss my situation. This seemed a little harsh, but I was in no fit state to argue. What was I going to do with a hundred and eighty-odd days at home?

I could get myself out of bed, washed and dressed by the end of the week, so Gay decided it was safe to leave me on my own for at least part of the day, which would allow her to return to work. I could get to and from the kitchen ok, so I thought I'd start to build up my exercise levels with a walk around the garden, that would do me good. I ventured out of the back door into the garden and shuffled the fifteen meters to the paddock gate. A journey that would usually take a second or two took several minutes. By the time I reached the paddock I was exhausted. I sat down on a rock and looked out across the expanse of ground. I barely noticed next doors dog yapping, as I studied the length the grass had grown to. The large garden that had once been the source of a lot of pleasure was now feeling like an acre of liability, littered with semi derelict outbuildings.

The Icarus Game

Sitting in the living room looking around me, I made a mental note of all the repairs and improvements I wanted to do while I was off work. Then I started sorting them into the order which I thought my recovery would allow me to carry them out. Initially it was going to be very slow, but I was sure that once I got moving things would improve quickly.

The first week or two was busy with phone calls from friends, relatives, and work, all concerned about my health and curious how I'd managed to 'give myself a coronary'. Like it was a matter of choice, or from associating with infected people. All the focus at this point was on getting better, and back to work.

Flybe allocated me a 'management friend' who was to be my primary contact with work. Dave was my base manager and lived close by. I'd known him for a while and we shared an interest in old motors. His interest was classic cars, mine, motor bikes, so we had plenty to chat about. He is an easy going and sociable chap, I looked forward to his regular visits. It was a chance to catch up on the crew room gossip.

His first visit was entertaining for me, less so for Dave. We were discussing my condition, the diagnosis process and prognosis. I was being very graphic with the details, and may have used the words blood and muscle tissue once or twice too often. Dave, it seems has an aversion to blood and all bodily functions that should remain unseen.

When I put my angiogram video on the computer, pointing out the blood flowing through the arteries in my heart, along with a detailed description of the bits that had silted up and failed, it was all too much. The colour drained from his face and he had to support himself on the fireplace. I looked up at him whilst I was giving my ad hoc anatomy monologue. He looked like a corpse. I sat him down and made him a fresh brew. After that the conversation was reverted to chrome plating and camshafts.

Filling in my time was no problem for the first few weeks. Watching TV and drinking tea suited me just fine. Having spent most of my time working odd hours, I hadn't seen a lot of the programs, so it was a bit of a novelty. Cooking and engineering shows were my preference, but as engineering was going to have to wait until I was stronger, I decided to give cooking a bash. I got pretty good at baking bread, and a steady supply of freshly baked crusty loaves was nice to have.

Looking longingly out of the windows at the tumbledown outbuilding in the paddock, I wondered if I was fit to restore it. Once it had been a cottage, pre-dating the house by a hundred years or so. When it was somebodies home it had a suspended floor above stalls where the livestock lived. The original structure could be seen in the walls and floor. I had pulled the rotten roof down, to prevent it falling in shortly after we bought the property. Now the walls needed repairing and a new roof and new floors had to be installed to finish the job off, making it watertight once more. I started slowly, half an hour a day was all I could manage. Gay was resigned to the fact I wasn't going to sit around and wait 'till I had recovered before I got started. She wasn't happy with my refusal to relax.

Steadily, I worked my way round the walls. Repairing the brickwork and replacing the woodworm infested, ancient lintels with concrete ones. I was proud of my brick laying and it improved quickly. With the walls finished I had to concede that putting on a tiled roof was beyond me. Running up and down ladders with piles of concrete roof tiles would end badly. It was time to call on my builder mate Steve.

Steve and his workmate started on the roof a couple of weeks later and I was promoted to teaboy. As the roof was a large area I incorporated a solar panel array into the build, it seemed a good idea at the time. Unfortunately, with pitiful feed in tariff rates I was never going to recover the extra cost. Lesson learned, do your sums before you spend your money.

I came out of the house one morning with tea and bickies, to find my builders up their ladder cursing and hurling abuse at next doors yapping dog. The thing was undoubtedly a nuisance, but I was surprised how quickly it got under the builder's skins. Once the effin' and blindin' had died down, we had a brew. Then I went to talk to the neighbours.

Alan was in his office, so I explained very carefully, quietly, and rationally that his dogs' constant noise was not acceptable. It was annoying me and my builders. Could he please make some effort to keep it under control? His response was predictable. "It's a dog, what can I do. I'll try, but that's all I can promise". What a lot of used car dealer bullshit. That discussion made no difference whatsoever.

Returned to my building site I told the guys what had been said. Steve volunteered, "No problem, I'll crack it's head with a shovel and bury it for you." I like builders, they're very practical. I had previously used this tactic on a rat, and that ended badly. It only took a second of thought to dismiss the shovel idea. I settled for leaving another message on the local Environmental officers' answerphone. A pointless exercise, but I felt a little better afterwards.

With the structural work finished, I carried on with the build and soon the derelict outbuilding became my mancave. It was fantastic. I filled it with my motorbikes and other boy's toys. Of all the things at Rose Cottage my mancave was without a doubt my favourite. It was used frequently, for everything from machining engine parts to brewing beer.

Time was passing by and six months had gone in a flash. I was feeling in good form, so I contacted the CAA to start the process of recovering my class one medical. I knew this was going to be complex and the sooner I could get things started the better.

First, I needed a cardiology report, so I found a cardiologist at the local hospital and booked an appointment. By the time I arrived I had a list of the tests and procedures the CAA required to be done. Things started easily with some form filling and vital statistics, then it was onto the treadmill with an ECG machine wired to me. Half an hour later I was puffing and sweating, but the ECG readout said I was still alive.

The last test on the list was a 'stress echocardiogram.' I had no idea what this involved. When I found myself in a treatment room wearing a hospital gown, with a cannular stuck in my arm, I was wondering how badly I really wanted to go back to work. The echocardiogram part was straight forward enough. I was laid on a treatment table with the doctor sat behind me, working on my chest with an ultrasound scanner. I could see the monitor and was following the procedure. Heart rate, blood pressure and a real time moving image of my heart. The doctor was taking measurements of valves and arteries.

Then came the fun part, dobutamine was injected into my arm via the cannular. My heart rate started to climb from around sixty beats per minute, as it increased, I asked the doctor what rate he was aiming for. "About double your resting heartbeat. A hundred and twenty to a hundred and forty beats a minute will be fine." Steadily more dobutamine was injected, my heart rate stabilised at a hundred and fifteen beats a minute. More dobutamine, no change. The drug was then switched to atropine, an armful of that did the trick. As my heart rate climbed through a hundred and thirty the doctor started to take more readings from the echocardiogram. As my pulse rate passed a hundred and fifty, he enquired to the nurse if she had any beta blockers handy.

The short answer to that question was "No.". The feeling was quite surreal, I was laying on a bed putting in no physical effort at all. My heart was racing like I had just finished a hundred-meter sprint. I could feel it pounding harder and harder in my chest. My heart rate continued to climb, as it passed a hundred and seventy beats', things were getting more tense. The doctor jumped down off the table and started going through the drawers in the treatment room. "Beta blockers, beta blockers, where are those beta blockers." I was chuckling to myself and thinking of the Mad Hatter from 'Alice in Wonderland'. By the time he found the drugs and returned to the table my own adrenalin had joined the atropine, and helped push my heart rate into the high hundred and nineties.

I don't know which of us was more relieved when the 'Mad Hatter' pumped the beta blockers through the cannular, my pulse rate finally started to return to normal. Although I had done very little, I was exhausted whilst I sat in the waiting room to recover. Before I left the hospital, I had the pleasure of paying for this experience, six hundred quid lighter I headed for my car.

Knowing from the outset the process of returning to work was going to be a pain in the neck, it became more so later that week. I got a phone call from Flybe telling me that my six months on the sick was up and they were no longer going to pay me. Cheers guys!

A week later I received a letter from 'Handbrake House' (CAA HQ) telling me that their cardiologist had reviewed my results. Once I had renewed my regular class one medical, I was fit to resume work. This was followed up by a phone call from the CAA cardiologist who sounded dumbfounded that I wanted to return to work. "Most people call it a day after a heart attack, just cash in your loss of license insurance".

At only fifty-one, I still had a few years to go until I had planned to retire. Besides, nobody at Flybe had mentioned early retirement as an option, let alone explained the details of what was available to me. Essentially, I was going back to work due to a lack of information about my choices. This is not too surprising as Flybe was, and likely still is, desperate for experienced pilots.

The decision to return to work as a pilot, is one that in hindsight I would change. Although I was considered fit to do my job by the medical world, the physical demands of being a pilot were accompanied by a lot of stress, long hours of high concentration and fatigue. All exacerbated by irregular sleep patterns and extended stints of isolation. So, it was with some trepidation that I contacted work to arrange my retraining.

Chapter 42

Back to Work.

With the ink still wet on my freshly revalidated medical certificate, I arrived at Flybe's training facility. The first job was to renew my LPC (Licence Proficiency Check). A quick refresher and test in the simulator, job done in a week. Then it was time to start line training.

This proved to be more fun and was going to last a couple of weeks. Flying around the network with a Training Captain occupying the FO's seat is an easy way to fly. Generally, first officers are very capable, they start out knowing the basics and develop over time, the downside is that, as soon as they really get the hang of the job, they are promoted to captain, and I never got to fly with them again.

Having made a reasonable job of getting back into the swing of things, I only made one minor mistake in Amsterdam. I'd turned onto the wrong taxiway, taxied against the one-way system. Me and my trainer in our little Dash ended up stopping and looking ahead at a Malaysian 747 coming towards us. It only took the controller a couple of seconds to sort this heavily biased game of chicken out. When taxiing the captain does the steering and looking out, the FO does the map reading, so technically it was my trainer's mistake. I have broad enough shoulders to accept my portion of blame though.

The handling agent boarded the plane in the Isle of Man looking very stressed, we had thirty odd passengers to take to Birmingham. They were all checked in and sat in the departure lounge. Flybe Op's had come up with a masterplan and it was a corker. We had a contract with Brussels Airlines, one plane ran between Bristol and Brussels several times a day. It had developed a technical problem and was stuck on the ground in Bristol. This meant financial penalties for Flybe, to avoid letting our new contract partner down, the Isle of Man passengers were about to be tossed under a bus.

We were to fly our Birmingham bound passengers to Bristol, stick them on a coach and send them up the motorway to Birmingham. The plane would then be available to take over the Brussels route. The agent went back to the departure lounge to explain this change of fortune to the passengers. He was also going to give them the option of not traveling on this flight at all. The passengers were understandably pissed off with all things purple and Flybe shaped. This was my Final Line Check before returning to normal flying duties, so I had a regular first officer flying with me and the Trainer occupied the jump seat and observed. My heroic Trainer made himself scarce, hiding in the rear galley, thanks for your support at this difficult time.

The passengers boarded, scowling at the cabin crew member stood in the doorway, she was doing her best to welcome them aboard. The aggression in the cabin was at a high level, so I felt an apology was in order. Apologising is one thing, telling the passengers why they were being treated so badly, something else. Thick skinned I may be, suicidal, I'm not. I walked down the cabin so that everybody could hear clearly what I had to say. The pertinent point being, that the crew had no part in this decision, and could do without the hassle it was going to cause.

'Will you be travelling to Birmingham on the bus as well?' A perfectly reasonable question, with a simple answer. 'No. We get to stay in Bristol.' 'You bastard!' chimed out one of the disgruntled travellers. I'd been called worse, so I just carried on, thanked everybody for their understanding, reiterating that the cabin crew were not to blame for this situation. 'Please email or call Flybe customer services with your grievances.' (They're even thicker skinned than me, so good luck with that one.)

By the time we'd transferred our grumpy passengers onto a bus to Birmingham, the plan for us had changed again. The broken plane, that Flybe hoped would eventually be repaired, so that we could position it (and us) to Birmingham, was not going to fly again that night. We were bundled into a taxi to Brum. I was feeling very ragged around the edges by now, was this the best way to be recovering from a heart attack? Probably not, I passed my Line check though.

My mate was a local councillor, we both enjoyed doing boy's stuff. Playing with power tools, welding, eating, and drinking. We were in the waste ground next to my garden, cutting back some overgrown trees with our chain saws, creating a lot of noise and dust. Alan had climbed up into a huge walnut tree and was chain sawing through a particularly robust branch. It fell with a crash, right on top of my shed. The shed moved, and my home brewed stash of beer fell off the shelves. Several gallons of beer poured across the floor, out of the door and soaked away into the dirt. We were gutted. We had to stop for a pint to console ourselves for the loss.

Having downloaded a decibel meter onto my phone, I was curious to know if it worked. My chainsaw running flat out at a meter away was registering a hundred and eight decibels. Next doors dog was out yapping as normal, from my fence about three or four meters away it registered one hundred and seven decibels, how did it not send itself deaf?

Although physically I was doing ok, I was feeling stressed at work. Going back after a six-month break was an uphill struggle. Some of the procedures we used were very different to what I'd been used to and had to be learnt from scratch. Flying as second nature in a familiar environment is one thing, having to think hard about everything you do is exhausting. I found the early starts, late finishes, and unfamiliar techniques very tiring. By the end of the week, I was done in.

Some days circumstances were just so bizarre, that it was hard to separate real life from fiction. Unfortunately, it was all very real. We were flying for Brussels Airlines; I was operating the Brussels to Manchester flight. The passengers had boarded, and we'd just started pushing back off stand. The cabin crew were getting ready to do their safety demo when there was a lot of noise in the cabin. Voices started to raise, and things deteriorated to pandemonium in a second or two.

The passengers had seen a trolley parked just off the left wingtip, on it were suitcases that belonged to some of them. The prospect of arriving in Manchester with no luggage wasn't going down at all well. Luggage space on the Dash is at best limited and the flight was rammed full. Every spare cubby hole had been stuffed with baggage. Unfortunately, the handlers didn't have the foresight to cover up the bags on the trolley, or better still, put them out of sight. The passengers started behaving like two-year olds that had just had their favourite teddy taken off them. They unfastened their seat belts, stood on their seats, and started yelling.

The rules for me are clear, if your load is insecure, you can't take off. Simple. I stopped the pushback and got the No1 on the interphone. She explained what was going on. So, I had the start crew tow us back onto stand. I don't speak any form of Belgian or enough of any other language to deal with a stand-up protest on my plane. I got on the radio to Brussels Airlines. 'Can you send a customer services manager out to the plane, to settle your passengers down please?' I shut the engines down and waited. We had just started our shift and already the delays were starting, they would only mount up, this is bad.

Airlines are all about management and statistics. On time flights are what everybody wants. So if your flight is running on time, the airline will do everything it can to keep that good statistic. If your flight runs late, then you are already a black mark on the stats board. If you're a bit late or massively late, it makes no difference to the stats. You're late. It therefore makes perfect sense for the airline management to have a few flights very, very late, rather than a lot of flights just a bit late. My passengers had just put us onto the naughty, late step. This was only going to get worse as the day progressed.

The Icarus Game

Once the management gets involved it's only going one way, the bigger deal they can make of a situation, the more smarty points they accrue. The customer services manager diligently listened to each and every passenger's complaint. 'That's my bag, it contains lifesaving paracetamols.' Everybody has a good reason not to be separated from their luggage. The fact remained, that there wasn't enough space on the plane, for each passenger to carry their entire retinue in one go. After I'd had a couple of coffees and paid a visit to the toilet, the manager had sorted out the issues and left us to it.

My next P.A. was totally predictable. 'Ladies and gentlemen, this is the captain. Now that the baggage situation has been resolved I'm afraid I have more bad news for you. We have now missed our airways slot, the next take off time available to us is in two hours. Please feel free to use your phones if you have calls to make. If there is any improvement to our circumstances, I'll let you know straight away.' Then I called up the No1 and asked for more coffee and a cake.

Chapter 43

That Bloody Dog.

I had already contacted the Environmental Health department at Daventry District Council, this resulted in an exchange of a lot of answer phone messages but was otherwise pointless. Over the preceding five or six years the Boddingtons dog had been a constant nuisance. It had turned our idyllic country retreat into an unusable millstone. My efforts to talk reason into Alan and Alison Boddington had been fruitless.

It was a scorching hot day, I was sweating in my paddock, weeding the vegetable patch, next doors dog was yapping like crazy, as usual. After a couple of hours, I walked over to the boundary fence and the nuisance creature ran over and started yapping at me. I simply leant over the fence and picked it up. From there the die was cast. Five years of annoyance and harassment were going to end.

On Monday teatime me and Gay went for a walk along the canal. As we passed the local pub, we saw Alan with his mate in the beer garden. I crossed the lock gate to talk to him. He was clearly upset, and I had nothing that I could tell him that would improve the situation. I could hardly tell the truth at this point. I had just dumped his dead dog in a hedgerow and walked away. It was unlikely its demise could have been linked to me. Suspicion and proving something are very different things.

The Icarus Game

The next thing we heard about the disappearance of the dog was on the Monday night. A police officer knocked on the door. This was when Gay discovered what I had done. At first, I tried to deny any involvement. Gay took one look at my face and knew I was lying. PC Lawson also knew this was clearly not true, asking to see in the boot of my car. I opened it for her, and she pulled out some dog hairs, I had not thought this through at all. I hadn't even bothered to fabricate a cover story. This resulted in me having no explanation for them being there. She pressed the point and I admitted taking the dog. I came up with an improbable story that I had let it loose in the countryside. Another lie.

How did the police know where to look? That's simple, the Boddingtons had told them. After we'd seen Alan in the pub he had gone home. He and Alison then broke into my car. When the police asked him how he'd got into my boot, he tried to tell them that it was left unlocked. Bullshit. The car was a top of the range VW, if you left it without the key fob for more than a couple of minutes it locked itself. Alan is a used car dealer, has been for a lot of years. More pertinently, I bought the car from him. Had he retained a key for my car, was that how he did his business? Did he have some other means of breaking into cars? Either way, he certainly did not have my consent to access the boot of my car.

Alison and Alan bragged on social media about breaking into my car and taking photos, like they were ace detectives. When they were questioned by the police about their crime, they didn't have any satisfactory answers. The way public opinion was swinging, the police didn't have any incentive to pursue the Boddingtons. The bad news was starting to stack up against me.

PC Lawson said she would need to talk to me further about the missing dog, but as I would be away working until Thursday evening, she would return for a statement then. Me and Gay discussed what I had done at length that night. She was shocked and horrified. Whilst I was away over the next two evenings we discussed the situation further over the phone, and we both knew that I needed to make a full and honest statement to the police. This was the first clear thought that I had relating to the madness of the previous days, and the first time any real clarity entered my head.

On Friday morning I went to Daventry Police Station and gave a full statement to PC Reid, and another officer, who was present at the interview. He immediately started following up on what I'd told him.

I recovered the dog, and PC Reid and an RSPCA officer arrived at my home. Shortly after the interview it was removed for a post-mortem, to be carried out by the RSPCA. Whilst they were there, I showed PC Reid and the RSPCA officer exactly what had happened and answered their questions.

It wasn't until this time that it entered my dense skull that I needed a lawyer.

If I thought that being honest with the police was going to aid my situation, I was deluded. Any chance of making amends for what I had done went up in smoke as soon as I had made my confession. The internet went crazy, people's imaginations were running wild. The slightest suggestion of a fact was embellished, exaggerated, and recycled. As far as I was concerned, the vexatious comments on social media were being made so that sanctimonious individuals could feel good about themselves. It's all about self-gratification, like masturbating.

The Boddingtons clearly felt that they now had the moral high ground, they would use this to justify any acts of criminal damage, harassment, threats, and abuse. The hysteria spiralled, the situation became more and more cynical. The Boddingtons played the distraught, bereaved parents joker in public at every opportunity. If it wasn't the dead dog, it was their dead disabled daughter, they milked it for all it was worth. Pretty soon Alison had swapped her aging Audi for a new Mercedes sports car.

I contacted Nigel Weller, a criminal lawyer who specialised in defending RSPCA cases. 'Have you made a statement to the police?' 'Yes, I've given them a full and honest account.' 'Oh dear, that's not going to be very helpful.' I arranged to go down and visit him in his office. After I went through the details of what I'd done, Nigel rolled his eyes and brushed his beard. 'What on earth were you doing. Were you trying to dispose of the evidence or preserve the bloody thing?' 'The main thing now, is to try and keep you out of prison.'

Acts of petty vandalism were becoming more frequent, talking to the police made no difference at all. My car was attacked and covered in paint. Eggs and tomatoes were thrown at my house, paint was daubed on walls. At first, I thought this must be the work of animal rights activists, it wasn't. I came home from work late in the evening to find a capping stone from the garden wall on the ground in front of the house. Looking more closely it was clear that it had been thrown at Gays' car, the windscreen was smashed, and the bonnet dented.

Knowing only one person who had a track record for attacking women alone in their homes, I checked the CCTV and there he was, large as life. We called the police, showed them the video footage, and made a statement. The police questioned our neighbours, they denied any involvement, they weren't even in the area at the time, they said. He was arrested, questioned, and bailed. Eventually the police decided not to press charges, apparently my video evidence wasn't good enough for them.

By the time I appeared in court for the first time, the social media storm was whipping itself into an evangelical frenzy. I was in the waiting area with Gay and my lawyer when I spotted a friend from work. 'Hi Stu, what have you been up to?' 'I'm not up in court, I'm here to support you, you twat.' That was unexpected but very welcome. As it turned out, all I did was enter a guilty plea, and confirm my name and address. The Boddingtons and their rent a mob crowd turned out on-mass, they'd even had t-shirts made for the loony protesters.

The second court appearance turned out to be totally pointless for me. It was just a means for the RSPCA to delay the proceedings, to raise more public awareness for their cause. It very quickly became apparent, that this was a massive fund-raising exercise for them. They needed to employ expert witnesses from every corner of the animal welfare state. How much cash can you throw at a dead dog? If the returns are exponential, a lot, it would seem. My case was adjourned. There would be a hearing to 'establish the facts' and carry out sentencing in six months. Six months! I'd killed a nuisance of a dog, even the RSPCA were going to struggle to expand on that.

For now, I was still at work. All the court appearances had fallen on days off. Flybe knew what was going on at every stage, I'd told them. There was no indication that it was affecting my ability to do my job. Some of my colleagues were foaming at the mouth over the whole thing, some were more understanding, most just got on with their jobs.

The circus had finally come to town, Corby magistrates court was packed. There wasn't a dry gusset in the room amongst the Boddington's supporters. What they didn't know was that despite six months of preparation, the RSPCA had totally failed to put together a case.

Their expert witness, Ms Millington, a vet from Nuneaton, had written an emotive essay describing the immense suffering and emotional turmoil the dog had experienced during drowning. This was based on a single experiment done in 1879 by Paul Brouadel. Although highly emotive it lacked credibility and when it was challenged, it was immediately withdrawn. They hadn't even done the most rudimentary of autopsies on the body that I had returned to them, the cause of death was taken from my statement.

Alison was hoping to gain more capital by linking the dead dog to her deceased, disabled daughter, yet again. She was itching to get onto the stand. No doubt she had her best Emily Bronte black veil and lacy handkerchief to hand for added drama. Her distraught parent mannerisms practiced to perfection. She didn't get the chance, a letter to me from her son explained the dog belonged to him and not their deceased daughter. It was disclosed to the RSPCA lawyer and he would not allow her to perjure herself on the witness stand, all of her testimony was withdrawn.

The RSPCA brought literally hundreds of animal cruelty cases to court each year. The total number of accusations were second only to every case brought by the Crown Prosecution Service during the same period that year. They relied on very narrow areas of evidence to secure convictions. If they are challenged, they soon cave in. They rely on their cases not being properly defended, to raise massive amounts of money through criminal prosecutions. Most people simply cannot afford a defence team, and the RSPCA know this; they capitalise heavily on it.

After my barrister had been through their evidence, piece by piece, they were left with no case whatsoever. Their lawyer Kevin McCole was visibly nervous by the time he stood up and read out a short excerpt from my statement to the police. This was the only evidence they presented to the court.

The magistrate was seriously unimpressed when the RSPCA tried to claim more than £10,000 in costs. They were told in no uncertain terms by the court that they had done nothing to warrant this amount. The award of the court was £2400 which was the costs the RSPCA had incurred up to the previous hearing, five months before. In the view of the court this latest fiasco was pointless in prosecuting the case, they had proved nothing.

Their lawyer had lived through a bad day, he looked shell shocked as he left, literally shot down in flames. Had I not gone to the police and confessed, there would have been absolutely no case against me. Note to self, don't admit a single thing to the police again. 'No comment' is the only answer you need.

Flybe became the target of the animal rights campaigners now. After a mediocre result in the courts, they were after my job. The press coverage became international, and my picture was plastered everywhere. The internet went into another frenzy, my case was unbelievably high profile. Flybe couldn't cope with the negative comments and images that they were being bombarded with. My place in history was guaranteed, the animal rights protesters had built a huge cyber statue of me on the World Wide Web, and it will be there forever. I'm sure if Beelzebub has a social media account, he'll be waiting for me.

Being targeted by the loony lefties was disconcerting at first, but quickly I worked out that they had very little to say. Variations on the 'He's a hateful person.' and assorted threats, were posted in more and more graphic terms by a group of armchair bound imbeciles, foaming at the mouth. They had just learned how to use the 'cut and paste' function. I scanned through the comments at first, but soon found I had to cover a lot of ground to find anything original.

Flybe held a couple of disciplinary hearings to decide what to do with me. Although they eventually concluded there was no issue with the way I did my job, they insisted that I had brought the company into disrepute.

This was the same company that floated on the stock exchange for £215 million and collapsed after less than ten years, worth about £2 million. I was being judged by the managers who had misused this money over the previous years. They had squandered £212.8 million and were now being all self-righteous over a nuisance of a dog.

As I had no control of the internet comments or the news reports, I felt this was a little harsh.

I turned up for the disciplinary hearing with my union, BALPA's, senior man, their National Officer was defending me. His advice was pitiful. 'Steve, you may as well give up now, they're going to fire you anyway, you're screwed.' This guy was supposed to be a defence barrister, specialising in employment law. Even worse, he was supposed to be on my side. My unions representation was ineffective at best, kow-towing to Flybe at worst. 'I'll give you a sheet of my legal chambers headed paper to write your resignation on.' Was the best he could manage.

That was an abrupt end to my airline career, over ten thousand hours of flying. Thousands of tonnes of freight, one hundred and twenty-five thousand passengers carried, all finished. I left the disciplinary feeling empty. I had no plans, and no idea what the future held. This was going to be a tough situation to pick myself up from.

My professional experience should have lined me up to find a responsible job, my criminal conviction and internet profile ruled that out. If I couldn't find another job, I'd create one for myself.

Chapter 44

Epilogue.

After the stress of the court case, we sold our dream home and moved. That ideal was as dead in the water as the irritating dog. The one that had caused the aggravation in the first place. In truth the property had turned into a liability, and we were glad to see the back of it. With no job and no prospect of finding another one, we figured a fresh start was what we needed. I still needed to fill in my days usefully. Property renovation and repair had always been a hobby, I decided to try and make it into a business.

On a Thursday afternoon I was sat in a meeting arranged by the DSS, in lieu of hard cash. Across the desk was Julia, a woman who was going to advise me on starting my own company. She went into detail about the support available, local experts for mentoring, legal and financial advice. 'When do you intend to start?' 'Monday.' I replied.

She gave me a patient look and rolled her eyes, 'You can't just start a business like that, it takes planning.' I pulled out one of my flyers and passed it to her. 'Oooh, you're a handyman, can you fix leaking roofs, get rid of wasps nests, trim hedges?' 'Yes, I can do all those jobs for you, on Monday.' She was away the next week, so I turned up the following morning, Friday.

I had started 'Steve's Handyman Service.' Doing maintenance and building work, it kept me busy for a couple of years. I trimmed Julia's bush for her and sorted out her leaks. First job done, from that day on I never looked back.

The Handyman business went from strength to strength. 'Can you lay a patio? Can you fit a kitchen? Can you hang wallpaper. The requests for my long list of talents just kept coming in. One job rolled into the next. I was dividing a large bedroom into two smaller rooms, when a stroke of luck dropped into my lap. The house's owner saw me putting in his new radiators. 'That's a neat job you're making of the copper pipework, I could have a job for you, if you're interested.' It turned out he was the manager of an engineering company and had a contract to install a couple of kilometres of copper pipe in a factory, and no one who could or would do the soldering. Happy days for me.

We thrashed out who was paying for what, this was a huge job by my usual standards, so I would need staged payments. I turned up at the site, met the engineers, went through the blueprints for the job, and off I went. It was heavy, physical work, up and down scaffolding with tonnes of copper piping, fittings, and tools. The freezing cold barely registered. After six weeks all my pipework was installed, and the cash eventually landed in the bank.

There was only one downside, I felt like shit. I'd taken a break from fitting a couple of en-suit bathrooms to do the factory installation. I'd arranged to take a break from them after the first one was done. I picked up where I had left off and carried on working. The shit feeling got worse. Even the house owner I was doing the work for, asked if I was ok.

Deciding I wasn't ok at all, I went to the doctors. He had a poke around my abdomen, asked about the symptoms and referred me for an ultrasound scan. This was where the bad news started. I half expected something horrid from the sideways glances the ultrasound operator kept giving me, checking I wasn't going to fall off my perch on her slab.

My GP had the results on the screen in front of him. 'You've got a lump in your stomach. About the size of a large hen's egg. Christ! He referred me to the Gastroenterologist at Coventry. If you ever find yourself waiting for ages to see a specialist, be thankful. If they see you straight away, you're up shit creek. My appointment with the consultant was made over phone by his secretary for the next day. The first job was to get a camera down my throat, to look inside my stomach. This was booked in for the start of the following week. For now, a blood test would do to get the ball rolling.

The following day I was back at work, finishing off the en-suite. It was Friday afternoon when my phone rang. 'Steve', it's the Gastroenterologist. 'A bed is booked for you at Coventry, you need an emergency blood transfusion, your red blood cell count is dangerously low. Get there as soon as you can.' That's a phone call to sharpen your senses. I made my excuses to my customer and knocked off an hour early. By the time I got to the hospital they were waiting.

The transfusion would take all night, my endoscopy had been brought forward to first thing the following morning. Things were moving so fast I could barely keep up. After the blood transfusion I felt a million dollars. I can see why athletes use these to enhance their performance. Once I had my new blood, I was sent downstairs for the endoscope. Not pleasant, but not too bad. The doctor that did it thought he was looking at a ruptured ulcer and was very delicate when he took the biopsies.

The Gastroenterologist looked at the results, then at the video of the biopsies being taken. He decided that it had all been too gentle, so the procedure would need repeating, this time, by himself. Right now. Crikey this guy was a force of nature. In truth he knew what was wrong, he just needed the evidence to back up his diagnosis. This time, even with a sedative, things were a lot less polite. 'I'm sorry Steve, but this is going to hurt.' He was right. I left the treatment room feeling ragged, then the sedatives kicked in. I spent an hour asleep in a random office, on a desk, somewhere in the endoscopy department. The news was not good. 'You have a GIST, it's a gastro-intestinal stomal tumour.'

This earth-shaking news was followed by a CT scan, followed by a PET scan, followed by an MRI scan, followed by worse news. 'It's spread, it's in your liver, spine, and pelvis. For fucks sake, how much worse can this get. Until now neither myself nor Gay had taken the time to let this monumental, terminal diagnosis sink in.

'You may want to think about getting your affairs in order.' Is not how you want an appointment with your consultant to end. 'I'm referring you to a gastrointestinal surgeon and an oncologist. Their team will take the best care of you. From being the captain of an airliner, followed by being self-employed and self-reliant, it was a sharp shock to find my life was now in somebody else's hands. The good news was, the bad news couldn't get any worse.

The Icarus Game

I met up for breakfast with my mate 'Awkins. Detailing to him in graphic detail, how by carting tonnes of copper pipe around on scaffolding, I'd ruptured the cancerous tumour in my stomach. This had bled profusely into my intestines, aided by the blood thinning and anticoagulant drugs I was prescribed after my heart attack. As he masticated on his bacon and sausage, he gave me the benefit of years of paramedic training and ambulance driving. 'So basically, you was a walking black pudding eh. If I were you, I wouldn't start any long books mate. Is there any mustard?'

The meeting with the surgeon was brief and to the point. 'The best way to deal with this type of cancer is to cut it out. If it comes back, we'll cut it out again.' Every time he used the word, cut, and he used it a lot, the surgeon made a chopping action with his hand. His enthusiasm for cutting stuff out, along with the graphic demonstration of his trade skills got him nicknamed Chop Chop by me and Gay. 'Any questions for me, Mr Woodhouse?' 'You will be using a nice new, sharp blade for all this cutting out, won't you?' My big gob again. 'Of course, and while I'm in there I'll have a good root about and get some biopsies out of your liver.' Buy one get one free, result.

Coming out of the anaesthetic, I was the proud owner of two thirds of a tumour free stomach. Along with a scar that ran over a foot, from one side of my abdomen to the other. Chop Chop had done his name proud and started the long road to extending my life. The epidural was dulling the worst of the pain and the morphine was giving me the weirdest hallucinations. Even with my eyes closed. I was floating in limbo under the surface of a lake of blood, looking up at the bright sky above. While the meniscus of my liquid tomb was covered in insects skating in and out of view. This was with the good quality, medical grade morphine. How anybody can think taking the back-street shite is fun, is totally beyond me. I was completely out of action for two months.

The next meeting with my Oncologist was the cruncher. Because the cancer was metastasising, they had to decide whether there was any benefit to carrying out further surgery. The problem was the skeletal metastases, these were beyond treatment. 'Where are the tumours on my skeleton?' 'One's at the base of your spine, the other is on the right side of your pelvis.' I showed her the scar on my hip, the one where the bone graft harvesting had been done for my neck repair, years before. 'Does that explain the pelvic lesion?' 'Maybe.' She took it to the next cancer team decision meeting and they restudied my scans, deciding during that team meeting, to give me the benefit of the doubt.

The next surgeon started sharpening his scalpel, he was the Hepatologist. The meeting with him was also a shocker. 'You need a liver resection.' This much I knew. 'It's a lot bigger operation than your stomach resection.' This bit I hadn't bargained on. The previous surgeon had removed two small tumours for histology from my liver, as part of his BOGOF deal. That left three larger, harder to access tumours for the Hepatologist to deal with. Two at the fat end of my liver, one at the skinny end.

After the procedure, I would need an intensive care bed. This was a problem. On the day I turned up for my operation the intensive care ward was full. There had been a pile up on the M6 and the hospitals ICU was overrun with Road Traffic Accident bodies. I was not at all sympathetic towards the idiot drivers, playing dodgems on the motorway and screwing up my life saving surgery.

The following week I was done. When I came to, in the intensive care ward I really didn't care whether I'd survived the surgery or not. I don't ever remember feeling so totally fucked. The nurses fortunately did care, they had their wards' survival averages to keep up. The surgical team had spent six hours slicing up my liver. Removing the three tumours we knew about was just the start. They then had an ultrasound scan done directly onto the surface of my liver and found another two tumours, which were also cut out. These hadn't shown up at all on the previous scans. In all I'd lost three kilos of liver, about forty percent of the whole thing.

This was now eight tumours removed from my body in total, the surgery was being backed up by a form of chemotherapy. Gists, until recently had only been treatable with aggressive surgery. Radiotherapy made them grow and metastasise even quicker, as did traditional chemotherapy. A clever person then suggested using the drugs that were used to treat leukaemia, as Gists spread through the blood system, rather than via the lymphatic system like other cancers. It showed promise and is still used today.

A couple of weeks later I staggered into my post-operative check-up. It was done by a nurse from the hepatology team. This was the only time so far in my illness I've felt I was getting second rate treatment. She waffled on about my fatty liver. The one that was now half the size it used to be. This from a woman who was barely contained by her XXL uniform. I couldn't get past thinking; the NHS really should get its own house in order, before preaching a healthy lifestyle to the rest of us. When I pointed out the huge, rugby ball sized lump on my stomach, she said it would probably go down in time. She had completely misdiagnosed a hernia, a foot long and four inches wide, from which my intestines were trying to escape. She really should be sent to Specsavers.

At the next appointment with my Oncologist, a quick look at my hernia was all she needed before she booked me back in for more surgery. This time for a hernia repair. This was not an unexpected complication of the previous surgery, because the chemotherapy drugs I take really hinder the healing process and scar tissue formation. This repair had to wait six months though, to allow my body to recover sufficiently to withstand another round of major surgery.

This latest turn of events has been an epiphany for me. After all, I had reached the heights of an airline pilots' career, then crashed down to the lowest point of my life with a criminal conviction. This had seemed somehow inevitable. Success, it seems, is only transient. Now I can look back at the good times in my life with pride and immense satisfaction. I also realise that bad times and challenges are there to amplify and allow me to appreciate the successes I enjoyed.

Now, I ironically owe my life to a dead nuisance of a dog, and its self-centred owners. Along with everybody else who forced me into quitting flying for a living. It was only when I left that sedentary life and took up a physical line of work, that my cancer came to light. As it was, it was touch and go whether, or not, it could be treated.

The Icarus Game

Had I continued flying, even for a short time, my tumour would never have ruptured, my cancer would have continued spreading undetected. And by now, it would certainly have been inoperable. That, or I would more than likely be dead already. Funny how life works, innit.

Steve Woodhouse

Note from the Author.

At the beginning of 2022 the country was coming out of lockdown. As a follower of the markets, I had worked out for myself that the future was not going to be all unicorns and rainbows.

The government had printed an eye watering amount of money and tossed it about like confetti. At some point, I reasoned they would want this cash back, with interest.

There was an exodus of people leaving the built-up cities in search of some space in the country, it wouldn't be long before this drove up rural housing costs.

By now, I was already retired and we both felt it was the right time for Gay to retire as well. So, we hatched a plan. We would sell our house, buy a motorhome and do a bit of travelling.

I worked for months, doing all the jobs the property needed, refurbishments, improvements, and redecorating it from top to bottom. We got it on the market in mid-2022. Getting a lot of interest, multiple bidders, it sold almost immediately. Completing just before Christmas.

Inflation hit the news, utility costs had spiralled, and interest rates headed north for the first time in a generation. Talk of a housing price crash started to infiltrate the media.

We spent the first nights in our motorhome in the depths of winter, and we loved it. We now look forward to a year or two of drifting where the fancy takes us. The only fly in the ointment is my medical issues, but so far we have been able to work around these.

Our new nomadic lifestyle has another bonus. Time, and lots of it. This allows us to concentrate on the good things in life. Exploring as far and wide as we wish. It's given Gay free time to dedicate to her hobbies. And it's allowed me to finish this book, the one I started writing way back in 2017.

2022 has been an incredibly busy time for us, but very productive. No doubt we will buy another house at some point, but we have no idea where or when. For now, we are focussing on a fruitful and fulfilling 2023.

What Goes Around Comes Around.

I was editing this manuscript this morning, enjoying my breakfast, and listening to the radio. When the news came on, it cheered me up immensely.

Flybe, my former employer had gone into administration, again. For the second time in just five years 'Britain's favourite regional airline' had gone bust.

I was so delighted by this act of karma; I made a point of watching the evening news on the TV to catch up on the full story. Not a mention. Nothing.

They weren't even worth a by-line on the national news. As their least favourite ex-employee, I managed a full story.

The Icarus Game

Annex 1.

Crash Report Prepared by the: Air Accidents Investigation Branch.

Lockheed L188C Electra, G-LOFD, 21 March 2001 at 1948 hrs

AAIB Bulletin No: 8/2001 Ref: EW/C2001/3/5 Category: 1.1

Aircraft Type and Registration: Lockheed L188C Electra, G-LOFD

No & Type of Engines: 4 Allison 501-D13 turboprop engines

Year of Manufacture: 1961

Date & Time (UTC): 21 March 2001 at 1948 hrs

Location: Prestwick Airport, Scotland

Type of Flight: Training

Persons on Board: Crew - 2 - Passengers - None

Injuries: Crew - None - Passengers - N/A

Nature of Damage: Damage to left main landing gear, left propellers, left flap and tailplane

Commander's Licence: Airline Transport Pilot's Licence

Commander's Age: 39 years

Commander's Flying Experience: 6,130 hrs (of which 560 were on type)

Last 90 days - 57 hours

Last 28 days - 42 hours

Information Source: AAIB Field Investigation

History of the flight

The first officer was undergoing night flying exercises for his conversion training to the Electra aircraft and was in the right seat with the commander, as training Captain, in the left seat. He had flown two normal night visual circuits, followed by an asymmetric power circuit and a go-around for a further circuit and landing on Runway 13 with No 1 engine retarded. The aircraft weight was about 68,600 lb and VAT (threshold speed) was 'bugged' at 120 kt on the air speed indicator; the final approach was flown at VAT + 20 kt.

The approach was normal and the aircraft was configured with the landing gear down and full flap. On short finals, the controller gave a surface wind check of 090°/12 kt. The aircraft crossed the threshold at VAT and initiated the flare. However, the commander then considered that the first officer had held the aircraft in the flare for too long an interval and, in the light crosswind from the left, had allowed it to drift to the right of the centreline. The commander therefore took control and applied left rudder, left aileron and slight back pressure on the control yoke to regain the centreline and land. During the touchdown the left mainwheel touched first, followed by the right mainwheel and then the nosewheel.

The touchdown appeared normal, but the commander was then immediately aware of a directional control problem. The aircraft was veering to the left to such an extent that he had to use full right rudder, in addition to asymmetric reverse thrust, to maintain the centreline. However, directional control became progressively more difficult as the aircraft decelerated. Because the Electra has no anti-skid facility, the wheel brakes are not normally used until the speed falls below 60 kt; in the event the commander thought that the speed had decreased to about 50 kt when he first applied the brakes. It then became apparent that the aircraft might leave the paved runway and so the commander applied full braking and maximum reverse thrust on all four engines to stop the aircraft on the left side of the paved surface. The aircraft came to rest about 10 feet from the edge of the runway and heading some 70° left of the runway direction.

The first officer pulled the four 'E Handles' to shut down all four engines and isolate their associated systems. Both pilots were not injured and vacated the aircraft through the main door.

The Airport Fire Service (AFS) attended the aircraft with four vehicles. Although there was no sign of fire the AFS deployed hoses, sidelines and dry powder media as a precaution.

Inspection of the aircraft on the runway

Runway 13 is 2,987 metres long and 46 metres wide, and has a displaced threshold with an elevation of 38 feet amsl. The concrete/asphalt surface of the runway is bordered by a hard surface for most of its length, and the aircraft had come to rest to the left of the runway edge on this border, some 1100 metres from the threshold. Initial examination of the aircraft showed that the lower (piston) oleo cylinder of the left main landing gear leg had fractured just above the axle, allowing separation of the axle and the two wheel/brake assemblies as a unit, as shown in Figure 1. The latter wheels assembly had caused relatively minor damage to the left flap and left tailplane after it had separated, and flash fires had occurred on the runway as hydraulic and oleo oil had been released from the broken gear leg and ignited by the friction sparks caused by contact of the fractured leg with the runway.

The upper section of the piston cylinder had remained in the upper leg as the aircraft had decelerated and its fractured end had initially generated an intermittent groove in the runway surface which had progressively become more continuous as the aircraft had slowed. Just before the end of the ground roll, the stub of the left gear piston cylinder had struck and destroyed a runway edge light before crossing over a recessed drain aperture. As this occurred, the left wing had momentarily lowered further and caused all eight propeller blade tips on the left side of the aircraft to contact the runway surface.

Fractured piston cylinder examination

As described above, the upper fractured surface of the failed piston cylinder had been ground down by contact with the runway and so only the lower half of the fractured surfaces was available for examination. After recovery of the piston cylinder lower end, axle and wheels assembly to the AAIB facility at Farnborough, the unit was stripped down in preparation for detailed metallurgical examination.

The fractured surface was cut from the bottom section of the piston cylinder and examined visually. It was readily apparent that the fracture had initiated within the lowest area of the piston outer surface, close to the limit of normal travel of the piston (which was clearly indicated by the lower boundary of the polished area of the chromium plated surface). This location was on the inboard side of the piston and was characterised by corroded arcs on the fractured surface which extended some 2.5 mm into the material from the outer surface, as shown in Figure 2. Visual examination also revealed the presence of some parallel secondary cracking adjacent to the main fracture. Examination of the fracture initiation zone in a Scanning Electron Microscope (SEM) revealed that the chromium plating on the surface exhibited brittle cleavage cracking and that the underlying steel in the corroded arc regions showed intergranular cracking, as illustrated in Figure 3. Beyond and between these areas the steel section had failed in overload.

Various non-destructive inspection techniques, including dye penetrant and magnetic particle tests, were used to examine the material around the fracture surface for evidence of additional cracking. Several areas of cracking of the steel substrate were found, and within the chromed surface on the front side of the leg, from 25 mm above the normal limit of travel to below this limit, a pattern of fine vertically orientated cracks were observed over the least worn regions. Almost all of the cracking in the steel was directly associated with cracks in the chromium plating, which was generally about 100μm thick in this area. Remote from the fracture initiation zone, the chromium thickness was reduced to between 25 and 40μm, probably due to wear. Some cracking in the plating was apparent in both the vertical and horizontal orientations, but this was not generally fully penetrating. Evidence of some remaining grit blasting debris was present in the chrome/steel interface, but the plating was strongly adherent to the parent steel substrate. Chemical analysis of the piston material showed it to conform to the required specification of AISI 4340 steel, and hardness testing confirmed that it was of the required strength.

Discussion of the fracture mechanism

Hydrogen embrittlement and stress corrosion cracking (SCC) are two main causes of intergranular cracking in high strength steels. Cracking due to hydrogen embrittlement (caused by hydrogen diffusion into steel during plating processes) can result in a fracture surface very similar in appearance to that resulting from stress corrosion, but in this case SCC was considered the most likely cause. This was because most of the cracks identified were present in the regions of the piston routinely exposed to the general environment, rather than throughout the material examined which would have been more indicative of hydrogen embrittlement involvement. SCC failures usually result from a field of cracks produced in a metal alloy under the combined influence of tensile stress (residual and/or applied) and a corrosive environment. The alloy is not attacked over most of its surface, but a system of intergranular cracks initiates at the stress corrosion site and propagates through the material grain structure over a period of time. Stress levels that produce SCC are well below the yield strength of the material and this mechanism is influenced by the level of stress, alloy composition, the type of corrosive environment and temperature.

The multiple orientation of the cracks evident on the failed piston indicated that internal stresses within the steel material were likely to be involved, as opposed to tensile stresses resulting from purely externally applied loads. The latter would result primarily from bending loads on the gear leg and it appeared that this mode of loading had propagated the final overstressing failure of the piston cylinder, after it had been weakened by the SCC propagation from the outer (cracked) chrome surface. The distribution of the cracking detected in the chromium plating by NDT was consistent with excessive loads having been generated in the plating by grinding wheel operations during manufacture/refurbishment of this component. Whilst it is not unusual for some cracks to form in chromium 'as-plated', the many cracks observed were considered to have resulted from a combination of the plating process used and excessive grinding action. These cracks in the chrome surface had then allowed the underlying high strength steel to be exposed to corrosive conditions, inducing SCC.

Landing gear history

Records held by the aircraft manufacturer indicated that four previous gear leg piston cylinder failures had occurred during service operation of the Electra type which were similar to this failure on G-LOFD. Metallurgical examinations carried out on three of these failures had found that two could have been initiated by stress corrosion and/or hydrogen embrittlement cracks. The other failure was determined to have resulted from SCC. Improper thickness of the external chrome plating, and overhaul procedures which induced hydrogen embrittlement, were considered contributing factors.

The manufacturer stated that the Electra main landing gear was not fatigue-critical and that at the time that this aircraft type had initially been certificated there were no requirements to establish safe lives for the landing gear components. The high strength steel material was, however, acknowledged to be susceptible to corrosion and subsequent SCC, but proper maintenance and correct plating procedures during overhaul were deemed sufficient to inhibit such cracking. In the latter context, the manufacturer had issued Electra Service Information Letter (SIL) 88/SIL-88A in October 1974 to address related stripping and plating procedures and believed that all operators were in possession of this SIL.

The authorised overhaul life for the main landing gear on G-LOFD was 16,000 flight hours. This component had achieved 15,400 hours since its last overhaul. The aircraft had flown for a total of 49,500 hours, with some 22,300 landings. It had been on the UK register since 1997, prior to which it had been operating with a Norwegian company. No re-working of this landing gear has been carried out since the aircraft had been on the UK register.

The Icarus Game

This charming individual thought throwing a brick through my wife's car windscreen whilst I was at work was acceptable. He was arrested on suspicion of criminal damage and bailed by Northamptonshire police. He was never charged.

The Icarus Game

Steve Woodhouse

•••○○ Sprint 🔒 11:35 AM 47% 🔋
datalounge.com

Pilot drowns neighbor's dog for barking too much

Is it really wrong for me to be on the pilot's side? He's sort of a hot daddy, by the way.

Flybe pilot drowned neighbour ›
Stephen Woodhouse was so angry about the noise made by Meg,...

The Icarus Game

Thank you for buying my book.

More thanks still for taking the time to read it.

I hope you found it entertaining, thought provoking, and challenging.

Now, if you feel that you have something to contribute, please do so, by adding your review of my efforts to the Amazon listing for this publication.

Reviews are massively important, and the lifeblood of future sales.

The Icarus Game

www.ingramcontent.com/pod-product-compliance
Lightning Source LLC
Chambersburg PA
CBHW071213080526
44587CB00013BA/1354